The Iraqi Kurds and the Cold War

Examining the effects of the Cold War and regional politics on the Iraqi Kurds between 1958 and 1975, this study demonstrates how regional and international powers sought to exploit the Iraqi Kurds in their quest for statehood. The research draws on a plethora of British and American archival documents and select Soviet and Iranian sources integrated with Kurdish authoritative and eyewitness accounts.

The work explores the Iraqi Kurds on three levels: Firstly, on a national Iraqi level, starting with the Iraqi Revolution in 1958 to the collapse of the Kurds' liberation movement in 1975 under Mela Mustafa Barzani. Secondly, it considers the issue on a regional level by examining the political dynamics between Iran (under the Shah), Iraq, Egypt (thus Nasserists) and other regional states, with a focus on these states' relations and tensions. Thirdly, it scrutinises the impact of the Cold War on the politics and history of Iraq, focussing on the effects on the Kurds in particular.

Complementing the existing literature, this volume builds a chronological narrative through historical analysis. It is a key resource for students, scholars, policymakers and regional experts interested in Kurdish history, foreign policy, politics and security in the Middle East.

Hawraman Ali is a lecturer at the Department of International Relations and Diplomacy of Tishk International University, Erbil. He completed his PhD in Middle Eastern Studies at the University of Manchester, UK, in 2017.

Routledge Studies in Middle Eastern Politics

93. Power Sharing in Lebanon
Consociationalism Since 1820
Eduardo Wassim Aboultaif

94. Israel in a Turbulent Region
Security and Foreign Policy
Edited by Tore T. Petersen

95. Women in Turkey
Silent Consensus in the Age of Neoliberalism and Islamic Conservatism
Gamze Çavdar and Yavuz Yaşar

96. The Decline of Democracy in Turkey
A Comparative Study of Hegemonic Party Rule
Kürşat Çınar

97. Ethnicity and Party Politics in Turkey
The Rise of the Kurdish Party during the Kurdish Opening Process
Berna Öney

98. Religion and Hezbollah
Political Ideology and Legitimacy
Mariam Farida

99. Erdoğan's 'New' Turkey
Attempted Coup d'état and the Acceleration of Political Crisis
Nikos Christofis

100. The Iraqi Kurds and the Cold War
Regional Politics, 1958–1975
Hawraman Ali

For a full list of titles in the series: https://www.routledge.com/middleeaststudies/
series/SE0823

The Iraqi Kurds and the Cold War
Regional Politics, 1958–1975

Hawraman Ali

LONDON AND NEW YORK

First published 2020 by Routledge

2 Park Square, Milton Park, Abingdon, Oxon OX14 4RN
605 Third Avenue, New York, NY 10017

Routledge is an imprint of the Taylor & Francis Group, an informa business

First issued in paperback 2021

Copyright © 2020 Hawraman Ali

The right of Hawraman Ali to be identified as author of this work has been asserted by him in accordance with sections 77 and 78 of the Copyright, Designs and Patents Act 1988.

All rights reserved. No part of this book may be reprinted or reproduced or utilised in any form or by any electronic, mechanical, or other means, now known or hereafter invented, including photocopying and recording, or in any information storage or retrieval system, without permission in writing from the publishers.

Notice:
Product or corporate names may be trademarks or registered trademarks, and are used only for identification and explanation without intent to infringe.

Publisher's Note

The publisher has gone to great lengths to ensure the quality of this reprint but points out that some imperfections in the original copies may be apparent.

British Library Cataloguing-in-Publication Data
A catalogue record for this book is available from the British Library

Library of Congress Cataloging-in-Publication Data
A catalog record has been requested for this book

ISBN: 978-0-367-34574-7 (hbk)
ISBN: 978-1-03-217425-9 (pbk)
DOI: 10.4324/9780429326646

Typeset in Times New Roman
by TNQ Technologies

To my parents, Ning and my late grandparents

Contents

List of Events		viii
List of Figures		x
List of Acronyms		xi
Preface		xii
Introduction		1
1	1958–1962: Iraqi Revolution, Kurdish hostilities	22
2	1963–1965: Seeking allies	49
3	1965–1971: Politics and struggle	75
4	1971–1975: Hope and betrayal	106
Conclusion		146
Bibliography		153
Index		159

Events

August 1920—the Allies and the Ottomans signed the Treaty of Sèvres, paving the way for Kurdish statehood.

July 1923—the Treaty of Lausanne annuls the Treaty of Sèvres, reneging on promises made by Sèvres regarding Kurdish self-determination.

1922, 1931, 1937, 1943 and thereafter—major Kurdish revolts take place.

August 1946—the Kurdish Democratic Party is established.

July 1958—the monarchy in Iraq is ousted.

September 1961—major hostilities break out between Kurds and Qasim's regime.

February 1963—Qasim's regime overthrown, Ba'athist government vows to make peace with the Kurds.

June 1963—fighting resumes; Kurdish appeals for US backing prove futile.

November 1963—the Ba'ath is overthrown, and pro-Nasserite Nationalists take power—Iran alarmed.

June 1966—the government in Baghdad offers the Bazzaz Declaration through Prime Minister Abd al-Rahman al-Bazzaz.

July 1968—the Ba'athists overthrow the Nationalists.

January 1969—the Ba'ath government resumes the war in Kurdistan.

March 1970—the KDP and the Ba'ath sign the March 11 Accord.

September 1971—the Ba'ath attempt to assassinate Barzani.

April 1972—Iraq and Soviets sign the Soviet–Iraq Treaty of Friendship and Cooperation.

May 1972—King Hussein of Jordan offers complete backing for Barzani albeit secret.

May 1972—Nixon and Kissinger visit Iran, after the Moscow Summit.

July 1972—high-ranking US officials agree to meet Kurdish leaders.

August 1973—Nixon authorises limited covert backing for the Iraqi Kurds.

March 1974—Saddam Hussein gives ultimatum to Kurdish leaders.

August 1974—the Ba'ath government launches all-out military action in Kurdistan.

Events   ix

March 1975—Saddam Hussein and the Shah of Iran reach an agreement in Algiers, which also includes selling out the Kurds by Iran. Kurdish pleas with the US not to abandon them immediately after this agreement are all futile, with Israel also backtracking on its promises.

April 1975—Kurdish leaders with their Peshmerga decide to abandon the War, disperse or take refuge elsewhere—Turkey uses troops to prevent Kurds' feeling, even to Iran via the Turkish border.

Figures

1.1 Kurdistan and areas with a majority Kurdish population and their proximity to the Soviet Union, i.e. showing the 'land bridge', according to the CIA (CIA, 1986).   32

3.1 The Kurdish majority inhabited area as contiguous territory (CIA, 1992). The Pershmerga controlled most of the rural Kurdish area in Iraq as shown, including the Iran–Iraq border.   96

Acronyms

CENTO	Central Treaty Organisation
CIA	Central Intelligence Agency
CUP	Cambridge University Press
DDRS	Gale's Declassified Documents Reference System
DNSA	Digital National Security Archive
DOD	Department of Defence
FO	Folder
FRUS	Foreign Relations of the United States
GOI	Government of Iraq
ICP	Iraqi Communist Party
IPC	Iraqi Petroleum Company
ISIS	Islamic State of Iraq and Syria
KDP	Kurdistan Democratic Party
NEA	Bureau of Near Eastern and South Asian Affairs of the State Department
NSC	National Security Council
OPEC	Organisation of the Petroleum Exporting Countries
OUP	Oxford University Press
PUK	Patriotic Union of Kurdistan
RAF	Royal Air Force
SALT	Strategic Arms Limitation Treaty
SAVAK	*Sāzemān-e Ettelā'āt va Amniyat-e Keshvar* (Organization of Intelligence and National Security)
UAR	United Arab Republic
UKFO	United Kingdom Foreign Office
UNHCR	United Nations High Commissioner for Refugees
UNSC	United Nations Security Council
USG	US Government
USINTS	United States Interest Section
VP	Vice President
WPLUSD	WikiLeaks Public Library of US Diplomacy

Preface

Since the making of the modern Middle East and the dismantling of the Ottoman Empire, the Kurdish question has remained one of the longest unresolved issues in the region. Indeed, in terms of longevity, it surpasses other significant issues in the Middle East such as Arab–Israeli disputes. Today, however, the Kurdish question is not settled for good any better than in the twentieth century. The most advanced progress in terms of peacemaking between the Kurds and the states that essentially rule over them has been in Iraq. Even this is very fragile and not set.

As this book will show, intermittent peace periods between the Iraqi Kurds and the rulers in Baghdad have taken place a number of times in the twentieth century. Nevertheless, each time this has only been temporary, and the peace ended whenever the government in Baghdad felt confident enough that it could overcome the Kurds militarily. In other words, as demonstrated in this work, peace or talks thereof have been directly related to the changes in the balance of power between the Iraqi Kurds and the central government in Baghdad. Whenever this has changed in favour of Baghdad, Baghdad has chosen to use military means to *resolve* its Kurdish Issue. Further, this balance of power has been, and still is, profoundly affected by factors outside of Iraq.

In addition to the historical period of the issue covered in this book, the impermanent nature of peace is evident by the aftermath of the ill-fated advisory Kurdish Referendum on independence—held on September 25, 2017. After the referendum, Iraqi forces and Popular Mobilisation Shia militias, with the consent of both Iran and Turkey, if not the direct involvement of Iranian troops, attacked Kurdish fronts and expelled Kurdish Peshmerga forces from what are called disputed territories between the Kurdish autonomous region and the central authorities in Baghdad. The Kurds had initially liberated these lands and protected its inhabitants from ISIS rule. These territories were subjected to an Arabisation campaign under former Iraqi governments. After the demise of Saddam Hussein's regime, the Kurds insisted on having their lands back, from which they had been expelled in pre-2003 Iraq.

This book endeavours to go into the roots of these and to offer a detailed account of much of this history in terms of the Cold War, regional and national Iraqi politics, and the effect of these on the Iraqi Kurds. Compelled by the need to detail, the focal point of the book is from the founding of the republic of Iraq in 1958 to the conclusion of yet another tragic chapter in the Kurds' history in 1975.

When the attitude of the post-referendum context of the US and other powers are considered—doing nothing—and in fact colluding with the Iraqi army and militias to attack the Kurds, one cannot but recall the 1975 bitter history that the Kurds have with the US and Iran in particular, and also Israel to some extent. This is as if history is repeating itself. What is particularly striking this time, also, is that pro-Iranian Iraqi militias known as Popular Mobilisation Units were on the back of US armoured vehicles forcing through Kurdish front lines, in some cases rolling over Kurdish Peshmerga members who were powerless to stop the advanced US-made armour, and the US being aware of this, and their plans, while doing nothing, with President Trump stating that the US will not be involved in this fight. In fact, one may argue that the Trump administration, or the US, supposedly allied with the Iraqi Kurds, gave tacit approval to Iran to eliminate Kurdish hopes of statehood in Iraq, and lose over 50% of the territory the Kurds were administrating, including the oil-rich city of Kirkuk. These are all while no single American service member has died on Kurdish lands so far from hostile action and that the Iraqi Kurds were central in containing ISIS and the eventual clearance of Mosul from ISIS. Mosul city was cleared by the Iraqi army and its allied Shia militias, but nonetheless the Kurdish Peshmerga played a pivotal part in the initial encirclement of that city.

It is not the intention of this book to study the Iraqi Kurds in the above context, but what it does is to offer a solid background on the Iraqi Kurds' issue within Iraq, with the effect of Iraqi, regional and Cold War politics on this issue in an earlier chapter of Kurdish and Middle Eastern history. The basics of this history, however, one may assert, has remained unchanged when it comes to regional and international effects of politics on the status of the Iraqi Kurds. And this brief mentioning of the recent post-referendum developments here is evident of this. It may be suggested that to understand the Iraqi Kurdish Issue within Iraq, and the latest developments, it is important to go back to an earlier time and see why an enduring peace has failed so far and is likely to also fail in the future unless the two sides, and indeed the international community, offer the last say to the ordinary Kurdish people within Iraq to decide on their own political future, or for this issue to be resolved through an impartial international tribunal in accordance with international law concerning self-determination of peoples, allowing both sides equal representation.

Introduction

The lands that the Kurds inhabit straddle primarily four countries: Turkey, Iran, Iraq and Syria. Since the end of WWI and the demarcation of the current borders of the Middle East, successive Kurdish generations have strived for self-rule and/or statehood in one or the other of these countries, sometimes contemporaneously, sometimes across borders and often resulting in armed conflict and rebellion.[1] This book presents a study of a part of that often bitter history, the *Kurdish Issue*, comprising a political narrative of the Iraqi Kurds between the years 1958 and 1975. Specified by breath of focus, a number of issues may be identified as addressed in this history (i.e. in respect of the effects on the Iraqi Kurds), namely, (1) regarding the *Cold War*, US and Soviet policies, focusing in particular on those of the former; (2) at the regional level, issues such as Iran–Egypt tensions, Iraq–Iran tensions and the Arab–Israeli wars; and (3) in *Iraq*, tensions within the Iraqi political class.

Regarding the periodisation, the year 1958 is selected as the starting point because this was when the monarchy in Iraq, installed with the British Mandate, was overthrown and a republic established. It was a consequential year not only for the country, but also, and more broadly, in the region, with profound implications for Middle Eastern politics and the Cold War in the Middle East.[2] Within Iraq, the Kurdish liberation movement developed and, from 1961, the Kurds' September Revolution, their *Şorrşî Eylul*, ensued. This was to outlive three governments in Baghdad while enduring successive Iraqi attacks bringing such death and destruction that charges of genocide can be raised. Then, in 1975, came the Algiers Accord, selected as the end-point here since it constituted the abandonment of the Iraqi Kurds by Iran, followed by the US and Israel and consequently the catastrophic collapse of the revolution.[3]

In terms of geopolitics, the superpowers (US and the USSR) and the regional powers of Israel, Egypt and Jordan, as well as Turkey, Iran and Iraq all had a stake in the Kurdish Issue in one way or another during the 1958–1975 period. This was further to internal Iraqi and inter-Kurdish politics, which comprise another and interrelated side of the Kurdish Issue there. Due to this complexity, clearly, it is not possible to elaborate on every single question that can be raised in respect of the relations between the above-mentioned actors. Attention is generally limited, therefore, to developments that impacted *on* the Iraqi Kurds, that is, on political

2 Introduction

relations *external* to them. This research is *not* a study of the Iraqi Kurds themselves, that is, and nor of their relations with Baghdad or Middle Eastern politics or the Cold War per se. Conversely, a number of issues *are* studied at national, regional and international levels.

At the international level, as indicated, US and Russian policies insofar as they affected the Iraqi Kurds are determined. At the regional level, tensions and insecurities between Iran and Arab nationalism, largely spearheaded by President Nasser in Egypt, and including Iran–Iraq relations and the effects of these on the status of the Iraqi Kurds are explored. And further, at country level, the impact of Iraqi and also intra-Kurdish politics are considered (i.e. while not a focus in their own right, these are considered insofar as they bear on the narrative).

Aim of this book

In a nutshell, this book seeks to investigate a little-covered topic with original source material that properly incorporates a Kurdish input. Unpacking and explicating that, first, one should note that of all the works on the subject (as cited in the following pages) and at the time of writing this book, the only one that is wholly dedicated to the present concern and period is the book by Bryan Gibson, and even that is largely a study of US policy towards Iraq rather than of the Iraqi Kurds.[4] Indeed, the lack of coverage of the issue under discussion, the under-representation of the Kurds in Middle Eastern politics generally and during the Cold War in particular, is well recognised. This becomes apparent when one consults texts that include these subjects, such as Gibson's, or when one studies the large volumes of primary sources, as is the case here.

In relation to US foreign policy and the Kurds, for example, Marianna Charountaki has stated that 'it is impossible to discuss a generalized US foreign policy towards the Kurds since each Kurdish cause is different'.[5] This implies that 'each Kurdish cause' in the four different 'parent states' does, indeed, merit a dedicated study of its own, due to the differing compositions and hierarchies of the actors involved. Gunter has also observed that 'The United States does not really have any grand foreign policy strategy towards the Kurds because they live in four separate states'.[6] The indication is that general studies of the Kurds do not do justice to the issue due to its complexity and that specialised, finely focused studies are necessary, which is surely correct.

Focusing on the Iraqi policy of the George W. Bush administrations in his doctoral thesis and in connection to the scarcity of such specialised studies, Mohammed Shareef also observed that:

> [...] little can be found focusing solely on US Iraq policy. Furthermore, within this context, even less can be found on US policy towards Kurdish Iraq. *Modern scholarship fails heavily in describing accurately the highly significant and parallel US interaction with Iraq's Kurds.*

Introduction   3

and

> The Kurdish aspect of US Iraq policy *is heavily under-researched...*
> [emphasis added].[7]

Gibson has also commented that the 'historiography—or the history of [the] evolution of a historical debate—of US-Iraqi relations during the Cold War is still in its infancy'.[8] Along these lines also, Kenneth Osgood has remarked that 'We know more about the 1991 Gulf War than we do about US-Iraqi relations during the five decades of the Cold War that led up to it'.[9] There appears to be a broad consensus in published scholarship testifying to a lack of literature in this area.

Regarding the second main reason for this book, the issue of the sources—most importantly—fundamentally, in fact, the Kurds' side of the story has been left out by some writers who have most closely studied the subject. Doubtless, this is in part language-related. The present work, authored by a native speaker of Kurdish, is at an obvious advantage and thus able to assist in developing a fuller picture. Actually, there are a number of primary Kurdish sources of great significance for the topic at hand that have not previously been considered.

As well as the issue of language barriers, this omission has also been due to the specific interests of scholars addressing different research questions, as in the case of Mohammed Shareef and Marianna Charountaki.[10] Although these authors have conducted a good number of oral history interviews and an admirable work in their own research frameworks, Shareef and Charountaki's works only briefly cover the period of the present topic and the actors involved (see below). Simply put, they were not much concerned with the same matters as those that occupy the present enquiry. Moreover, on the issue of sources generally, there are other, non-Kurdish data sources now available that previously were not. There are literally thousands of recently declassified US and also UK archives, relevant materials that have been largely unexplored, especially for the purposes of the focus here. Regarding this issue, it was only in 2014 that Shareef remarked thus:

> Due to the contemporary nature of this study, my research has been profoundly handicapped by the lack of unclassified documents allowing a greater and detailed assessment of US Iraq policy under the George W. Bush administration. It has been additionally hampered by the lack of unclassified documents from previous administrations.[11]

And in 2011, Charountaki also noted that:

> The dearth of literature on the research topic [that she had studied] results from the fact that the Kurdish Issue is still in flux. Additionally, the release of official US documents relevant to the theme under examination has occurred only recently from around 2005 or a bit early 2003. I tried to fill the gap through reference to an extensive collection of scholarly writings on the Kurds as a nation, Kurdish history and the current status of the Kurds. Most

4   *Introduction*

of my primary information was drawn from the interviews, US government electronic sources and US congressional records and reports.[12]

The present study has not faced such obstacles; on the contrary, it has had the luxury of being able to make use of a large number of American archives, enjoying access to the declassified materials to which Shareef and Charountaki allude as well as to additional materials that have been further declassified since they wrote. In other words, the current work brings the contemporary scholarship up to date.

Clearly, the varying research concerns and timing of archive release may be considered technical factors that bear on the telling of any recent history; there is always a value in the development of new perspectives and updating information. The issue of language and source material, however, is a little different, since it concerns structural issues in narrative presentation. Where native language sources go un- or under-employed, there then develops an urgent need for work making use of these and the perspectives they bring. In some cases of the existing literature, an overly heavy and sometimes near exclusive reliance on American sources has meant, for example, that claims made by the Shah and relayed to the Americans by Iranian sources have not been cross-checked. Findings have been stated without the recourse to confirmatory evidential triangulation. Due to the conflict of interest between what Kurds view as national liberation and the states that have control over them view as separatism and secession, one just cannot substitute Iranian for Kurdish sources. Without the triangulation, one simply cannot know whether the conclusions are correct; there is only partial evidence which is neither confirmed nor denied. In other words, even where this book effectively reiterates rather than revises perspectives that are already in the public domain, it still has a value in converting their suppositions to knowledge, or changing what is thought to be known to what can really be said to be known.

There *are*, however, revisions to the history here, and *primarily* because even among studies focusing on the Kurds, the most substantial sources in relation to the period covered by this study *are* lacking in appropriate primary Kurdish references. Roham Alvandi's otherwise excellent work, for instance, one may suggest, is influenced by Iranian sources—the Shah or his inner circles—and thus appears to attempt to vindicate the Shah for his betrayal of the Kurds, accepting his claim that the Kurds had already been defeated and thus the narrative of the Shah having had no other choice but to scavenge whatever he could out of their fate in return for an Iraqi compromise on the Shatt al-Arab issue in 1975.[13] Kurdish sources strongly dispute and dismiss this.

For the Kurds, the Shah simply sold them out, and there was no justification for this as would later be claimed by the Shah—and taken up by Alvandi. In Chapter 4 of the present work—based on an examination and integration of Kurdish sources—it is argued that the reason why Saddam Hussein yielded to the Shah's demands regarding disputes in the Shatt al-Arab was precisely the opposite because of the failure of *Iraq's* military (in a major offensive intended to finish off the Kurdish resistance and quell the independence movement), which caused

Introduction 5

Saddam to resort to his undeclared *plan B* (i.e. to meet the Shah's demands). The question here, of course, is not whether or not Kurdish sources are more credible than Iranian ones, or vice versa, but to ensure that the different sides' accounts are all taken into consideration in aiming at something like an objective assessment of what really transpired—to which endeavour this book aims to contribute.

In addition to the English language translation of a memoir of Kurdish leader Masoud Barzani employed by Alvandi, this study uses Barzani's three other Kurdish memoir-series publications, which include rich documentary sections and cover the subject to 1975.[14] These Barzani memoir-series publications are only available in Kurdish and Arabic, which presumably explains their lack of employment until now. Similarly, there are a number of audiovisual materials in which eyewitnesses—former Kurdish officials—narrate much of the history this work covers. These interviews of a historical nature are produced by the Kurdish TV station *Rudaw* in a programme series that focus on the making of (Kurdish) history and are only available in Kurdish. These are essentially lengthy interviews of people who were very closely and actively involved in the events covered in this book. One such person, for instance, was a former Iraqi minister who enjoyed close relations with both Saddam Hussein and the USSR and who was also a high-ranking Iraqi Communist Party (ICP) figure; another was a Mustafa Barzani confidante, one of the highest trusted emissaries, who met with the Shah at critical times. What is clear, therefore, is that the Kurds' side of the story is largely neglected, and for the most part this is due to language barriers as Kurdish is not a widely spoken language by non-native speakers. This research, conducted by a native Kurdish speaker, intends to bring the Kurds' side of this history into light.

Positioning and context

With the literature in the field still in development, in its infancy even, and unexplored sources needing to be introduced and cross-checked, in particular to develop a more balanced narrative (i.e. by introducing Kurdish language sources), this book aims to take its place among a range of publications on the Kurds, particularly in Iraq, as well as on Middle Eastern politics and its international relations more generally (including bilateral state relations, such as between Iraq and Iran) and on the Cold War in the Middle East. The literature on the Kurds has flourished in recent times, which have witnessed the establishment of the field of Kurdish studies.[15] In this context, well-established contributions that are highly pertinent to the subject at hand include, in addition to those already cited by Marianna Charountaki and Michael Gunter, works or parts of works by Douglas Little, Lokman Meho, David Mack and Francis Ricciardone.[16] Recently, these have been joined by the books of Mohammed Shareef, Roham Alvandi, and Bryan Gibson as mentioned.[17] A book by Peter Hahn, like Kenneth Osgood's (mentioned), also focuses, albeit briefly, on the Iraqi Kurds in addressing broader US–Iraq relations.[18]

Among the other works and published materials on the Kurds and Kurdish politics and history are some that also touch upon US relations, although these are

6 *Introduction*

mostly not scholarly studies or else they briefly touch on the position of the Kurds in the Cold War, in US or USSR foreign polices in that period, or they do so in the context of a larger theme without making significant contributions to these relations, *or* else they focus on a time period outside of that covered here. Examples of such publications include works by Jonathan Randal, Quil Lawrence, David Mack, Francis Ricciardone, Aram Rafaat, Lokman Meho, Edmund Ghareeb, David Romano, Nader Entessar, Ofra Bengio, Edgar O'Ballance and David Kimche, Wrya Rahmani. Additionally, there are also works on US relations with Iraq that only very briefly look at the Kurds' struggle or place in this in the period of interest here.[19] Examples of these are the works by Peter L. Hahn (cited) and David Ryan with Patrick Kiely. Further, the contributions cited by Mack and Rafaat also comprise examples of works that concentrate on the post-1990s, alongside Stansfield's *Iraqi Kurdistan: Political Development and Emergent Democracy*, which focuses on the political developments in Iraqi Kurdistan from 1991,[20] so these may be taken as contextualising the present work by continuing the narrative from where these end.

Ricciardone briefly looks at US policy and the Kurds.[21] Similarly, the books by Meho and Rehmani are collections of documents from the US and other sources on issues pertaining to but not specifically focused on the subject at hand. Rehmani's Kurdish work also has an introductory addendum by the collector in which he interviews and explores a number of important sources, in particular, regarding Iran's use of the Kurds, and from them constructs a narrative of the events. David McDowall's *Modern History of the Kurds* may also be cited as another excellent book, and one that has informed the present work.[22]

In reviewing this extensive literature, the present work ought to be contextualised in relation to and, as appropriate, with critical consideration of the most well-known relevant works in the field as well as those that are particularly pertinent to the subject. These may be listed as those by Charountaki, Entessar, and Shareef, together with Gunter, Little, Alvandi, and Gibson, paying particular attention to the latter four.

First, investigating the 'role of the Kurds in US foreign policy from World War II until Gulf War III (March 2003) and its aftermath', Marianna Charountaki focuses on two central questions, namely, 'whether the Kurds have influenced US foreign policy, and if there is such a thing as a relationship between US foreign policy and the Kurds in the form of an interaction between a state and "non-state" actor'.[23] In Chapter 4, 'US foreign policy towards the Kurds, 1945–1990', Charountaki finds that there was no relationship as such between the Kurds and the US in the 1950s because the US was more preoccupied with preventing the USSR from attaining regional domination.[24] Thus, the present work starts from that beginning point in charting the development of the Iraqi Kurd–US relationship within the Cold War and the regional political affairs.

Next, Nader Entessar has written on issues of present interest but in a broader period and looking at international relations in the Middle East in relation to the Kurds, including the Iraqi Kurds, so somewhat in the reverse perspective to that taken here.[25] Importantly, I think, Entessar recognises that there was essentially a

Introduction 7

cold war between Nasser and the Shah due to their respective alliances with the Soviets and with the West, as a result of which each viewed the other as a threat. Indeed, this is a theme that also runs through the present work, with its impact on the Iraqi Kurds closely analysed. Entessar further notes that the 1958 Iraqi Revolution gave a new impetus to the Kurdish Issue in Iraq, as essentially changing the political dynamics of the region, thus confirming the significance of the year 1958, taken as the starting point here.

For his part, Mohammed Shareef seeks to address the issue of change and continuity in US policy towards Iraq.[26] While largely taking 1979 as its starting point, the book does, however, include a section in a chapter on US–Iraqi Kurdish relations, 'The Iraqi Kurds in US Foreign Policy: From Kennedy to Obama', that covers the 1961–1975 time period investigated here.[27] Noting that his work from Chapters 1 to 5 focuses on US policy towards 'Arab Iraq',[28] Shareef also recognises that:

> [w]hat contemporary scholarship largely fails to address is US relations with Iraq's Kurds, the second largest ethnicity in Iraq, who were largely absent from government in Baghdad until the toppling of Saddam Hussein in 2003.[29]

Indeed, that is a major topic here. In considering the impact of regional and Cold War politics on the Iraqi Kurds, of which US policy is only one aspect—albeit a major one given the US position as a superpower and its active role in the Middle East—the present work may thus be seen as extending Shareef's in this respect, regarding both subject matter and, clearly, detail (the 1961–1975 section in Shareef's book only occupies about ten pages).

Moving to works that require a fuller consideration, we can start with Michael Gunter, who has generally been concerned with the complexity of the Kurdish Issue and the division of Kurdish territory. In the (2011) *Five Stages of American Foreign Policy Towards the Kurds*, however, he develops an analysis of the relevant history of US relations, noting also 'foreign influences' in the struggle with Baghdad under Barzani's leadership. The first of Gunter's five stages starts from WWI and Woodrow Wilson's Fourteen Points and runs to the early 1970s, while his second moves from there to the Kurdish revolution and the capitulation of 1975. In addition to the above article, the most relevant part of a book that he has authored consists of six pages.[30] The present work, therefore, may be read in the light of this staged development and as focusing on what, again, is only touched upon in the context of rather different concerns.

Crucially, Gunter recognises the Shah's role in bringing in the US to back the Kurds, albeit symbolically, as part of a strategic game played for its own— Iran's—purposes. Indeed, the recurrent theme of external interests is the lack of a genuine intention to support the cause of the Kurds as worthy in itself, in Iraq or elsewhere, which is especially the case for the regional actors with sizable Kurdish populations of their own. Gunter looks at the Pike House Committee Report—the Committee being a Congressional investigation established to

8 *Introduction*

investigate illegal CIA activities—and considers its mentions of US involvement in the Kurds' war with Iraq. In so doing, Gunter ties covert US support to the Kurds to a number of reasons, the most important of which being, first, the US responding to the calls of one of its allies (the Shah) to contain Iraq (a Soviet ally) in the Cold War and, second, a US tactic of preoccupying Iraqi troops with problems at home so that they would be unable to participate in any future Arab–Israeli conflict. In other words, US support for the Iraqi Kurds was based on its twin strategic interests related to Russia and Israel (opposing one and supporting the other). That made the Kurds disposable.

Gunter also states that US aid to the Kurds was given in response to Barzani's desire for US involvement so that it would act as a guarantor for them and thus prevent the Shah from summarily abandoning them when it suited. And he further proposes that the US supported the Iraqi Kurds basically to secure access to their oil and thereby benefit from that. Barzani is quoted as saying that he 'would turn over the oil fields to the United States' if it supported the Kurds in their bid for independence.[31]

However, the US was well aware of the landlocked geography of Iraqi Kurdistan and, indeed, the hostile concurrent geopolitics of the region in relation to any Kurdish statehood. The only way America would have been able to make use of Kurdish oil would have been through Iran or Turkey, and it is widely recognised (including by Gunter) that the Shah's support for the Kurds was tactical, as he aimed to use the Iraqi Kurds to bring Iraq to submit to Iran's Shatt al-Arab demands.[32] For the Shah, friendship with the Iraqi Kurds was primarily just a means to this end. Iranian warmth certainly did not extend to the birth of any form of a Kurdish entity in Iraq, Gunter argues, which would give succour to his own, Iranian Kurds—again, a perspective developed in the present work. Gunter subsequently goes on to review the relationship between the Iraqi Kurds and Israel, so the relevant part of his book is another good indicator, albeit brief, of the effect of regional and international politics on the political status of the Iraqi Kurds in 1958–1975 (and beyond).

Among Douglas Little's contributions to the general subject area considered here, his 2010 article on *The United States and the Kurds* is key, examining as it does 'three key episodes', which are all directly related to the Kurds in Iraq. These are (1) secret backing given to Kurds by both the Eisenhower and Kennedy administrations intended to weaken the Qasim regime; (2) the 'cynical covert action launched by Richard Nixon and Henry Kissinger in Iraqi Kurdistan, with help from Iran and Israel',[33] after the Treaty of Friendship and Cooperation in 1972 between Iraq and the USSR; and (3) the half-hearted US attempt to use the Kurds to foment regime change in Iraq in the early 1990s. Little states that 'In each case the US government exploited long-lasting anti-Arab resentments among the Kurds' and 'secretly supplied US guns or dollars or sometimes both',[34] but adding that it pulled back when the situation escalated. Little also examines the connection of the Cold War to the Kurdish Mahabad Republic as well as Barzani's return from the Soviet Union after the Iraqi Revolution of 1958.

Introduction 9

Essentially, Little argues that the US saw the Kurdish Issue through the Cold War prism and examines the issue within this context. He makes an innovative contribution in examining the relationship between the Iraqi Kurds and the Cold War when it comes to the US. However, a number of points need to be raised, and clarifications are needed, particularly in light of the variety and large volume of data accessible and employed in the present research.

Firstly, as noted, Little states that the work examines three major episodes—the Eisenhower and the Kennedy administrations' backing for the Iraqi Kurds and Nixon's covert operations in Iraqi Kurdistan—and, '*In each case*, the US government exploited long-lasting anti-Arab resentments among the Kurds, secretly supplied US guns or dollars or sometimes both, and helped ignite an insurrection in Kurdistan' (emphasis added).[35] However, the argument presented is not convincing in showing how, during the Eisenhower and Kennedy eras, the US 'secretly supplied' the arms and money. In fact, the evidence examined by the present study suggests the contrary, that the Kennedy administration, at least, supplied munitions to Iraq to be used *against* the Kurds. This will be examined in Chapter 2 of this book.[36]

More recently, Roham Alvandi (2014), who describes his book *Nixon, Kissinger, and the Shah* as 'a study of Iran's impact on how the United States fought the Cold War', has looked, in the third chapter, at how and why both the Shah and Israel were involved in arming Barzani's Kurdish Peshmerga against Iraq in the 1960s.[37] Alvandi finds that the two parties pursued this tactic for different reasons and thus with different strategies. Unlike the Israeli governments, he notes, the Shah was not interested in the Iraqi Kurds winning any sort of autonomy; rather, he was seeking to preoccupy the Iraqi army in Iraqi Kurdistan so that it would not pose a threat to Iran in its territorial disagreements with Iraq. Recalling the Mahabad Republic of 1946, in which Barzani himself served and fought to defend, Alvandi makes the point that the Shah would not have wished a Kurdish entity within Iraq as the shockwaves of this would have affected the Kurds of Iran and thus Iran itself. Alvandi explains all this as an extension of the Cold War for Iran, in combination with its territorial disputes with Iraq.

Alvandi also states that the US, throughout the 1960s, refused to be dragged into the Kurds' conflict with Iraq. This clearly contradicts the argument presented by Little that the Kennedy and Eisenhower administrations assisted them. Instead, according to Alvandi, and correctly so, the US saw this issue as an entirely internal Iraqi matter.[38] Thus,

> the Americans were suspicious of Barzani's ties with Moscow and feared that a civil war within Iraq would not only generate instability that the Iraqi communists could exploit, but also make Baghdad more dependent on military assistance from the Soviet Union.[39]

Further light on this matter is shed in the present work.

Alvandi also presents a history of how Iran and Israel's relations with the Iraqi Kurds developed from the early 1960s, focusing on the role of the Shah and the

10   *Introduction*

nature of his relations with the Kurds. He also covers the internal Iraqi political affairs leading up to the March 1970 Accord between Iraq and the Kurds, together with Iran and Israel's continuing assistance as well as their interest in the continuation of the war in Kurdistan—but somewhat briefly.[40]

Also of concern to Alvandi, and especially related to this present book, is how the Shah managed to sell the Iraqi Kurds' cause to the White House in the mid-1970s as one of fighting the Cold War and preventing a pro-Soviet coalition government between the Ba'ath Party, the Iraqi Kurds and the ICP. This is studied in detail in the present work in Chapter 4. Like Gunter, Alvandi highlights the Shatt issue and how the Iraqi Kurds were essentially only a means to an end.[41] Primarily concerned with the influence of the Shah on the US in the Cold War, Alvandi thus examines the Shah's role in this and how he managed to draw it into the conflict.[42]

Reflecting on the chapter in Alvandi's book—*Iran's Secret War with Iraq*—that concerns the Iraqi Kurds and is thus relevant here, we see that not only does it allude to the impact on them of regional politics and the Cold War, a major part of the focus here, but also presents commendable original work employing an array of primary sources in relation to Iran–US involvements in Iraqi Kurdistan, in particular, in respect of the period from 1969 to March 1975 (notwithstanding a lack in respect of Kurdish sources, as critiqued earlier in this book). However, the overall subject of Alvandi's work is a study of relations between the Nixon administration and the Shah, and it is only from this perspective that he introduces the Iraqi Kurds.

Finally, the most recent scholarly addition to this category of relevant literature is Bryan Gibson's (2015) *Sold Out? US Foreign Policy, Iraq, the Kurds and the Cold War*. Gibson 'underscores the reactive nature of US foreign policy during the Cold War, while assessing America's policies towards Iraq'. He explains that 'As a study of the Cold War', his book is 'situated within a wider debate about superpower intervention in the Third World'. Gibson shows that 'America's intervention in Iraq—a Third World nation—at the height of the Cold War contributed to the country's political and economic destabilisation and its continual national upheavals and agonies'.[43] This indicates the nature of Gibson's work and its relationship to the Iraqi Kurds, and it is indeed a major contribution not only to the study of US foreign policy towards Iraq but also to the Kurds' position in this matter.

Moreover, Gibson shows how the US 'moved from being an unsophisticated observer of events in 1958–59 to becoming a direct protagonist in Iraq during 1972–75 through its own covert programme to support Iraq's Kurdish rebels'.[44] One important point to note is that Gibson recognises the significance of the Iraqi Kurds as an *actor* in regional and Iraqi affairs and has sought to explain the implications of this, calling the Kurds' conflict with Baghdad the 'Kurdish War'.[45] Indeed, the present work acquiesces with the use of the 'Kurdish War' as a more accurate term for the fight between the Kurds and the central Iraqi governments in Baghdad than words such as 'conflict' or 'rebellion'—for the simple reason that there were protracted hostilities on a large scale that often involved the

Introduction 11

bulk of the Iraqi army. With regards to this terminology, David Kimche has also observed that 'By 1965, the Kurdish insurrection had grown into a full-scale war'.[46]

Overall, Gibson's work examines a number of issues related to the Kurds as well as to the wider region in reference to America's policy. In Chapter 1, in narrating US foreign policy towards Iraq from 1958 and the consequences of the Iraqi Revolution both on regional polices and those of the superpowers, he refers to the Iraqi Kurds, from the Eisenhower administration to Kennedy. The roles of Egypt's President Nasser and Iraq's Qasim, army leader of the revolt that established the Republic and its first leader, are also linked to US concerns about communism by Gibson, who explores a large number of US archives and secondary sources. In seeking to show how Iraq had become a 'Cold War battleground'[47] by 1958 and how the US and the Soviets both sought to exert influence on successive Iraqi governments and ensure that the country did not join the other side, Gibson extensively analyses the American and also Russian policies towards Iraq and, within this context, as related to the Iraqi Kurds.

However, since Britain's role in the Middle East frequently enters as a major theme in Gibson's work, the inclusion of British governmental archives would have strengthened it, a point that applies similarly to Kurdish sources. Importantly in this respect, the author has relied on secondary sources and US archives in order to draw his conclusions on the Kurds and Britain's stance on the whole issue. One disadvantage of relying so heavily on American sources is that American diplomats primarily tended to report what they had heard from the Iraqi government and Iran's sides rather than directly from the Kurds. There is, thus, a lack of balance, which does not allow the presentation of an accurate picture of events, particularly given the conflict of interest between the established states and the Kurds around the issue of Kurdish self-determination. Accordingly, given the perception of the state actors (Iran, Turkey, Iraq and Syria) of any Kurdish autonomy as an existential threat to their territorial integrity, one cannot have expected the US to have heard anything positive about the Kurds from these states. The aspect of sources is expanded upon in the next section. There are a number of other points, generally related to this, that should also be noted here.

First, the evidence for a number of claims made by the book is not convincing. For instance, the author states that 'throughout the spring of 1963, the Kennedy administration pressed the Ba'ath Party to make reasonable concessions to the Kurds [but] without much success'.[48] In fact, however, the Kennedy administration approved a $55 million arms deal to provide Iraq with arms, despite US officials themselves having recognised that there was an element of truth in the Soviet's charge of genocide in Kurdistan, as raised in the UN by the USSR in July 1963.[49] In other words, US decision-makers were aware that the arms would end up being used against the Kurds and the destruction of Kurdistan.

Furthermore, according to Gibson, under the Johnson administration, Britain as well as Iran and Israel 'were all giving the Kurds military and economic support to destabilise the pro-Nasser Arif regime'.[50] However, the evidence available to the present research in the form of large volumes of British state national archives

12   *Introduction*

unfolds that not only was Britain not aiding the Kurds but that in fact it was playing an *adverse* role with regards to the Kurdish national liberation aspirations. Britain supplied Hawker Hunter bombers to Iraq with devastating effects in Kurdistan; it also imposed *informal* conditions on the visas of visiting Kurdish emissaries, requiring abstention from public activities such as talking to the media since, according to the Foreign Office, it 'could be embarrassing to us both in our relations with Iraq and vis-à-vis public opinions here in the context of our decision to supply arms to Iraq'.[51] Equally, Britain spearheaded the West's effort to derail Soviet attempts at the UN to discuss 'Genocide in Kurdistan' due to the connection of this to the Cold War and the regional politics.[52] The evidence that exists showing Britain's negative attitude towards the Kurdish national liberation movement from 1958 to 1975 is conclusive, and, in contrast, there is no evidence to show that Britain backed the Kurds by any means. These matters are considered here in detail in Chapters 2–4 of this book.

While providing a detailed narrative of the Kennedy administration's policies towards Iraq until the end of Qasim's regime in February 1963, Gibson also states that the Soviets had offered 'limited degree of diplomatic and military assistance' to the Kurds after the breakout of war in June 1963 between the Ba'ath and the Kurds.[53] However, in light of alternative evidence, the present work disputes the idea that the Soviets provided 'military assistance'; rather, according to informed Kurdish sources, what they have offered to the Kurds was limited financial assistance with which they could attempt to procure arms themselves in the black market, which is rather different. Chapter 2 will elaborate on this further.

Overall, Gibson has examined US policy towards Iraq, as a superpower, and whether this can be explained by Cold War considerations, finding that it can be, and it is within this context of US policy that he looks at the affairs of the Kurds.[54] Gibson emphasises that Cold War considerations dominated US thinking in its relations with the Iraqi Kurds, while also examining other, related regional issues, such as the Arab–Israel conflict and Israel's stake in assisting the Kurds and the US interest in these. Indeed, my doctoral research—the predecessor of this book—was conducted concurrently (it seems) but independent of Gibson's research and concurs that Cold War politics had a fundamental effect on US policy in relation to how they saw the Iraqi Kurdish independent movement. Further, the US was not the only global power whose views of the Iraqi Kurds were profoundly affected by the Cold War, but the UK, as a long-time hegemon of the Middle East, is another example. What is left to say in relation to Gibson's notable work is that it may thus be the most detailed account of the history of US relations with the Iraqi Kurds within the timeframe to date. However, its specific focus along with issues regarding source material leave many matters to be further considered, as explained in the next section.

A second category of relevant literature consists of works focusing not on the Kurds but on the wider international relations of the Middle East, on politics among the states of the region and on its Cold War politics, yet which may be applicable here for their coverage of the Kurds as used by the powers to advance their local and regional interests, and/or because they introduce related issues and

Introduction 13

perspectives. Good examples of such publications are the works written or edited by Trita Parsi, Louise Fawcett, Fred Halliday, Beverley Milton-Edwards with Peter Hinchcliffe and volumes edited by L. Carl Brown and Raymond Hinnebusch with Anoushiravan Ehteshami, in addition to another work by Hinnebusch and pieces by David W. Lesch, and Yezid Sayigh with Avi Shlaim.[55]

Parsi's book on relations between the US, Iran and Israel in the Middle East includes a consideration of the undisclosed dealings of these countries with the Iraqi Kurds featuring a number of interviews with US and Israeli officials that were closely involved at the time. Again, Parsi seeks to explain each actor's particular interests and essentially how Iran betrayed the Kurdish movement in Iraq in 1975. Noting the difficulties and challenges involved in studying the international relations of the Middle East, Fawcett notes both an internal Middle Eastern studies aspect and the external international relations dimensions, with the latter impacting on the former and the two only begun to be integrated towards the end of the twentieth century and the international relations dimensions largely observed from the outside. Such analysis, one may argue, is also applicable to the Kurdish Issue, with the broader dimensions concerning US–Russian involvement (here, historically the Cold War), or rather, the complicating impacts of this.

Brown's edited volume considers the international relations of the Middle Eastern powers as well as the policies of the major world powers, including the US and UK, towards the Middle East, while Hinnebusch and Ehteshami look at the Middle East in the context of international relations as a regional system, taking into account the foreign policies of a number of countries, including Iraq, Iran and Turkey. Hinnebusch's own work is another example of a comprehensive study of Middle Eastern affairs, in which he notes that the Middle East is 'the epicentre of world crisis, chronically war-prone and the site of the world's most protracted conflicts'—an observation that is as true today as it was when he made it, a decade and a half ago, and which is highly relevant here.[56] As well as addressing, among other things, issues of identity, sovereignty and foreign policymaking, along with, in relation to the Kurds, the incongruity of identity and territory in the Middle East, Hinnebusch notes that the Kurds 'have been regularly used by their host states', while, in their turn, they have also sought to exploit the inter-state rivalries to their own ends.[57]

Milton-Edwards and Hinchcliffe are concerned with 'the nature of conflict in the Middle East'[58] and putting these conflicts in their wider context, which includes coverage also of 'the forgotten Kurds'.[59] There are also country-specific works on Iran and Iraq which offer historical overviews that are relevant to the present work, such as Nikki R. Keddie and Ervand Abrahamian on Iran, and Charles Tripp and Gareth Stansfield on Iraq.[60] Sayigh and Shlaim's book is an example of the rich texts on the Cold War in the Middle East and the Middle East during this post-WWII period.

Regarding the Cold War itself, an excellent eclectic text by Arne Westad looks at its historical evolution, origins in the Third World (under which nomenclature, of course, the Middle East fell) and how and what motivated the superpowers to intervene there. The CIA involvement in Iraqi Kurdistan in the mid-1970s is

14   *Introduction*

covered as among the various superpower interventions, but only minimally. In the journal *Diplomatic History*, Douglas Little remarks that 'Nowhere has the story of American covert action in the Middle East since 1945 been shrouded in greater mystery than in Iraq'.[61] Other articles pertaining to the region, its states and the Cold War include one by Alvandi and another by Little, as well as by Eric Jacobsen and Brandon Wolfe-Hunnicutt.[62]

Among the relevant contributions on broader US–Middle East relations and politics, Matthew Jacob's book on the Middle East and American Foreign Policy until 1967 examines the evolution of US views of the region through half of the twentieth century; Ray Takeyh and Steven Simon study ten significant crises in the Middle East during the Cold War to show the successes of America's strategy; and Burton Kaufman surveys US policy towards the Arab world. Other scholars among whose publications the present work is positioned or whose works have been consulted in the developing stages of this present study and that have enlightened this study include Yakub Halabi, Joyce Kaufman, Robert J. Pauly and Patrick Kiely, Roby Barrett, Michael J. Hogan, and Thomas G. Paterson; Bruce W. Jentleson; Thomas M. Kane; Richard Jackson and Matt McDonald.[63]

Primary sources and methodology

In addition to the literature on the Kurds, the Middle East and the Cold War as reviewed and which included recourse to the fruits of a comprehensive search through publication databases covering ETHOS, Index Islamicus, Thesis.com, ProQuest and COPAC together with the *Journal of Cold War Studies* and *Cold War History*, the information types and databases that this research has utilised can be broadly categorised into American, UK, and Kurdish sources, with others, all of which were of a primary nature.

The American databases employed hold well over two million governmental documents in total, from which the documents from the Foreign Relations of the United States (FRUS) has proved invaluable. FRUS contains archives from the 'Presidential libraries, Departments of State and Defense, National Security Council, Central Intelligence Agency, Agency for International Development, and other foreign affairs agencies as well as the private papers of individuals involved in implementing US foreign policy'.[64] Also documents from The WikiLeaks Public Library of US Diplomacy's 'The Kissinger Cables' have been explored for this research. The Digital National Security Archives (DNSA), Gales Declassified Documents Reference System (DDRS), and memoirs and newspaper publications from the US, among others, have also all been informative in producing this work.

When it comes to UK documents, time spent at the British National Archives in Kew was rewarded with an extensive amount of documents on the Kurds which proved to be an integral part of this research. The UK was still heavily involved in the Middle East during the period in question and, of course, it was also a leading member of the Western Bloc during the Cold War. In addition to the US and UK

Introduction   15

sources, primary Kurdish sources are also looked into. The Kurdish sources comprise memoirs and documentary interviews in Kurdish with people who had first account information on the Kurds' side related to the issues covered in this book. These are in addition to a personal interview. I have also used sources originating in Iran and the USSR.

Regarding the Kurdish interviews, I have incorporated accounts given by a number of prominent figures who were core members of the Kurdish leadership and thus closely involved in much of the history covered here. First, I telephone interviewed Dr Mahmoud Othman, a prominent Kurdish politician for this study, via Skype. Mahmoud Othman was Mustafa Barzani's confidante and the head of the Kurdish delegation for the negotiations that led up to the March 1970 Accord between the Kurdistan Democratic Party (KDP) and the Ba'ath Iraqi government. He was also one of the two Kurdish representatives that for the first time met high-ranking US officials in 1972 in Washington (Chapter 4).[65] Dr Othman also met the Shah of Iran on a number of occasions and at decisive times for the Kurds. He was one of the Kurdish leaders that met the Shah for the last time in March 1975, after the Algiers Accord, in which the Shah told them what he had in store for them as a result of the Accord.[66]

Second, regarding the documentary interviews, I have used a series of detailed audiovisual interviews in which Muhsen Dizaei, Mohammed Aziz, Omar Othman and Mukaram Talabani each separately share their accounts of this history. Dizaei is the only other living member of the Kurdish delegation that negotiated the 1970 Accord and was also made Minister for the Development of the North in 1968 under the Ba'ath Party rule. Mohammed Aziz was director of Mustafa Barzani's headquarters and also deputy head of the KDP's intelligence agency, *Parastn*, when the Kurdish national movement under Mustafa Barzani collapsed as a result of the Algiers Accords. Mukaram Talabani is a former high-ranking Kurdish ICP official and became an Iraqi Government Minister in 1972 when the ICP joined the Ba'ath in the National Front Government. He also had close and lasting relations with Saddam Hussein—with whom he met on numerous occasions and had extensive discussions—as well as the Ba'ath leadership and the Soviets.[67]

Masoud Barzani's (Kurdish language) memoirs, as indicated, have been another major Kurdish source of information. Masoud Barzani, Mustafa Barzani's son, was the head of the *Parastn* when Iran and Iraq signed the Algiers Accord of March 1970. Similarly, Jalal Talabani's Kurdish memoir in the form of a dialogue with the author of that book has also proved to be instructive. Talabani was also often a chief representative of the KDP in the 1960s, including a meeting with President Gamal Abdel Nasser of Egypt regarding the Kurdish Issue in Iraq. He went on later to became Iraq's first Kurdish president between 2006 and 2014, and was head of one of the two main Kurdish political parties in Iraqi Kurdistan (the PUK) before his death in 2017. There are simply no other better and/or living Kurdish sources than these. Broadly speaking, this book introduces these sources into the literature for the first time in this field of study and it also tells the story from the Kurds' side as they saw it.

16　*Introduction*

Additionally, the Mitrokhin Archive, which is a Soviet archival source, the memoir of Asadollah Alam, Minister of Iran's Royal Court and a number of other sources have been exhausted.[68]

Structure

The book is divided into four chronological periods, corresponding to the four main chapters of the book. Following an introductory history of the early days of the Cold War and brief background, Chapter 1 'Iraqi Revolution, Kurdish hostilities' covers the period 1958–1962. The first main section of this chapter then shows how the development of the Cold War and its effects on regional politics negatively affected the Iraqi Kurds and how regional powers hostile to Kurdish self-rule played a significant role in this. This is then followed by coverage of the Iraqi Revolution of 1958 and its impact on superpower politics, on the region and ultimately on the Kurds. Next, the outbreak of hostilities in Iraqi Kurdistan and the perspectives of the two superpowers and the major regional powers on the Iraqi Kurds are analysed, along with the development of US and USSR policies towards the Iraqi Kurds and the link between global US policy in the Cold War and its effect on the Iraqi Kurds.

Chapter 2 'Seeking allies' covers the years 1963–1965. Within this period, the policies of the first Ba'ath regime, the regional aspects of this and superpower politics are studied, followed by further analysis of the US and the USSR's policies in the area. The heighted regional tensions between President Nasser of Egypt and the Shah of Iran, with the implications of this for Iraq and consequently on the Iraqi Kurds, and US policy from Kennedy to Truman make up further sections of this chapter.

Chapter 3 'Politics and struggle' covers the years 1965–1971. It looks at the Kurds' appeals to the US for help and how Cold War politics took precedence over the plight of the Kurds when it came to their war with Baghdad. The change of government in Baghdad upon a military coup is then considered, followed by further investigation of the Kurds' endeavours to obtain outside support. Another change of government in Baghdad and then Britain's withdrawal from the Gulf with the tensions arising from this are also covered in this chapter.

Chapter 4 'Hope and betrayal' concludes by addressing the topic for the years 1971–1975. This chapter explores how an opportunity was missed to remove the Ba'ath Party from power after US reluctance to back the plan, followed by consideration of the strengthening of Soviet–Iraqi relations, Iran's perception of insecurity and the use of its *Kurdish card* and the renewal of the war in Kurdistan and the various parties' interests in this. The chapter concludes by looking at the betrayal of the Kurds by their supposed allies together with observation of US foreign policy under Nixon and Ford in order to assess the link between US Cold War strategy and its impact on the Iraqi Kurds.

Finally, the conclusion reviews the main chapters. This comprises an outline of the major details, themes and arguments of the narrative as arranged by chapter.

Notes

1 For a detailed background, see, for example, Ghareeb, Edmund, *The Kurdish Question in Iraq* (New York, NY: Syracuse University Press, 1981), pp. 1–28; McDowall, David, *A Modern History of the Kurds* (London: I.B. Tauris, 2004); O'Ballance, Edgar, *The Kurdish Struggle, 1920–94* (Basingstoke: Macmillan, 1995); Romano, David, *The Kurdish National Movement; Opportunity, Mobilization and Identity* (New York, NY: Cambridge University Press, 2006); Entessar, Nader, *Kurdish Ethnonationalism* (Boulder, CO: Lynn Rienner Publishers, 1992).

2 See, for example, Gibson, Bryan R., *Sold Out? US Foreign Policy, Iraq, the Kurds and the Cold War* (New York, NY: Palgrave Macmillan, 2015), pp. xiv–31; Osgood, Kenneth, 'Eisenhower and Regime Change in Iraq: The United States and the Iraqi Revolution of 1958', in *America and Iraq: Policy-Making, Intervention and Regional Politics*, ed. by David Ryan and Patrick Kiely (London: Routledge, 2009), pp. 4–27; Aburish, Said, *Saddam Hussein: The Politics of Revenge* (London: Bloomsbury, 2001), pp. 36–44.

3 In contrast to words such as *rebellion* or *revolt* to describe Kurdish insurrections, Kurds usually refer to their attempts to achieve autonomy from the 'parent state' as *Şorrş* in Kurdish, which equates to *revolution* in English. See, for instance, the English and Kurdish titles of two of the volumes of Masoud Barzani's memoir series; while the actual contents of these works (the main texts) are in Kurdish (except one, which is in English), their titles are given in English too, where 'revolution' is employed, thus: Barzanî, Mes'ud, *Barzanî Û Bzutnewey Rizgarîxwazî Kurd: Bergî Sêyem, Beşî Yekem 1961–1975* [Barzani and the Kurdish Liberation Movement, Part iii, Vol. i: The September Revolution 1961–1975] (Hewlêr: Çapxaney wezaretî perwerde, 2004[?]); and Barzanî, Mes'ud, *Barzanî Û Bzutnewey Rizgarîxwazî Kurd: Bergî Sêyem, Beşî Duwem 1961–1975* [Barzani and the Kurdish Liberation Movement, Part iii, Vol. ii: The September Revolution 1961–1975] (Hewlêr: Çapxaney wezaretî perwerde, 2004[?]). See also Shareef, Mohammed, *The United States, Iraq and the Kurds: Shock, Awe and Aftermath* (Oxfordshire & New York, NY: Routledge, 2014), p. 137.

4 Gibson, op. cit.

5 Charountaki, Marianna, *The Kurds and US Foreign Policy: International Relations in the Middle East since 1945* (London & New York, NY: Routledge, 2011), p. 202.

6 Gunter, Michael M., 'The Five Stages of American Foreign Policy Towards the Kurds', *Insight Turkey*, 13 (2011), p. 93.

7 Majeed, Mohammed Shareef Jalal, 'President George W. Bush's Policy Towards Iraq: Change or Continuity?', (PhD, University of Durham, 2010), pp. 5 and 241.

8 Gibson, op. cit., p. xvi.

9 See Osgood, op. cit., pp. 4–7.

10 Shareef, op. cit.; Charountaki, op. cit.

11 Shareef, op. cit., p. 242.

12 Charountaki, op. cit., p. 3.

13 For example, Alvandi, Roham, *Nixon, Kissinger, and the Shah: The United States and Iran in the Cold War* (New York, NY: Oxford University Press, 2014, p. 110): 'The Shah's *only choice* was to use the winter lull in the fighting to secure a deal with Iraq, while the Kurds were still on their feet' (emphasis added); 'The Shah's faith in the Kurds' fighting ability was clearly wavering'.

18   *Introduction*

14   Barzanî, Mes'ud, *Barzanî Û Bzutnewey Rizgarîxwazî Kurd: Bergî Yekem 1931–1958* [Barzani and the Kurdish Liberation Movement, Part i: 1931–1958] (Hewlêr: Çapxaney wezaretî perwerde, 2012); Barzanî, Mes'ud, *Barzanî Û Bzutnewey Rizgarîxwazî Kurd: Bergî Duwem 1958–1961* [Barzani and the Kurdish Liberation Movement, Part ii: 1958–1961] (Hewlêr: Çapxaney wezaretî perwerde, 2012); Barzanî, op. cit., Part iii, Vol. i; Barzanî, op. cit., Part iii, Vol. ii.

15   The recent launching of the Transnational Press (London) journal *Kurdish Studies* brings to three the number of dedicated periodicals currently publishing (the others being the *Journal of Kurdish Studies* and the Kurdish Library (NY) *International Journal of Kurdish Studies*).

16   Charountaki, op. cit., pp. 77–84; Gunter, op. cit., and *The Kurds of Iraq: Tragedy and Hope* (New York, NY: St. Martin's Press, 1992); Little, Douglas, 'The United States and the Kurds: A Cold War Story', *Journal of Cold War Studies,* 12 (2010); Meho, Lokman, *The Kurdish Question in US Foreign Policy: A Documentary Sourcebook* (Westport, CT & London: Praeger, 2004); Mack, David L., 'The United States Policy and the Iraqi Kurds', in *Kurdish Identity: Human Rights and Political Status*, ed. by Charles G., *et al.* (Gainesville, FL: The University Press of Florida, 2007); Ricciardone, Francis J., 'An American Diplomats Perspective', in *Kurdish Identity: Human Rights and Political Status,* ed. by Carole O'Leary, *et al.* (Gainesville, FL: The University Press of Florida, 2007).

17   Shareef, op. cit.; Alvandi, op. cit.; Gibson, op. cit.

18   Hahn, Peter L., *Missions Accomplished? The United States and Iraq since World War I* (New York, NY & Oxford: Oxford University Press, 2012), pp. 38–62; Osgood, op. cit.

19   Randal, Jonathan, *Kurdistan: After Such Knowledge, What Forgiveness?* (London: Bloomsbury, 1998); Lawrence, *Invisible Nation: How the Kurds' Quest for Statehood Is Shaping Iraq and the Middle East*; Mack, op. cit.; Ricciardone, op. cit.; Rafaat, Aram, 'US-Kurdish Relations in Post-Invasion Iraq', *MERIA: The Middle East Review of International Affairs,* 11 (4) (2007); Ghareeb, op. cit.; Romano, op. cit.; Entessar, Nader, *Kurdish Politics in the Middle East*, Rev. ed. (Lanham: Lexington Books, 2010); O'Ballance, op. cit.; Bengio, Ofra, *The Kurds of Iraq: Building a State within a State* (Boulder, CO: Lynne Rienner Publishers, Inc., 2012); Kimche, David, *The Last Option: After Nasser, Arafat & Saddam Hussein: The Quest for Peace in the Middle East* (London: Weidenfeld and Nicolson, 1991); Hahn, op. cit.; Meho, op. cit.; Rehmany, Wirya, *Şorrşî Eylul Le Bellgename Nhêneyekanî Emrîkada* [The September Revolution in the Secret Documents of America] (Tehran: [no pub.], 2013).

20   Stansfield, Gareth, *Iraqi Kurdistan: Political Development and Emergent Democracy* (Abingdon: Taylor & Francis, 2004).

21   Ricciardone, op. cit., pp. 246–251.

22   McDowall, op. cit.

23   Charountaki, op. cit., p. 1.

24   Ibid., pp. 126–152.

25   Entessar, Nader, 'Kurdish Politics in Regional Context', in *Kurdish Politics in the Middle East* (Lanham: Lexington Books, 2010), pp. 155–170.

26   Shareef, op. cit., p. 2.

27   Ibid., pp. 135–191.

28   Ibid., p. 135.

29   Ibid.

Introduction 19

30 Gunter, Michael M., *The Kurds of Iraq: Tragedy and Hope*, pp. 25–31.
31 Quoted in ibid., p. 28.
32 The shallow, 127-mile-long Shatt al-Arab waterway located at the confluence of the Iraqi Tigris and Euphrates rivers was the site of two of Iran's main oil terminals and cargo ports, Abadan and Khorramshahr, as well as Iraq's only maritime outlet to the Persian Gulf and the Arabian Sea; Iran wanted the boundary to be drawn down the middle of the Shatt, but a 1937 treaty between the two countries had left it mainly on the eastern bank of the river estuary, and the waterway thus in Iraqi hands.
33 Little, op. cit., p. 64.
34 Ibid.
35 Ibid.
36 Among the other points made by the article that may be questioned are the claims on page 69 that Barzani had essentially insisted on Kurdish autonomy with the Ba'athists in 1963 as a reward for helping to weaken Qasim; similarly, page 70 gives the impression that US envoys tried to broker a deal between the Kurds and the Ba'athists.
37 Alvandi, op. cit., p. 4.
38 Ibid., pp. 65–73.
39 Ibid., p. 73.
40 Ibid., pp. 73–77.
41 Ibid., pp. 63–125.
42 Ibid., pp. 77–84.
43 Gibson, op. cit., p. xiv.
44 Ibid., p. xiii.
45 Ibid., p. 163.
46 Kimche, op. cit., p. 189.
47 Gibson, op. cit., p. 80; see pp. 1–30.
48 Ibid., p. 80.
49 Ibid., pp. 69–80.
50 Ibid., p. 84.
51 'FO371/170429: 1963' (United Kingdom: The National Archives, n.d.).
52 Ibid.
53 Gibson, op. cit., p. 67.
54 For example, ibid., p. 197.
55 Parsi, Trita, *Treacherous Alliance: The Secret Dealings of Israel, Iran, and the United States* (New Haven, CT: Yale University Press, 2007); Fawcett, Louise, *International Relations of the Middle East* (Oxford: Oxford University Press, 2013); Halliday, Fred, *The Middle East in International Relations: Power, Politics and Ideology* (Cambridge: Cambridge University Press, 2005); Milton-Edwards, Beverley and Hinchcliffe, Peter, *Conflicts in the Middle East since 1945* (London: Taylor & Francis Routledge, 2004); Brown, L. Carl, 'Diplomacy in the Middle East: The International Relations of Regional and Outside Powers' (London: I.B. Tauris, 2004); Hinnebusch, Raymond and Ehteshami, Anoushiravan, *The Foreign Policies of Middle East States* (London: Lynne Rienner Publishers, 2002); Hinnebusch, Raymond, *The International Politics of the Middle East* (Manchester: Manchester University Press, 2003); Lesch, David W., *The Middle East and the United States: A Historical and Political Reassessment* (New York, NY: Westview Press, 2007); Sayigh, Yezid and Shlaim, Avi, *The Cold War and the Middle East* (Oxford: Clarendon Press, 1997).
56 Hinnebusch, op. cit., p. 1.
57 Ibid., p. 56.

20 *Introduction*

58 Milton-Edwards, Beverley and Hinchcliffe, Peter, op. cit., p. i.

59 Ibid., pp. vii and 72.

60 Keddie, Nikki and Richard, Yann, *Modern Iran: Roots and Results of Revolution* (New Haven, CT: Yale University Press, 2006); Abrahamian, Ervand, *Iran between Two Revolutions* (Princeton, NJ: Princeton University Press, 1982); Tripp, Charles, *A History of Iraq* (Cambridge: Cambridge University Press, 2007); Stansfield, Gareth, *Iraq: People, History, Politics* (Malden, MA: Wiley, 2007).

61 Little, op. cit., p. 694.

62 Alvandi, Roham, 'Nixon, Kissinger, and the Shah: The Origins of Iranian Primacy in the Persian Gulf', *Diplomatic History,* 36 (2012); Jacobsen, Eric, 'A Coincidence of Interests: Kennedy, US Assistance, and the 1963 Iraqi Ba'th Regime', *Diplomatic History,* 37 (2013); Wolfe-Hunnicutt, Brandon, 'Embracing Regime Change in Iraq: American Foreign Policy and the 1963 Coup D'état in Baghdad', *Diplomatic History,* 39 (2015); Little, Douglas, 'His Finest Hour? Eisenhower, Lebanon, and the 1958 Middle East Crisis', *Diplomatic History,* 20 (1996); McGlinchey, Stephen, 'Richard Nixon's Road to Tehran: The Making of the US-Iran Arms Agreement of May 1972', *Diplomatic History,* 37 (2013).

63 Jacobs, Matthew F., *Imagining the Middle East: The Building of an American Foreign Policy, 1918–1967* (Chapel Hill, NC: University of North Carolina Press, 2011); Takeyh, Ray and Simon, Steven, *The Pragmatic Superpower: Winning the Cold War in the Middle East* (New York, NY: W. W. Norton, 2016); Kaufman, Burton I., *The Arab Middle East and the United States: Inter-Arab Rivalry and Superpower Diplomacy* (New York, NY: Twayne Publishers, 1996); Halabi, Yakub, *US Foreign Policy in the Middle East: From Crises to Change* (Farnham: Ashgate Publishing Limited, 2009); Kaufman, Joyce P., *A Concise History of US Foreign Policy* (Lanham, MD: Rowman & Littlefield, 2006); Pauly, Robert J, 'US Foreign Policy During the Cold War', in *International Relations Theory and US Foreign Policy,* ed. by Pauly, Robert J. (Farnham: Ashgate Publishing Limited, 2010); Kiely, Patrick, 'Through Distorted Lenses […]', in *America and Iraq: Policy-Making, Intervention and Regional Politics,* ed. by Patrick Kiely and David Ryan (London: Routledge, 2009), pp. 36–55; for example, Barrett, Roby, *Greater Middle East and the Cold War: US Foreign Policy under Eisenhower and Kennedy* (London & New York, NY: I.B. Tauris, 2010); Hogan, Michael J. and Paterson, Thomas G., *Explaining the History of American Foreign Relations* (Cambridge: Cambridge University Press, 2004); Jentleson, Bruce W., *American Foreign Policy: The Dynamics of Choice in the 21st Century* (New York, NY: Norton, 2004); Kane, Thomas M., 'Realism', in *New Directions in US Foreign Policy,* ed. by Parmar, Inderjeet, *et al.* (Oxfordshire & New York, NY: Routledge, 2009); McDonald, Matt, and Jackson, Richard, 'Constructivism, US Foreign Policy and the War on Terror', in *New Directions in US Foreign Policy,* ed. by Parmar, Inderjeet Miller, *et al.* (Oxfordshire & New York, NY: Routledge, 2009).

64 FRUS, 'About Us – Office of the Historian' (United States: US Department of State).

65 The other was Idris Barzani, who is deceased.

66 Mahmoud Othman, in 'Telephone Interview B from the UK', by Hawraman Ali (October 15, 2015).

67 Dzaei, Mohsin, 'Muhsîn Dzeyî – Nwênerî Pêşûy Mes'ud Barzanî – Beşî Duwem' [Muhsin Dzeyi –Masoud Barzani's Former Representative – Part Two], in *Pencemor,* ed. by Emin, Kawa (Kurdistan, Iraq: Rudaw, 2015); Dzaei, Mohsin, 'Muhsîn Dzeyî – Nwênerî Pêşûy Mes'ud Barzanî – Beşî Sêyem' [Muhsin Dzeyi – Masoud Barzani's

Former Representative – Part Three], in *Pencemor,* ed. by Emin, Kawa, op. cit.; Aziz, Mohammed, 'Mhemed 'Ezîz- *Pencemor*', in *Pencemor,* ed. by Emin, Kawa, op. cit.; Aziz, Mohammed, 'Mhemmed 'Ezîz – Beşî Sêyem' [Mhemmed Eziz – Part Two], in *Pencemor,* ed. by Emin, Kawa, op. cit.; Othman, Omar, 'Umer Usman, Endamî Serkirdayetî Partî' [Umar Usman, Member of the KDP Leadership Committee], in *Pencemor,* ed. by Emin, Kawa (Kurdistan, Iraq: Rudaw, 2016); Talabani, Mukaram, 'Mukerem Tallebanî 3', in *Pencemor,* ed. by Emin, Kawa (Kurdistan, Iraq: Rudaw, 2015).

68 These are Mitrokhin, Vasili and Andrew, Christopher, *The World Was Going Our Way: The KGB and the Battle for the Third World* (New York, NY: Basic Books, 2005); Alam, Asadollah, *The Shah and I: The Confidential Diary of Iran's Royal Court, 1968–77* (London: I.B. Tauris, 1991). And for instance: Faiaz, Mae'hd, *Beşêk Le Bîreweryekanî Mam Celal* [Some of Mam Jalal's Memories] (Erbil: Aras Press, 2009).

1 1958–1962: Iraqi Revolution, Kurdish hostilities

Background

In the aftermath of WWI, on August 10, 1920, the Treaty of Sèvres was signed between the Allies and the Ottoman Empire. Among other things, the Treaty stipulated that a referendum should be held on self-determination for the Kurds under the rule of the Ottoman Empire, which was obliged to respect its outcome. Sèvres also laid the ground for 'the voluntary adhesion to such an independent Kurdish State of the Kurds inhabiting that part of Kurdistan, which [had] hitherto been included in the Mosul vilayet [i.e. Iraqi Kurdistan]'.[1]

However, with the birth of the new Republic of Turkey, Sèvres never materialised. Instead, it was annulled and replaced by the Treaty of Lausanne of 1923, which demarcated the borders of the new Turkish republic. With control over eastern Levant already ceded to Britain at the San Remo conference in April 1920 as a League of Nations mandate over the then Mesopotamia, Mosul was included in what became the State (later Kingdom) of Iraq, a British client territory in which the House of Hashim was established (the Iraqi kings Faisal I, Ghazi I and then Faisal II). Thus, denied the opportunity for self-rule, the Kurds of what was the old Ottoman province (*vilayet*) of Mosul rebelled, with major revolts and uprisings in 1922, 1931, 1937, 1943 and thereafter. Each time, Britain intervened, supporting the Iraqi forces in forcibly subduing the Kurds.[2] Britain, however, did hold a referendum to legitimise the Hashemite accession, but, as Nader Entessar has noted, the 'Kurds either boycotted the referendum or voted against Faisal'.[3] After Faisal's accession, Britain was more concerned with installing and maintaining a pro-British monarchy in a viable Iraq than it was in autonomy for the Kurds, regarded now as lost, like the Treaty of Sèvres, to history.[4]

The 1943 uprising was led by Mustafa Barzani, also known as Mullah—or rather Mela (in Kurdish)—Mustafa, later to become a pivotal figure in the Iraqi Kurds' national liberation movement until his death in 1979.[5] Outnumbered and outgunned, the 1943 rebellion crumbled in the face of RAF bombings and the Iraqi army onslaught, and Barzani and his fighters retreated across the border into Iran's Kurdistan. In Turkey and Iran too, various Kurdish uprisings took place, but all were crushed by the use of military force and the leaders usually executed.

1958–1962: Iraqi Revolution   23

The Kurds of Syria did not have a better fate, and in all these countries, the Kurds faced forced assimilation in one way or another.[6]

From the beginning of the new arrangements imposed on the post-WWI Middle East, therefore, regional and international politics had a profound effect on the status of Kurds. This included what were now the Iraqi Kurds, who never settled with the new order of rule from Baghdad. After WWII, the impact of the wider political environment on the Kurds was to evolve further with the transition from imperial conflicts to the Cold War. Following their crossing into Iran, Mustafa Barzani and his fighters joined the Kurdish Mahabad Republic (January–December 1946), before it, too, was crushed (by Iran) and its founder (Qazi Muhammad) hanged. Barzani and his fighters then made their way and sought refuge in the Soviet Union.[7]

In connection to the Cold War, perceiving any sign of Kurdish nationalism as a nemesis and thus seeking to demonise it, as early as November 20, 1945, the Turkish ambassador in Moscow conveyed to the Americans that Barzani was 'in Moscow being provided with a printing press and propaganda to be distributed to the Kurds in Iraq and Turkey'.[8] Thus, Kurdish aspirations for independence became entangled with international relations and alliances as determined by the growing tension between the US and USSR.

By August 1946, the Iraqi Kurds had established the Kurdish Democratic Party in Baghdad, in the absence of Mustafa Barzani himself, who was, nevertheless, appointed as its chairman. The Party was later renamed the Kurdistan Democratic Party (KDP) in 1953.[9] When, in July 1958, the monarchy in Iraq was ousted by a group of officers led by Brigadier Abd al-Karim Qasim, the KDP declared its support for the new regime and the interim constitution. According to that constitution 'Arabs and Kurds are partners in the Homeland, and their national rights are recognized within the Iraqi entity'.[10] Qasim also invited Barzani back from exile, but this was primarily just to balance his adversaries. Consequently, the honeymoon was short-lived, and a combination of factors led to the outbreak of major hostilities between the Iraqi Kurds, led by the KDP, and the Iraqi government, in September 1961.[11] Hostilities continued intermittently until 1975, when Iran ended its support for Mustafa Barzani's Kurdish movement, to be followed by the US and Israel.

The 1961 hostilities broke out in the shadow of a number of regional struggles and issues, including a global one. At the regional level, one may name the regional powers of Iran, Egypt and Turkey, among others, as well as the perceived threat of communism by the non-communists, while at the international level, the international powers of the USSR, US and UK all had a stake in the direction in which Iraq headed. Subsequently, the road taken by the new republic after the Iraqi monarchy was overthrown also impacted on the relations of these actors with the Iraqi Kurds.[12] This chapter, therefore, is concerned with analysing these interactions and the contributions this may make to the broader research of Kurdish, Iraqi and related international relations' issues. The chapter broadly focuses on the years 1958–1962.

24 1958–1962: Iraqi Revolution

The Cold War's regional delineation and the Iraqi Kurds: the exaggerated Soviet interest

Contrary to the impression that the literature conveys about the lack of US interest or knowledge regarding the Kurds in the early years of the Cold War, it is apparent that the US was taking a cautious interest in the Kurds from at least the late 1940s. A lengthy secret report produced by the CIA on December 8, 1948, provided thorough information to US policymakers not only on the Kurds' political circumstances and their relations to the 'parent state' but also on the Kurds' ancient history, socio-political composition and even, in a throwback to nineteenth-century anthropology, their physical characteristics.[13] The term 'parent state' was used by the CIA to refer to the countries that control Kurdish territories. Distributed to the Office of the President and the National Security Council (NSC), among others, this report comprised 21 pages and was presented in the form of a study. In fact, it might be better categorised as research on the Kurds' socio-political history than a mere intelligence report.

In terms of Kurdish unity and struggle, it is clear from the report that disunity hampered the success of Kurdish national aspirations, or at least that is how the CIA perceived it. The Agency saw a unity that would have to be on an unprecedented scale as 'necessary before any Kurdish uprising could achieve genuinely serious proportions'. Nevertheless, ominously to the Kurds, however, it also stated that 'The Kurdish question, as manipulated by Soviet agitation, is a disruptive force which will continue to threaten, sporadically, the delicate balance of the present Near East system'.[14] In other words, the Kurdish Issue was seen by the US in the shadow of the Cold War from the very start of the US involvement in the region. The report goes to some length in describing the Turkish government's assimilation policies and various Kurdish uprisings, as well as Kurdish organisations and the names of influential individuals and their ambitions in each of the so-called parent states. Undoubtedly, therefore, there was a degree of awareness of the Kurds' situation in US government circles, although any natural empathy there might have been for the desire of a people for self-determination was tempered both by realism (the Kurds' own divisions) and realpolitik (the overriding concern with communism and the power politics of regional domination).

Concerning the start of the Cold War and its relation to the region in the context of this book, various US documents from the period understood the Kurds in one way or another to have, as one put it, 'strong but unfulfilled nationalistic aspirations'.[15] In contrast, primary sources suggest that Iranian, Turkish and Iraqi diplomats and other officials played a significant role during the second half of the 1940s as well as the 1950s in attempts to convince the US that the USSR was intent on establishing a satellite Kurdish state in the midst of these countries.[16] Certainly, Soviet attempts to woo the Kurds ran counter to Kurdish aspirations, since they both augmented the states' apprehensions that the Soviets really were seeking to establish a client Kurdish state out of their Kurdish areas and were also indeed perceived by the US as dangerous. For example, *The Washington Post*

1958–1962: Iraqi Revolution 25

reported that a Soviet radio station broadcasting from Baku in September 1950 had 'appealed to the broad masses of the "Kurdish people" to be ready to fight "for peace and independence"'[17] while a CIA report on the matter concluded that 'Soviet propaganda continues directed agitation of the Kurdish tribes', that there were 'reports of greater Kurdish activity than in previous years', and the 'tribes' were 'not capable at present of causing serious trouble in Iran and Iraq without direct Soviet support'.[18]

There was, therefore, at least a suspicion at these times among various American organs that the Soviets were attempting to destabilise the post-Ottoman framework in the northern Middle East and establish a client Kurdish state there.[19] This belief seems to have influenced US views on the perceived risk that the Kurds posed, which must have contributed to the US policy of remaining aloof, cognisant of the Kurds' various attempts to self-rule and watching them closely, but with some apprehension. The US would not have consented to its number one antagonist, the Soviet Union, creating a Kurdish state from a territory at the geographical intersection of its allies of Iran, Turkey (and Iraq), and most especially not in the geopolitically significant Middle East.

In relation to the CIA's apprehensions, a question that arises is whether the USSR actually did have such an intention of supporting the emergence of a Kurdish state. On the one hand, the prevailing view among 'the diplomatic community' *on the West's side* of the Cold War immediately after 1945 was that the Soviets *were* intent on establishing what would be a satellite Kurdish state and thus adding a regional Soviet ally to the Cold War in the region that would thus significantly enhance Soviet power in the area.[20] On the other hand, however, the Soviet courting of the Kurds seems to have been at least partly due to its desire generally to exert pressure on Iran, Turkey and Iraq and also/or else to gain an additional (Kurdish) card at its disposal, should it need to use it. It is indeed true that, as stated in Talabani's dialogue, from the early 1960s, and especially after the death of Qasim and the successive government's suppression of the Iraqi communists, the Iraqi Kurds' leadership enjoyed such close relations with the USSR that as Talabani states 'we (the Kurds) were taking permission from the Soviets in everything that we were doing'.[21] However, first, this was post 1960, and second, this does in no way imply the Soviets planned to sponsor a Kurdish state per se as feared by adversaries. This research has found no evidence or indications of the Soviets actually considering the establishment of an independent Kurdistan; other than the fears of the Kurdish antagonist states—whether real, exaggerated or fabricated—there appears to be no good reason to postulate this.

Therefore, we may assume that the USSR's intentions were not to parent a Kurdish state, either generally in the region or, as is the concern of this study, specifically in Iraq. As Edmund Ghareeb has also observed, if the Russians really had sympathised with Kurdish aspirations, even in Iran, then the Kurds' status may have been different, but when, in 1941, the Soviets occupied northern Iran, they had other objectives. It was as a side effect of these, one may say, that they then encouraged Kurdish independent movements. This was to serve their own

26   *1958–1962: Iraqi Revolution*

interests rather than to sponsor a Kurdish state. The Soviets did not even attempt to avert the fate of the Kurdish state in Iran that was already declared.[22]

While it is correct to say that the Soviets provided both political and financial aid to the Iraqi Kurds from the early 1960s to early 1970s, as will be examined in due course, this was directly proportional to fluctuations in Soviet relations with the successive governments in Baghdad.[23] Soviet–Kurdish relations are considered throughout this book in different periods, but what is important to emphasise from the outset is that they were unsteady, changing with the dynamics of Cold War considerations and not at all evidencing any type of commitment to the Kurdish cause beyond the temporary, partial and instrumental.

The evidence that the regional states saw or at least portrayed the Kurds as being in the Soviet camp and therefore engaged and working with, in their view, ominous intent (i.e. to establish a Soviet Kurdish client state) is substantial. When Secretary of State John Foster Dulles in his May 1953 visit to Iraq met the then Iraqi Prime Minister Jamil al-Madfai and a number of his cabinet ministers, Nuri al-Said, then Minister of Defence, pointed out to the Secretary that 'Turkey was strong and ran less risk than Iran, which was weak, of being attacked' and that 'Kurds were being *trained in Russia under Mulla Mustafa*' (emphasis added). Also, according to Nuri al-Said, 'the Iran–Iraq frontier south of Turkey [essentially Iraqi Kurdistan] was therefore in great danger from international situation [communism]' and that to protect this area 'plans had been worked out with the British'.[24] In fact, al-Said had resigned as Prime Minster in 1944 due to the Kurdish Issue and shortly after that had stated in a report that 'some of the great powers want to exploit the Kurdish problem for their own interest'.[25]

It is evident that American intelligence must have at least believed that the Kurds *could* be a factor for destabilising its allies and susceptible to exploitation by the USSR. Therefore, Kurdish nationalism was not looked upon favourably by the US from the early periods of the Cold War. While any Kurdish state would have meant a major Soviet gain in the Cold War, insofar as this would have hugely negatively impacted on Iran and Turkey, as much as the US was concerned, a Soviet-client Kurdish state was unthinkable. The idea was that a Soviet-sponsored Kurdish state in Iraq presented the Soviets with an immediate opportunity that could be used, for example, directly for military purposes in the midst of US allies. It would also have given the Soviets an ally in the Middle East, one that would have been dependent on them for its survival and thus equating to a firm Soviet foothold and power base in the Middle East more generally.

This, essentially, is how the US appears to have perceived the dangers of a Soviet-sponsored state for the Kurds—even though there is no evidence to suggest that the Soviets did actually intend to create a Kurdish state or to assist the Kurds in doing so. Just the fear of undesired possibilities, one may say, ruled the day, without it having any particular grounding in reality. It was in this political environment and against this backdrop, therefore, that US perceptions of the Iraqi Kurds took form as the Kingdom of Iraq became the Republic of Iraq from 1958.

The 1958 Iraqi Revolution and the Kurds: the consequences of the revolution

The Iraqi Revolution of 1958 had a profound effect on the region as a whole as well as on Iraq. In relation to the Iraqi Kurds, one of its main effects was to cause Iran to reassess its relations with them.[26] The gradual change in Iran's relations with Iraq's Kurds in the years that followed had radical implications for the latter. There were a number of reasons behind this rethink of approach and policy on the part of Iran, as the evidence shows. These were:

(i) Iran sought to contain the new revolutionary Iraqi regime under Qasim, which it suspected to be at least a pro-communist regime under this leader.[27]

(ii) The Shah feared that the Iraqi Kurds could ask the USSR for assistance, resulting in a Kurdish state. Iran, therefore, needed to reassess its relations with the Iraqi Kurds not only to counter and contain the government in Baghdad but also to divert the Kurds away from the USSR by portraying Iran as preferable for them in order to forestall any alliance between the Soviets and the Iraqi Kurds that could result in a Kurdish state, as assumed by the Shah.[28]

(iii) The Shah was apprehensive about Nasser's influence over Iraq and thus also motivated to drive a wedge between the Kurds and Nasser; the Shah saw Nasser as in favour of an independent Kurdistan, which is something that he feared greatly.[29]

Regarding the last point (iii), Nasser had come to power himself through a military takeover of the state and abolition of the monarchy and was now enjoying unequalled popularity in the Arab world after his victory over the British and French in the Suez Crisis. Indeed, the Iraqi Kurds and Nasser also did enjoy warm relations—such that, according to Masoud Barzani

> The attitude of the deceased president Jamal Abd al-Nasser on the Kurdish Issue was that he was always with the just demands of the Kurdish nation, and has admitted to the right of self-determination of Kurds and had thought that this was also in the interest of the Arabs.[30]

Barzani also confirms not only Iran's but also Turkey and Britain's concerns of both a communist takeover of Iraq as a result of the Revolution and also of the strengthening of Nasser's hegemony in Iraq.[31]

Whether Nasser was genuinely supportive of the right of self-determination for the Kurds is uncertain and how he may have construed *self-determination* is unclear. What seems to be beyond doubt, however, is that he was forthcoming in his support, at least for some Kurdish rights, and enjoyed cordial relations with the Kurdish leadership. For instance, Nasser welcomed Mustafa Barzani to his home in 1958 when the latter was passing through Egypt on his return home from exile in the USSR after the Revolution. Similarly, the Kurdish movement had a representative in Egypt from 1961 until 1966 where he was expelled under pressure from the Iraqi government. However, Nasser also had an interest in developing

28   *1958–1962: Iraqi Revolution*

amiable relations with the Kurds in order to use them to influence Iraqi politics and counteract the Shah's influence. He did not want to *leave the Kurds* for non-Arab regional actors, lest they pit them against the Arabs under Nasser's control. Nasser was thus for a peaceful solution of the Kurdish Issue within Iraq.[32]

Contending with these factors and bearing in mind these considerations, the Shah engaged in an emerging alliance with the Iraqi Kurds, and by 1963, he was considering the Iraqi Kurds, in his own words, 'as weapons'[33] to be used as necessary against Nasser and his ambitions in Iraq. This not only referred to Iran's need to redefine its relations with the Iraqi Kurds, as explained, but was also to have a fundamental effect on the Iraqi Kurds' relations with the US.

After the overthrow of the monarchy in Iraq, one of the options that the pro-US regional states of Turkey, Iran and Jordan had, with the US's blessing, was to launch a military invasion to topple Qasim's regime. However, there was also a second choice. In his July 20, 1958 meeting with Edward Wailes, the US ambassador to Iran, the Shah 'felt strongly that Turkey should not at [the] present time invade Iraq' but nevertheless then suggested to the ambassador that if there was a lesser precipitous approach to the Iraqi situation then it would be to 'work with local tribes in Iraq, including the Kurds, to try to win them over to our side',[34] among other measures. The Shah's views as shared with the ambassador here are consistent with other sources in this section on this, which thus constitute one consequence of the Revolution regarding the Iraqi Kurds.

On July 23, three days after the meeting of the Shah with the US ambassador, the State Department instructed Wailes to meet with the Iranian leader again and provide the following response. In reference to the Shah's suggestion that Iran could work with 'local tribes including the Kurds' to win them to 'our side' and thus influence Iraqi politics, the Department 'agreed [that] that might be worthy of study as means of influencing developments'[35] insofar as it related to non-military action. Therefore, while the regional states most concerned with the Kurds were viewing them suspiciously along with the USSR's related strategy in the region, the evidence denotes the Revolution as marking the start of a partial change in Iran's ostensible policy towards the Iraqi Kurds, which was ultimately, by the early 1970s, to have profound implications for US views of the Iraqi Kurds, as the Shah ultimately drew the US in to back the Kurds in their war with Iraq. In addition, ultimately it also had a fundamental effect on the views of the other Cold War superpower—the USSR—when it came to the independent Kurdish movement in Iraq. These will be covered in Chapter 4 of this book.

After 1958, America and its regional allies were worried that the Revolution could pave the way for a Soviet push into the region or the takeover of Iraq by followers of Nasser or else communists; and as for the Shah, Nasser and the Nasserites were 'worse than the communists'.[36] The Shah was concerned that the collective defence (CENTO) planning put in place to stop Soviet expansion into the region, along with the details of the (1955) defensive (anti-Soviet) Baghdad Pact, would be shared by Iraq with the Soviets and Nasser, thus creating a security quandary. He feared isolation for Iran if more Middle Eastern countries fell into the 'enemy hand'. This, he noted, would put 'my people and country […] in

1958–1962: Iraqi Revolution 29

imminent peril'[37] unless the US acted promptly. The action the Shah was asking for, however, was directed against Iraq but rather took the form of military assistance for Iran. It is worth noting here that Qasim did, in fact, withdraw Iraq from the Baghdad Pact, in March 1959, and also that diplomatic relations between Iran and Cairo were later severed, in the summer of 1960. Such was the state of regional affairs, and of course, the Iraqi Kurds were caught in the middle of these regional power pillars. Britain was also a member of the Pact.[38]

In response to the Shah's worries, President Dwight D. Eisenhower confirmed to him by writing on July 19, 1960 that 'It is our purpose to help assure the political independence and integrity of your country as an integral part of those security arrangements'.[39] When it came to the Cold War and the Revolution, on the US side, the fear among the intelligence community was not only that Iraq could be lost to either communism or pan-Arab Nasserites and thus gaining the Soviets a victory in the Cold War in this sensitive region, but also that other pro-Western Arab regimes might follow the Iraqi example; especially if Iraq was to enter into any kind of a federation with Nasser's Egypt and its political union with Syria, which was the United Arab Republic (UAR), also established in 1958. The worry was of a domino effect, that opposition elements in other regional countries would take over and then either ally with communists (essentially, the USSR) or pay allegiance to Nasser. Such governments deemed to be at risk of instability and thus of falling to the leadership of Nasser or Nasserites with consequences for Iran included, in particular, Saudi Arabia, Kuwait and Sudan—not to mention Iraq itself, of course, which would have been a trigger for the others. These were the worries.

In July 1958 and in relation to the Kurds, a US inter-departmental Special National Intelligence Estimate stated that 'Kurdish nationalism, which is susceptible to exploitation by the Soviets and the UAR, might flare into revolt in north-western Iran'.[40] There is no reason why this special intelligence assessment of the Iranian Kurds was not also applicable to the Iraqi Kurds in the US view, since both Iraqi and Iranian Kurds harboured 'strong but unfulfilled nationalistic aspirations', as expressed by another CIA report, in 1950.[41]

In fact, it appears that Iran did shortly thereafter pursue a dual policy with the Iraqi Kurds, by which, on the one hand, it befriended and assisted the Kurds—to the extent that this empowered Iran with the means for an indirect interference in Iraqi politics—while, on the other, this assistance was restricted to a level that ensured the Kurds did not actually break away from Iraq or pose a threat to Iran itself.[42] As such, Iran's rapprochement with the Iraqi Kurds after the Revolution had specific strategic aims as explicated; and certainly, it was not about assisting the Iraqi Kurds to establish an entity of their own or for the sake of the Kurds themselves.

Adding to this complexity, Turkey was also concerned about a possible collaboration between Iraq and Egypt in fomenting unrest among the Kurds of Turkey and Iran.[43] Indeed, before the Revolution, the radio 'Voices of Kurdistan'[44] from Cairo was inciting Kurds to rise up against the Baghdad Pact powers and establish an independent Kurdistan. This led Iran to complain to Cairo

30   1958–1962: Iraqi Revolution

as well as to the US when the Shah met Eisenhower on June 30, 1958. The fact that Cairo wanted the Kurds to rise up against the Baghdad Pact powers again is evidence of the strong regional dimensions of the Kurdish Issue in the Middle East.

However, after the Revolution, even Turkey, which at times would officially deny the very idea of the Kurds' existence as a people distinct from the Turks, was in private considering the (Iraqi) Kurds as 'a factor to be held in reserve for possible use if the Iraq situation deteriorates'.[45] At least, this was the view expressed by its Foreign Minister Fatin Rüştü Zorlu in his meeting with US Deputy Assistant Secretary of State, Parker T. Hart, in Istanbul in 1959. Hart had visited Turkey and the region at the Turks' request primarily to discuss the Iraqi situation (i.e. Qasim's coup and the Revolution).[46]

The complication of the Kurdish Issue in the Middle East by the internal politics of and relations among the regional powers and the Russian and American interests within these, perceived and/or otherwise—and specifically these in respect of the Iraqi Kurds—can be traced back to the mid-1940s and the new world order post WWII. When it came to American interests, such complexity was intensified and brought into sharp focus after the fall of the monarchy in Iraq in 1958. Thus, for instance, a US NSC meeting in November 1958 unequivocally presented in meticulous depth the knowledge of American policymakers of the Kurds. While discussing US foreign policy towards Iran, the participants at this meeting, who included the President, again raised their worries of Soviet influence on the Kurds.

As part of Iran's rapprochement with the Kurds after Qasim's takeover, Eisenhower had been told by the Shah that it was desirable to establish an Iranian radio in Kurdish broadcasting with a 50-kW capacity to the 'Kurds living in Iran'.[47] The Shah had desired this because 'the Kurds were constantly bombarded by Soviet propaganda broadcasts',[48] which he wanted to counteract. In the NSC meeting, the US President wanted to learn the response to the Shah's requests, which included US assistance in setting up and programming the radio station. The US Information Agency (USIA) was concurrently working with the Iranians to establish this station and, more importantly, to also formulate broadcasts which 'the Kurds would respond to favourably'.[49] According to the Director of the USIA, however, this was not easy 'because the Kurds have always disliked the Iranians and probably could never be induced to like them'.[50] Manifestly, there was a keen awareness of the Kurdish Issue and Kurdish sentiment among US officials. This exchange also shows the extent of superpower involvement (by the US, in this case) in Kurdish affairs in their 'parent states'.

FRUS sources also suggest that while US officials were well aware of the Kurds' nationalistic desires, these desires were regarded as posing potential risks to US interests or those of its allies. From an American viewpoint, as mentioned, a Soviet-sponsored Kurdish entity could be exploited by the communists to destabilise Iran, Turkey and Iraq as well as afford the Russians a foothold in the Middle East. This represents a deeper knowledge and awareness of the Kurds and their potential role in the Middle East than is conveyed by much of the

1958–1962: Iraqi Revolution   31

literature—or rather, there is a lack of indications in the literature to show the depth of these. The literature gives the impression that the US was somehow simply ignorant of the Kurds, presumably because it did not have the imperial background or geographical proximity, and/or that it basically had no real interest in this people—for why should it? As shown here, however, that was simply not the case, and there was more going on here than superficial appearances or a sketchy reading of the situation would suggest.

Further evidence of this is provided in another memorandum. In their meeting on March 22, 1959, in Camp David focusing on how to counter 'Soviet probing for weak spots in the free world position', Eisenhower told the visiting British Prime Minister Harold Macmillan that 'the Soviet Union would make its next move in Iraq by organizing the Kurds'[51] and also that 'Iraq would be the next major trouble spot with the Soviets making use of the Kurds who live in four countries [Iraq, Iran, Turkey and Syria] and have never been assimilated into these'.[52] The CIA Director, Allen Dulles, also told the aforementioned leaders that he 'had always believed that the Russians were trying to develop an advance through the Kurds and Iraq', adding that 'If they succeeded they would have it made'.[53]

Thus, by January 1959, the US priority in Iraq, as elsewhere, was to respond proactively to the perceived threat of a communist takeover, as, should this occur, in Eisenhower's words (at another NSC meeting), 'the result would be to outflank both Iran and Turkey and to provide the Soviets with their long-desired land-bridge to the Middle East'.[54] In this meeting, President Eisenhower also 'expressed anxiety about a Kurdish uprising'[55] together with a potential communist move to seize power in Iraq, with all the assumed ramifications for the Cold War in the Middle East.

The reason for Eisenhower's 'Kurdish anxiety', based on all the sources examined so far, would primarily have been that, in the US view, a Kurdish uprising would have meant instability in Iraq. It was then presumed that this would give the Soviets greater opportunities to exploit in Iraq, with the resulting instability from a Kurdish uprising presenting openings for Iraqi communists to exploit (and hence a Soviet foothold in Iraq and the broader Middle East). The latter was precisely what the US was striving to avoid.

Moreover, short of dissecting Iran from Turkmenistan or passing through significant non-Kurdish territories of Iran, the Soviet 'land bridge' was assumed to have to go through Kurdistan, as the following map (Figure 1.1) illustrates.[56] The worry was that this 'land bridge' coupled with a communist Iraq, in addition to allowing the Soviets a gateway to the Middle East, would have involved eventual dismembering of Iran and Turkey to create an independent Kurdistan in the midst of these countries, both of which, of course, were US allies and were supposed to block the Soviet's march southwards towards the oil-rich regions of the Middle East.

For all these reasons, therefore, as Secretary John Foster Dulles stated in the aforementioned NSC meeting, 'the situation in Iraq [...] was very complicated indeed'.[58] Primary sources point to a considerable anxiety on the part of US

32 *1958–1962: Iraqi Revolution*

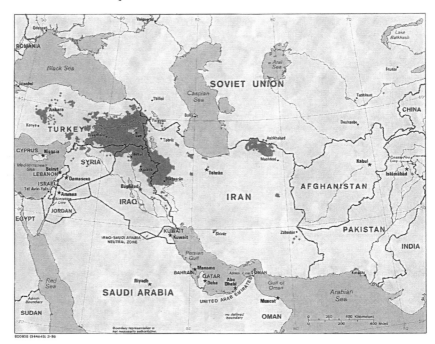

Figure 1.1 Kurdistan and areas with a majority Kurdish population and their proximity to the Soviet Union, i.e. showing the 'land bridge', according to the CIA (CIA, 1986). Courtesy of the University of Texas Libraries, The University of Texas at Austin.[57]

policymakers after the Revolution regarding the likelihood of the USSR exploiting the Kurds in order to further its regional—hence global—interests. This manifests the degree of the Cold War impact on US policy in the region and its perceptions of the Kurds. The Kurds were not communists as far as the US was concerned, but they could have been exploited by communism. Iran, Turkey and Iraq were the parties that largely convinced the US of this *Soviet Kurdish threat*, which demonstrates that not only the Cold War but also the regional politics in relation to the Kurdish Issue in the Middle East must be considered. American perceptions of the Iraqi Kurds, therefore, were shaped by the Cold War and also by regional politics from as early as the Iraqi Revolution of 1958, if not before that.

This section has shown the profound effects that the Iraqi Revolution of 1958 had on the minds of the regional policymakers and also on those of the US, with the Iraqi Kurds caught in this. It demonstrated that the Cold War and regional politics had a significant effect on the Iraqi Kurds and their aspirations for independence, whether they realised it or not. The regional powers hostile to Kurdish nationalism did their best to convince the US of a Soviet design to access the Middle East via Kurdish lands, and they inflated this. For its part, the US took this on board and perceived the Kurds in the 'parent states' as security

1958–1962: Iraqi Revolution   33

risks to the region liable to exploitation by the USSR. The Kurds were thus caught in a quagmire. However, as argued in this book, in fact, there is no evidence to suggest that the Soviets really ever did intend to *work* for the creation of an independent Kurdistan.

Ignition of hostilities in Kurdistan and the start of the race to exploit the Iraqi Kurds

By September 1961, the honeymoon between the Iraqi Kurds or the KDP and Qasim's government was over. Declared by the KDP, the initiation of hostilities in Kurdistan, known among Kurds as *Şorṣî Eylul* or the September Revolution, went by the motto of 'Democracy for Iraq and autonomy for Kurdistan'.[59] According to Masoud Barzani, besides the Kurds wanting democracy in Kurdistan, they also knew that only a democratic Iraq with all the other attributes that accompany such a system could assure respect for the Kurds' rights within Iraq—hence the 'Democracy for Iraq' motto. With the start of the Kurds' September Revolution, relations between the Iraqi Kurds and external powers also began to intensify. Essentially, external powers now had a strong card to play in Iraq against any undesired government in Baghdad, and they would exploit political instability in the country to advance their own agenda. What follows here is illustrative of this.

Kurdish sources reveal that in January 1961, Mustafa Barzani visited Moscow and was seen by high-ranking unnamed Soviet officials. The Soviets agreed to supply the Kurds with weapons and armaments. However, this was not implemented by the Soviets due to 'practical and political reasons',[60] but instead it was decided that the Soviets would provide some financial aid to the Kurds to buy weapons themselves on the black market. The majority of the weapons that the Kurds obtained via this means were of 'English and Czech'[61] origins. Between March and September 1961, 3,000 weapons were bought and distributed in Kurdistan. Mustafa Barzani was already anticipating political turmoil or a military coup in Baghdad; thus, the Kurds were preparing for war.[62]

In fact, from 1961 until 1972, the Soviets continued to give financial support to the Kurds consistently but in a limited, or what Dr Othman calls a 'symbolic',[63] way; this did not involve the direct provision of arms. The Soviets also told the Kurds not to trust Iran or America and advocated for a peaceful solution between the Kurds and Baghdad. Throughout this period, the Soviets wanted to exercise influence over the Kurds together with Baghdad so as not to allow the US or Iran an opportunity to exploit.[64]

According to Masoud Barzani, the financial side of the USSR's assistance to the Iraqi Kurds consisted of a quarter of a million dollars annually, gradually increasing to one million by 1972. This proved very useful for the Kurds, especially at the start. Therefore, in the period 1961–1972, the Soviets enjoyed warm relations with the Kurdish leader, Mustafa Barzani. As stated by Masoud Barzani, this relationship was especially nurtured by Yevgeny Primakov. However, with the 1972 signing of the Treaty of Friendship and Cooperation with Iraq, and the

34 1958–1962: Iraqi Revolution

USSR's insistence that the Kurds join the National Front Government together with the KGB's full disclosure of the Kurds' relations with the US, this relationship dwindled until it was eventually severed.[65] The signing of the stated treaty was a turning point in this era of Soviet–Kurdish relations (see Chapter 4).[66] Jalal Talabani, another Kurdish leader, confirms in his dialogue that the Iraqi Kurdish movement enjoyed close relations with the USSR during the 1960s.[67]

Soviet sources confirm these relations of Moscow with the Iraqi Kurds and also show its underlying intentions. According to the Mitrokhin Archive, in the summer of 1961, the KGB Chairman, Aleksandr Shelepin, devised a scheme to support 'a Kurdish rebellion' in Kurdistan and also informed Nasser that if the rebellion succeeded Moscow 'might take a benign look at the integration of the non-Kurdish part of Iraqi territory with the UAR on the condition of Nasser's support for the creation of an independent Kurdistan'.[68] This scheme was part of a strategy devised by Shelepin and approved by Khrushchev in the summer of 1961 in which the Soviets would support national self-liberation movements around the globe.[69] However, while the history and Nasser's amicability towards the Kurds may have been influenced by the Soviets, there is no indication to show that the latter actively pushed for a political Kurdish entity or for this strategy to have been implemented. Certainly, one may conclude, there was by no means anything like wholehearted support for the Kurds. The very fact of the small nature of the aid, as mentioned, was clearly vastly disproportionate, falling a long way short of the amount that would be required to seriously set about the task of establishing a Kurdish state by means of armed force. According to an authoritative Kurdish source, also, at no point did the Soviets provide any offensive military ordinance to the Kurds[70] or any kind of aid necessary for state-building.[71]

It therefore seems more plausible that, rather than the Soviets determining to sponsor an independent Kurdistan, as the West was concerned about, they may simply have alluded to Nasser that his *tolerance* of this *possibility* would encourage them to look sympathetically at the potential of Arab Iraq uniting with the UAR. In fact, it would be fair to say that the Soviets' relations with the Kurds fluctuated in the years until 1975, and that actually the Soviet approach tended to depend on the political environment in Baghdad. Overall, it appears clear that the Soviets did not go on the offensive to create an independent Kurdistan but, much like every other actor involved, operated to serve USSR interests—which, evidently, did not include this. The type and nature of support provided by the Soviets was simply far too short of what was needed to establish, let alone sponsor and sustain, a Kurdish state. On the other hand, Soviet-provided arms and munitions were continuously used by the Iraqi governments to destroy Kurdish livelihoods and villages in Kurdistan.

After the ignition of hostilities in Kurdistan and by late 1962, all the strategic locations on the borders of Iraq with Iran and Turkey had already been taken over by the Peshmerga. A memorandum from the Deputy Assistant Secretary of State for Near Eastern and South Asian Affairs, Grant, to the Under Secretary of State for Political Affairs, McGhee, in May 1962 indicated the possibility of a violent overthrow of Qasim by dissident forces—the result of which could be a regime 'somewhat less anti-Western'. It also suggested that the US policy towards

1958–1962: Iraqi Revolution   35

dealing with the new Iraqi regime after Qasim should not be affected by the Kurds or their demands for autonomy: 'the US should recognize the new government on the basis of the same criteria it would use were there no Kurdish complications involved, thus avoiding any appearance of support for Kurdish claims'; this is while the US, in consultation with the UK and Iraq's neighbours, was to offer covert support to non-communist Arab forces in Iraq if this ended in a confrontation between the communists and non-communists. It also described the situation thus:

> Qasim is currently engaged in a military action, using troops, artillery and planes against Kurdish tribal insurgents (supported by the leftist Democratic Party of Kurdistan and by city Kurds) in the north and northeast of Iraq along the Turkish and Iranian borders. This military campaign is politically damaging since Qasim has insisted that Iraq is a 'brotherhood' of Arabs, Kurds and other minorities, and Kurdish resistance highlights Qasim's estrangement from all Iraqis. Kurdish guerilla fighters are famously tough and elusive and the heavy strain on the Army has created discontent in the Iraqi forces.[72]

Meanwhile, it is also clear from the Shah's meeting with Kennedy on April 12, 1962, that Iran continued to perceive the Kurds as a source of threat. The Shah used the likelihood of the Kurds becoming Soviet pawns to explain to the US President that they posed a security risk to Iran and Turkey in order to, among other things, expedite US military support for Iran. This was in addition to his citing of the military strengths of Egypt and Syria as well as the Shatt al-Arab issue as additional reasons for his request.[73] The situation, with respect to the Iraqi Kurds, that is, comprised one of four reasons listed by Iran as impelling America to, in simple terms, sell it weapons. This also supports the reports (mentioned earlier) that the Shah sought to divert the Kurds away from the Soviet Union by offering Iran as their backer, thereby pre-empting closer relations between the Soviets and the Kurds that may have ended in the sponsorship of a Kurdish state. In this meeting with Kennedy, the Shah told him that all of the 'Kurdish tribes',[74] except one, were now united against Qasim and that if Qasim failed in controlling them, then 'great problems would arise':

> Although the Iranian Kurds are true Aryans, any minority can get restless, and the security of Iraq could be threatened. Turkey, which has a Kurdish minority of four million, could also be affected. Iran therefore needs more mobility for its ground forces and more aircraft. The Soviets have not intervened in the Kurdish problem, but they might well do so if the situation were to worsen. Many of the Barzani Kurds who have lived 15 years in the Soviet Union must be Soviet agents.[75]

What the Shah was arguing was that an eye needed to be kept on the Kurds, the Iraqi Kurds in this case especially, so as they could not be strong enough to

36   *1958–1962: Iraqi Revolution*

function as a Soviet Trojan. In order to account for this potential risk, the US also needed to strengthen the military capabilities of its allies (Iran in this case). The Shah, therefore, appeared to dread the possibility of the Kurds being backed by the Soviets in 1962—or, at least that fear was a card he played in attempting to leverage military support from the US—which, as we have seen, had to be combined with the possibility of Nasser enlisting the Kurds in a strategic alliance against Iran or of the Soviets, not so much backing the Kurds as merely making use of them for their own agenda, with the potential outcome of any of these being a Kurdish state.

A further indication of the state of affairs was the Shah telling Secretary Robert McNamara, after his meeting with Kennedy, that 'We must therefore be on our watch, especially since we have Kurds, as do the Turks'. Again, the reference to Turkey indicates the wider regional issue of security for America's allies, throwing up the image of a vulnerable order easily cracked and broken to the advantage of the Cold War enemy. The Shah again brought in the likelihood of the Soviets interfering in backing the Kurds, and being a self-appointed spokesman for the Kurds, the Shah continued to the Secretary that 'incidentally the Kurds are the purest Persians, pure Aryans, from their tradition, their language and their history'.[76] As for the Arab world 'perhaps it is pure prejudice, but I just don't like them'. Therefore, we have some apprehensions, particularly when we see them talk about the 'Arab gulf' and essentially because of their relations with the Soviets. This dislike, however, excluded Lebanon, Jordan and Saudi Arabia. The timing of these meetings with Kennedy and McNamara is crucial also, since they occurred some months after the beginning of the Iraqi army's offensive in Kurdistan in September 1961, when Qasim's attack had backfired, since, the Kurds were not only holding their own against the state power but actually advancing and taking territory.[77] This could have only worsened the Shah's unease about the likelihood of a Kurdish state, about the 'great problems' with which Iran would be presented were the Kurdish tribes to unite and Qasim fails to control them.

Summarising, it is evident from these entangled webs of relations and interests from the Iraqi Revolution of 1958 that by 1962 Iran was using the risk of a Kurdish statehood enabled by the Soviets to convince the US of the need to stand against such a development as potentially catastrophic for their strategy in the region. The Shah of Iran invoked this to gain more US support. At the same time, however, Iran and Turkey also saw the Iraqi Kurds as a valuable asset to influence politics in Iraq. Meanwhile, the Soviets had indeed extended both political and financial support to the Kurds from 1961, with whom Nasser also enjoyed warm relations. The Kurdish question in Iraqi also played a part in USSR–Egypt calculations. For its part, the US was clearly convinced that the Kurds posed a risk to its regional allies and thus had the potential to be a Soviet gateway to Iraq and beyond. By implication, so far as the US was concerned, this supposed political Kurdish entity, a Russian land bridge to the Middle East, would certainly have had serious consequences for the Cold War in the Middle East.

1958–1962: Iraqi Revolution   37

Evidently, a number of actors sought closer relations with the Iraqi Kurds, but their intentions were very well calculated. This does not mean that states such as Iran and Turkey no longer perceived the Kurds in general as a clear and present threat; on the contrary, there is plenty of evidence that they did. It is also important to note that many of the new developments in thinking and policy in respect of the Iraqi Kurds arose as a direct result of the profound change in Iraq following the Revolution of 1958.

The US and the Iraqi Kurds: the policy of 'the internal matter'

In 1962, the Iraqi Kurds aimed for their case to be heard by the UN and approached the US government for support. The response given by the latter reveals how the US government viewed the Issue in Iraq. On June 20, 1962, two Kurds—Kamaran Badrkhan and Jamal Abdullah—called on the State Department stating that they represented Mustafa Barzani, or, in the words of the Department, the 'tribal leader now fighting [the] GOI [Government of Iraq] army'.[78] Apparently, the Kurds asked for US 'moral support'—as a State Department telegram carefully quoted. This being, it explained, 'on humanitarian grounds' for the 'suffering' of the Kurdish people 'caused by Iraqi attacks'; the Kurds also asked the US not to be 'hostile' were the Kurdish question to be broached in a UN debate. The response the Kurds received was unambiguous: 'Kurds must through [their] own endeavours reach [an] agreement with GOI and that for US to indicate sympathy or interest, let alone support, would merely accentuate their problems with GOI'.[79]

Manifestly and unsurprisingly, the US was siding with the state actor, and for all the reasons and considerations listed, one assumes. The Kurdish intent may have been less obvious. It seems that this Kurdish endeavour was in preparation for an attempt by the Soviets or its allies to raise the Kurdish Issue at the UN—for the latter was indeed what ultimately occurred, in 1963 (see Chapter 2). The Department not only rejected the Kurdish plea but it decided to inform the government of Iraq but without naming the persons involved. The Kurdish representatives had apparently held talks with Justice William O. Douglas earlier.[80]

The US view of the Iraqi Kurds in June 1962, therefore, was that they would have to come to an understanding with the Government of Iraq and, for this if no other reason, the US could not support the Kurds because it would exacerbate the issue. Actually, Qasim had already, much earlier, accused the US of plotting against him; this had prompted the US ambassador to Iraq, Waldemar J. Gallman, to be instructed by the State Department on December 8, 1958, 'to convince Qasim that there was no truth to the allegations that the United States was encouraging or supporting dissension in Iraq'.[81] When Gallman met Qasim three days later, on December 11, Qasim told him that 'the Kurds in the Sulimaniyah area were being incited against his government' and that there was movement of individuals across the border with Iran.[82] These 'individuals', according to Qasim, included people of both American and other nationalities. Qasim was basically indirectly accusing the US of stirring up a revolt against him, including among the

38   1958–1962: Iraqi Revolution

Kurds, and that, moreover, US personnel were involved in this. The ambassador denied the allegation, including the involvement of any US personnel.

It needs to be recalled here that the view on Iran's side of the Iraqi Kurds in 1962 was that, if they were to unite, and in conjunction with Soviet support, this might provoke the Kurds in other countries and thence pose a threat to Iran.[83] When it came to communism among the Iraqi Kurds, it is certain that they were predominantly nationalists as opposed to communists or ideologues in general. This was made clear during another request for US assistance from the KDP. On September 20, 1962, an unnamed 'Kurd official' representing Mustafa Barzani met with an officer from the US embassy in Baghdad and pledged that Barzani would essentially purge communists in Kurdistan, share intelligence with the US and 'cooperate with conservative Arab Iraqi elements' and, according to the US Department of State, 'bring Iraq back into [the] Baghdad Pact if we [the US] wish'. Furthermore, 'this offer would [also] be binding on Kurds in Syria and Iran as well as Iraq'. Barzani was offering this to the US, apparently, as *quid pro quo* for 'money now and possibly arms later'.[84]

Mustafa Barzani's representative conveyed the Kurdish leader's view that the downfall of Qasim was imminent and that the USSR would be enticed into aiding the Kurds thereafter, but that Barzani preferred the West to the USSR 'which he does not trust'. However, the Kurds conveyed that they were not willing to 'burn all bridges to Russia' unless the US assured them of its support for their movement.[85] The carrot of cooperation was partnered by the threat of the Cold War enemy—and then impelled with urgency with the claim, as reported by the US Department, that 'all Kurds are nationalists, and must win autonomy now or be prepared for racial extinction, but before Kurds will permit this, they would take help from the USSR or from the "devil himself"'. The Kurds' relations with both Iran and the UAR were also confirmed by the emissary while describing the former as 'friendly but unhelpful' and the relations with the latter as 'close and friendly'.[86]

Despite the Kurds' offer, essentially to become a US client, and its covert threat or warning what might happen if support were not given, and quickly, the 'KDP official was clearly told that USG policy toward Kurdish rebellion has not changed'.[87] That policy was described in a memorandum on September 11, 1962, from the Director for the Office of Near Eastern Affairs, Robert C. Strong, to the Assistant Secretary of State for Near Eastern and South Asian Affairs (and also Chairman of the Iran Task Force), Phillips Talbot. The memorandum is crucial to the subject at hand and runs as follows:

> The United States considers the Kurdish problem in Iraq an internal matter which should be resolved internally. Our Government does not support Kurdish activities against the Government of Iraq in any way and hopes an early peaceful solution will be possible. It is our understanding that some of the Kurdish demands include requests for the reinstitution of certain constitutional guarantees. While the United States' position is clear on the desirability of democratic constitutional life, any comment on these demands

1958–1962: Iraqi Revolution 39

in Iraq would be an intrusion into that country's internal affairs. We believe the future well-being of Kurds in Iraq, as well as those in Iran and Turkey, is inseparably tied to the well-being of the countries in which they reside. We know Turkey and Iran share this view, and believe the Iraq Government feels the same way.[88]

This internal memo, therefore, captures the essence of US policy towards the Iraqi Kurds in September 1962 and perhaps prior to that, from the mid-1940s or the onset of the Cold War proper. Whether the policy was publicly declared or otherwise is not the issue here, since it is the very privacy of this message in the form of a clear statement of official position that is important. Indeed, it seems to read as an implied confirmation of that position with a superior in the US administration. Basically, a written policy existed as revealed, and it was an institutionalised policy. This policy was based on a rational self-centred calculation. The memorandum from Strong to Talbot and the NSC meetings referred to confirm that this policy went beyond the views of an ambassador or field diplomat here and there. The totality of the numerous official documents of US governmental bodies collectively cited here all testify as evidence to the general implementation of this written policy and the reasons behind it as analysed.

What is important to emphasise here, therefore, is that this US policy was calculated against the backdrop of the US regional and Cold War interests, as analysed, involving the US allies of Turkey and Iran, as well as Iraq itself in relation to a Kurdish state sponsored by the USSR. Thus, the regional political context examined and its relations to the Cold War, when it comes to the Kurds, not only affected the Iraqi Kurds but the Kurds in all the relevant states. Of course, such a distancing in this matter by the US, one of the two superpowers, has had serious implications for the Kurds in terms of turning a blind eye to flagrant human rights violations. A policy of no action, one may suggest, is itself an action, with consequences. The lack of response by the US to Kurdish rights' claims over the years was not an oversight, accident or due to ignorance; quite the opposite, it was a result of a deliberation, and in that sense quite intentional and calculated.

Moreover, since the Kurds essentially offered to be a US satellite and advance its interests in the region which the US refused, this also suggests to us that US–Kurdish relations cannot be explained by Cold War considerations alone, but it demonstrates the intertwined nature of the Cold War and the regional politics when it came to the Kurds. The US feared upsetting its Cold War regional allies, Turkey and Iran especially, if it was forthcoming to Kurdish pleas. The political considerations in play were strategic.

In addition to the US, according to Mela Mustafa's representative and as confirmed by the British Embassy in Baghdad, the Kurds had also asked Kuwait for assistance and Kuwait had refused. To the Kurds' misfortune, Britain was also playing an adverse role in their struggle, as the British Embassy in Baghdad confirmed that it had advised Kuwait to 'give no money to [the Kurdish] rebels'.[89] Israel had also offered assistance at this stage, but the Kurds had declined it,

40   *1958–1962: Iraqi Revolution*

reportedly not due to an unfriendly attitude towards Israel but because the Kurds were apprehensive that 'Israel might purposely' reveal information on this, which would harm the perception of the Kurdish movement in the Arab World.[90] The developments after 1962 would, in fact, confirm this analysis of Israel–Kurdish relations, that discretion was crucial for the Kurds.

In late 1963 and beyond, Barzani also sent multiple emissaries to London to ask the UK for any means of assistance. Again, they were to no avail because Britain was more concerned with the state actor and improving its relations with Iraq.[91] This is in contrast to a claim that Britain, together with Iran and Israel, 'were all giving the Kurds military and economic support to destabilise the pro-Nasser Arif regimes'.[92] The extensive volumes of UK state archives to which this research had access all show that Britain's role was detrimental to the Kurds, and for the entire time covered by this work. Given the generally close and arguably tightening relationship between the UK and US over these post-war decades, Suez, of course, being the exception, this further demonstrates the effect of the Cold War in conjunction with regional politics and the significance of this combination on the policy of the Western bloc as a whole in relation to the Kurds' national aspirations.

What also needs to be noted here is the fact that the Iraqi Kurds' leadership did not outrightly, on this stage, ask the US or even the UK to sponsor the establishment of a Kurdish state. In contrast, they appear to have been aware that there was no point in asking for that as the negative answer was known already. What the Kurds wanted more, realistically, was to acquire international backing to first alleviate their suffering, and second, to win a degree of autonomy and have their rights respected within Iraq. The Kurds essentially wanted the great powers to view their cause favourably. This, however, does not mean that they did not dream of establishing a state of their own, but it is clear that no international party was willing to extend any sort of meaningful diplomatic, financial or military support to that effect, and thus it was pointless for them to ask for any party to back the establishment of a Kurdish state at this stage, where no one was willing to give them any meaningful backing even in the primitive stages. Further, Mustafa Barzani insisted on winning the backing of the US for a combination of reasons. First, he had recognised that Iran and Turkey were both allies of the US and thus the Iraqi Kurdish movement would be seen as less of an enemy by these two powers if they side with the US, too, as opposed to the USSR, and that the US could use its position to that effect. Second, essentially Barzani thought that the US was too great a nation to betray a desperate people like the Kurds, that only the US was trustworthy when compared to Iran or the USSR.[93]

US foreign policy and the Iraqi Kurds in a wider context: from Truman to Kennedy

From the start of 1958, several significant events occurred both in the Middle East and globally that concerned the US in one way or another, to which the US responses were governed by certain tenets. These are the primary concern of this section. Among those significant events during the time period covered in this

1958–1962: Iraqi Revolution   41

chapter were the landing of US marines in Lebanon in 1958, purportedly to safeguard the independence of the country from *international communism*. The deployment of the US Navy in the Mediterranean, troubles elsewhere, such as in Jordan, Syria and, of course, Iraq itself in the form of the Iraqi Revolution, are among other examples of US and Cold War concerns. These were in addition to other significant issues involving the US outside of the Middle East, such as in Cuba, in Europe over Germany and in Vietnam.

On January 5, 1957, President Eisenhower addressed a joint session of Congress, in which, as Cecil V. Crabb has observed, he called for a 'fundamental reorientation of American policy towards the volatile Middle East'.[94] Eisenhower wanted Congress to collaborate with him on this or to essentially empower him with the authority required. Congress eventually passed a resolution on March 9, 1957, granting him a modified version of the authority he was seeking. This 'Middle East Resolution' came to be known as the Eisenhower Doctrine.[95]

Previously, during the period of the Truman Doctrine—by which the US sought to contain the Soviet Union, in particular by extending financial aid to Greece and Turkey, it had been believed that the Soviets were interested in the Dardanelles and thus seeking to pressure Turkey. The worry in Washington was that if Greece or Turkey fell to the Soviet Union or communism, then the Soviet Union would exert control over the entire surrounding areas, especially given Turkey's vital geopolitical position between Russia and the Mediterranean, on the one hand, and the Balkans, thus Europe, including the Soviet bloc, and the Middle East, on the other. US involvement in this and its aid to Turkey as enunciated by the Truman Doctrine indicates that Kurdish nationalism was already in contradiction with the Doctrine by way of its potential impact on Turkey, as seen by Turkey and the US and as a Cold War US ally and NATO member.[96]

The Eisenhower Doctrine, like that of Truman before him, was a response to threats that the US executive branch perceived the US as facing. While the locale of the Eisenhower Doctrine was shifted to the Middle East, the threat, like that of Truman's, remained 'international communism'. The Doctrine called for economic and military aid intended to bolster the independence of nations in the Middle East that requested such aid. More importantly, the Resolution, passed by Congress, empowered the President, if he determined to be necessary, to assert military power: '[T]he United States is prepared to use armed forces to assist any such nation or groups of nations [in the Middle East] requesting assistance against armed aggression from any country controlled by international communism'.[97] Thus, the purpose of the Eisenhower Doctrine, like that of Truman but more specifically, was to challenge the hegemony of the USSR in the Middle East. Although Russia did not have a direct physical connection to the region, it was increasingly tied politically through the dyad logics involved in nationalist and pan-Arab sentiments pitting the region against the Occident and in the Western support for Israel.

With the Eisenhower Doctrine, Congress had authorised the use of military force to help nations contain communism in the Middle East if the President deemed it to be necessary and when such help was requested. It should be stressed

42   1958–1962: Iraqi Revolution

here that the use of the word 'nation' in the language of US policy, such as that in the Resolution mentioned, actually denoted states (through the notion of *nation-states*) as opposed, that is, to the idea of a nation as a people. This, of course, distinguished rather pointedly those peoples that did not have a state of their own, such as the Kurds. Again, and evidently, there was no favourable place in the broader US policy for the Kurds, since the Soviets could have exploited them and the US itself could not help them as this would have offended the nation-states of Syria, Iraq, Iran and Turkey. This was the predicament that the Kurds found themselves in with regard to the Cold War. Any American aid or assistance to the Kurds would have risked building closer ties between the states concerned and the Soviet Union in order to counter the US act; or at least it would have given an opportunity to the Soviets to meddle. At least this is how it was perceived by the US, which determined the position of the Kurds in respect to the broader US regional and global policy at the time.

This state of affairs and America's anti-communism and obsession with international communism in the Cold War period was revealed when the rule of King Hussein of Jordan was threatened by anti-monarchy elements in the spring of 1957. Eisenhower's response was to order parts of the US Six Fleet into the eastern Mediterranean. Although events that followed in Jordan did not require US intervention, that just the possible risk of the loss of a friendly power brought such a reaction indicates the political and regional atmosphere insofar as it concerned the US and its interests, including safeguarding the security of its allies. The US seems to have preferred a stability that would keep the Soviets or communists out at all costs and would not risk this for anything. That was the overarching policy, with obvious implications for the Kurds generally.

In Syria, too, by mid-1957 there was the likelihood of an American intervention to prevent communists, or what Washington perceived to be communists, from taking power. Such was the seriousness of the situation that Khrushchev warned Turkey against intervening in Syria by declaring that 'If the rifles fire, the rockets will start flying',[98] while Secretary of State Dulles replied that if the Soviets attacked Turkey, the US would retaliate directly against the USSR.[99] Meanwhile, the situation in Lebanon was growing more acute. On July 15, 1958, at the request of its president, some 14,000 American marines landed in response to the charge that Syria and Egypt were fomenting a revolution. And this was just one day after the Iraqi Revolution of July 14, 1958.[100] These all demonstrate the delicate nature of the politics of the region, the high stakes involved and the two superpowers' competing interests in the Cold War.

Collectively, moreover, these events serve to confirm the preservation of the status quo as the priority for the US, as the preferred option rather than any change that ran the risk of communist gains. When the broader context is considered, therefore, where the US was concerned, it simply would not have put its Cold War allies of Iran and Turkey at risk. As much as the US was concerned, the Kurds could not be substituted for a country like Turkey, Iran, Iraq or any other Middle Eastern country. Basically, the Kurds did not have a state that could be of use, and it was this consideration that dominated, regardless of what the

1958–1962: Iraqi Revolution   43

Kurds could have offered America as a non-state actor. This demonstrates that the stage was already unfavourable for the Kurds, and this was the case at least from the Truman Doctrine.

When Kennedy became president in January 1961 conflict was already brewing in South Vietnam. Kennedy attached great importance to South Vietnam, fearing a domino effect on South East Asia were it to fall to communism. By the time of Kennedy's assassination, in November 1963, the US had sent 16,000 military advisers to Vietnam. The war in Vietnam was, in addition to the Bay of Pigs fiasco for the US in April of 1961, a disturbance in Europe over West and East Germany and the Cuban Missile Crisis, in October 1962. Kennedy, therefore, was facing multiple serious challenges, ranging from Latin America (Cuba) to South East Asia (Vietnam), and Europe (Germany) to Africa, where the US was seeking to win over newly formed, decolonised states. Regarding the latter, as new states gained their independence, the idea was to fill *the gap* by getting there first, as it were (i.e. before the Soviet Union).[101]

Against this backdrop—and again, much like the Eisenhower era—issues such as Iraqi bombings in Kurdistan or Kurdish national aspirations would not have been anywhere near Kennedy's list of concerns for America. War in a landlocked Kurdistan did not directly affect the US. From the US perspective, not only did Kurdish self-determination offer no obvious gain but lending a hand to the Kurds in their struggle against any of the parent states would have been counterproductive to its relations with that state, as was analysed.

It therefore seems that at this time, non-state actors, such as the Kurds, were completely overshadowed in the political arena by state actors; the exception of international communism being more of an ideology than a people. Therefore, regardless of how important the Kurds may have been in the politics of the region, or how strongly they may have felt about their national cause, because the US perceived them as posing risks to its allies, they could essentially be sacrificed, as part of the Cold War. It is thus entirely comprehensible why the combination of regional and Cold War politics had such a detrimental effect on the Iraqi Kurds' cause. This analysis is not to imply that neglect of the Iraqi Kurds' suffering was ethically justified, of course, but rather to convey how the US as a Cold War superpower saw the issue, together with its allies, and why this was the case.

The broader question of non-state actors in US foreign policy goes beyond the defined scope of this book. Nevertheless, Shareef also appears to agree that Kurdish statelessness has had a significant effect on the US views of the Kurds' status as compared to state actors such as Iran and Turkey—that is, as relatively unimportant and ultimately disposable.[102] Indeed, one may suggest, it was, in part, just such recognition, rights and stability in external relations gained *de jure* from a status legally enshrined in international statute that the Kurds were after.

Notes

1 HR-NET, 'The Treaty of Peace between the Allied and Associated Powers and Turkey Signed at Sèvres, August 10, 1920' (1995–2016).

44 1958–1962: Iraqi Revolution

2 For more on Kurdish nationalism at the turn of the twentieth century and an account of the post-WWI settlements as related to the Kurds, see Ghareeb, Edmund, *The Kurdish Question in Iraq*, pp. 1–7 and also 29–31.

3 Entessar, Nader, *Kurdish Ethnonationalism*, p. 51.

4 For more on these and the related politics, see Entessar, op. cit.; Allain, Jean, *International Law in the Middle East: Closer to Power Than Justice* (England & United States: Ashgate Publishing Limited, 2004); Ghareeb, op. cit.

5 Lawrence, Quil, *Invisible Nation: How the Kurds' Quest for Statehood Is Shaping Iraq and the Middle East*, pp. 13–17; Entessar, op. cit., pp. 49–80. The English language literature usually refers to 'Mullah' Mustafa, from the Persian/Urdu *mulla* following the Arabic mawlā (e.g. Randal, Jonathan, *Kurdistan: After Such Knowledge, What Forgiveness?*, p. 116; Charountaki, Marianna, *The Kurds and US Foreign Policy: International Relations in the Middle East Since 1945* (London & New York: Routledge, 2011), p. 9); in Kurdish, however, it is 'Mela', which will be used henceforth.

6 For more on the history of the Kurds in Iran, Turkey and Syria, see e.g. Allain, op. cit.; Eagleton, William, *The Kurdish Republic of 1946* (London & New York: Oxford University Press, 1963); Lawrence, op. cit.; McDowall, David, *A Modern History of the Kurds*; O'Ballance, *The Kurdish Struggle, 1920–94*; Randal, op. cit.; McKiernan, Kevin, *The Kurds: A People in Search of Their Homeland* (New York: St. Martin's Press, 2006); Refugees International, 'Buried Alive: Stateless Kurds in Syria' (2006).

7 See Entessar, op. cit., p. 56.

8 'Intelligence Summary–Red' (DNSA, December 10, 1945), p. 1.

9 See McDowall, op. cit., pp. 293–297.

10 Quoted in ibid., p. 302.

11 For a lengthy narrative of these events and the recommencement of hostilities, see ibid., pp. 302–313, and Ghareeb, op. cit., pp. 29–44 (the latter is perhaps slightly influenced by non-Kurdish Iraqi sources); see also the British Embassy in Baghdad, 'FO 371/157404: E1821/5 Confidential, Feb 1961' (United Kingdom: The National Archives, 1992), and Mhemed 'Ezîz- *Pencemor*; Muhsîn Dzeyî – Nwênerî Pêşûy Mes'ud Barzanî – Beşî Duwem.

12 See e.g. 'FO 953/1861; P10048/3: The Kurdish Problem, December 1958' (United Kingdom: The National Archives, 1989); Barzanî, Mes'ud, *Barzanî Û Bzutnewey Rizgarîxwazî Kurd: Bergî Duwem 1958–1961.*

13 CIA, 'The Kurdish Minority Problem' (DNSA, December 8, 1948).

14 Ibid., p. 2.

15 Daily Selected Intelligence Reports […] (DNSA, August 4, 1950), p. 4.

16 For Turkish and Iranian diplomats reports on the alleged Soviet aspirations, see e.g. Daily Selected Intelligence Reports […] and 'Intelligence Summary–Red' (DNSA, December 3, 1945); Intelligence Summary–Red (December 10, 1945); Washington Post, 'Ankara Quarters Fear Kremlin […] the Kurds', Editorial, *The Washington Post* (March 15, 1946); Washington Post, 'Reds Take Part In Kurd Talks, Iranians Say', Editorial, *The Washington Post* (May 01, 1946).

17 Washington Post, 'Rise and Fight, Russian Radio Exhorts Kurds', Editorial, *The Washington Post* (September 20, 1950).

18 'Situation Summary' (DNSA, September 1, 1950); Daily Selected Intelligence Reports […]. For the Washington Post report, see 'Rise and Fight, Russian Radio Exhorts Kurds', *The Washington Post.*

1958–1962: Iraqi Revolution   45

19 See, for example, the following cable: 'The Soviets have attempted for a number of years, without notable success, to establish a Kurdistan, embracing the Kurdish areas of Iran, Turkey, Iraq and Soviet Armenia' (Daily Selected Intelligence Reports [...]). The same cable also mentions that the Iranian military attaché in Ankara 'stated that the Soviets are stirring the Kurdish peoples to form an independent state'. Also see 'Memorandum From the Director [...] to Dulles, frus1958-60v7/142' (FRUS, November 15, 1959). This memo states that 'One result may be an increase in Kurdish restiveness, which the Soviets have been able to stimulate and exploit in the past, in the face of disunity among the Arabs in the country'. The latter refers to the implication of the arrest of Arif by Qasim's Iraqi government.

20 See e.g. Washington Post, 'Red Column Approaches Kurdistan [...]', Editorial, *The Washington Post* (March 16, 1946), where it is stated that 'The move [a Soviet troop deployment to the Lake Urmia area, in Iran] apparently gave support to a theory among many Iranian and foreign government officials that the Russians favour the establishment of an independent Kurdistan for the Kurds of Iran, Iraq and Turkey'. Also, see 'Intelligence Summary–Red'.

21 Selah reşîd, *Mam celal: dîdarî temen, le lawêtyewe bo koşkî komarî, beşî yekem* (Karo: Kurdistan; Iraq, 2017), p. 256 (trans. by author).

22 For more on this, see Ghareeb, op. cit., pp. 11–12; with regard to Soviet support for Mahabad, see e.g. Goodwin, Joseph, 'Russians Are Supplying Arms To Kurd [...]', *The Washington Post* (April 04, 1946). On the Mahabad Republic, see Eagleton, op. cit.

23 For the nature of this backing, see e.g. Barzanî, Mes'ud, *Barzanî Û Bzutnewey Rizgarîxwazî Kurd: Bergî Sêyem, Beşî Yekem 1961–1975*, pp. 30–31.

24 'Memorandum of Conversation [...], frus1952-54v9/32' (FRUS, May 18, 1953).

25 Quoted in Ghareeb, op. cit., p. 33.

26 For the implications of the Iraqi Revolution of 1958 on regional and Middle Eastern politics, see e.g. Osgood, Kenneth, *Eisenhower and Regime Change in Iraq: The United States and the Iraqi Revolution of 1958*, p. 5; Gibson, Bryan R., *Sold Out? US Foreign Policy, Iraq, the Kurds and the Cold War*, p. xvi; Aburish, Said, *Saddam Hussein: The Politics of Revenge*.

27 See 'FO 317/170456: EQ103134/9, Iraqi Relations with Iran, June 29 1963' (United Kingdom: The National Archives, n.d.).

28 Ibid.

29 See 'FO 317/170456: EQ103134/6, Kurds: Interview with the Shah [...] May 30 1963' (United Kingdom: The National Archives, n.d.); FO 317/170456 ..., June 29, 1963.

30 Barzanî, *Barzanî Û Bzutnewey Rizgarîxwazî Kurd: Bergî Duwem 1958–1961*, p. 117 (trans. by author).

31 Ibid., p. 117.

32 The following British archive folder is instructive on this: 'FO 371/170450: 1963' (United Kingdom: The National Archives); also Othman, Mahmoud, in 'Telephone Interview A from the UK', by Ali, Hawraman (October 14, 2015). For the Kurds' relations with Nasser see Barzanî, *Barzanî Û Bzutnewey Rizgarîxwazî Kurd: Bergî Sêyem, Beşî Duwem 1961–1975*, p. 196.

33 Quoted in FO 317/170456: EQ103134/9, Iraqi Relations with Iran, June 29, 1963. Also see 'FO 317/170456: EQ103134/8, Ambassadors talk [...] the Shah, June 19 1963' (United Kingdom: The National Archives, n.d.).

46   *1958–1962: Iraqi Revolution*

34 'Telegram From the Embassy in Iran […], frus1958-60v12/d244' (FRUS, July 20, 1958).

35 Quoted in footnotes of 'Telegram From the Embassy in Iran […], frus1958-60v12/d244'.

36 Quoted in 'Telegram From the Department […], frus1958-60v12/d243' (FRUS, July 19, 1958).

37 Quoted in footnotes of 'Telegram From the Department […], frus1958-60v12/d243'.

38 For more on the Baghdad Pact and such regional defensive measures, see e.g. Entessar, op. cit., pp. 114–115; Gibson, op. cit., pp. xv–18.

39 'Telegram From the Department […], frus1958-60v12/d243'.

40 'Special National Intelligence Estimate, frus1958-60v12/d27' (FRUS, July 22, 1958).

41 Daily Selected Intelligence Reports […], p. 4.

42 These sources are indicative of this: FO 317/170456: EQ103134/9, Iraqi Relations with Iran, June 29, 1963; FO 317/170456: EQ103134/8, Ambassadors talk […] the Shah, June 19, 1963.

43 'Operations Coordinating Board Report, frus1958-60v10/d322' (FRUS, November 19, 1958).

44 FO 317/170456: EQ103134/6, Kurds: Interview with the Shah […] May 30, 1963 and also '240. Memorandum of Conference With President Eisenhower, frus1958-60v12/d240' (FRUS, June 30, 1958)

45 See 'Memorandum for the Record, frus1958-60v12/d191' (FRUS, June 1, 1959).

46 Ibid.

47 'Memorandum […] of the National Security Council, frus1958-60v12/d256' (FRUS, November 13, 1958).

48 Ibid.

49 See ibid.

50 See ibid.

51 'Editorial Note, frus1958-60v12/d61' (FRUS, 1960[?]).

52 'Editorial Note, frus1958-60v19/d274' (FRUS, March, 1959).

53 'Memorandum of Conversation, frus1958-60v12/d62' (FRUS, March 22, 1959). Also see 'Editorial Note, frus1958-60v12/d198' (1959[?]).

54 'Memorandum of Discussion […] the National Security Council frus1958-60v12/d157' (FRUS, January 15, 1959).

55 Ibid.

56 The views of the Chairman of the Foreign Relations Committee, Senator J. William Fulbright, are a further indication of this; see: Kilpatrick, Carroll, 'Fulbright Says West Has No Policy On "Most Dangerous" Crisis in Iraq', *The Washington Post* (April 29, 1959).

57 CIA, 'Kurdish areas in the Middle East and the Soviet Union' [cropped from the original] (The University of Texas at Austin, 1986).

58 Memorandum of Discussion […] the National Security Council (January 15, 1959). Also from the discussion given in the memo, it is clear that the US was at this time open to a rapprochement with Nasser as the lesser of the two 'evils' and to contain the communism in the region.

59 See e.g. Barzanî, *Barzanî Û Bzutne012wey Rizgarîxwazî Kurd: Bergî Sêyem, Beşî Yekem 1961–1975*, pp. 104 and 117 (trans. by author); Muhsîn Dzeyî – Nwênerî Pêşûy Mes'ud Barzanî – Beşî Duwem; Mhemed 'Ezîz'; 'Umer 'Usman, Endamî Serkirdayetî Partî.

1958–1962: Iraqi Revolution 47

60 Ibid., p. 30.
61 Ibid., p. 31.
62 Ibid.
63 Othman, Mahmoud, in *Telephone Interview B* (trans. by author).
64 Ibid.
65 See Barzanî, *Barzanî Û Bzutnewey Rizgarîxwazî Kurd: Bergî Sêyem, Beşî Duwem 1961–1975*, p. 206.
66 Othman, in *Telephone Interview A*.
67 Selah reşîd, op. cit., p. 256.
68 Quoted in Mitrokhin and Andrew, *The World Was Going Our Way: The KGB and the Battle for the Third World*, p. 150.
69 See ibid., p. 150.
70 Othman, in *Telephone Interview B*.
71 The aids provided are listed by Barzani as stated earlier, see Barzanî, *Barzanî Û Bzutnewey Rizgarîxwazî Kurd: Bergî Sêyem, Beşî Duwem 1961–1975*, p. 206. There is no indication of any substantial aid.
72 'Memorandum From the Deputy Assistant Secretary of State for Near Eastern and South Asian Affairs (Grant) to the Under Secretary of State for Political Affairs (McGhee), frus1961-63v17/d262' (FRUS, May 3, 1962). For the criteria suggested, see the same source.
73 See 'Memorandum of Conversation, frus1961-63v17/d243' (FRUS, April 12, 1962).
74 Ibid.
75 Ibid.
76 Quoted in 'Memorandum of Conversation, frus1961-63v17/d247' (FRUS, April 13, 1962).
77 For more on why and how the Kurds were successful in this conflict, see Barzanî, *Barzanî Û Bzutnewey Rizgarîxwazî Kurd: Bergî Sêyem, Beşî Yekem 1961–1975*, p. 87. Barzani backs up his claims with copies of documentary evidence, such as letters exchanged between Kurdish commanders and commands and also admissions by army officers in retrospect.
78 This is the description the State Department gave to Barzani at the time; see 'Telegram From the Department of State to the Embassy in Iraq, frus1961-63v17/d305' (FRUS, June 22, 1962).
79 Ibid.
80 Ibid.
81 'Telegram From the Embassy in Iraq [...], frus1958-60v12/d147' (FRUS, December 11, 1958). Also, see 'US Denies Attempts To Win Over Kurds', *The Washington Post* (January 25, 1959).
82 'Telegram From the Embassy in Iraq [...]' (December 11, 1958); US Denies Attempts To Win Over Kurds.
83 See the Shah's visit to Washington and his meeting with US officials including the President: Memorandum of Conversation [B]; Memorandum of Conversation [A].
84 'Telegram From the Embassy in Iraq to the Department of State, frus1961-63v18/d49' (FRUS, September 20, 1962).
85 Quoted in ibid.
86 Quoted in ibid.
87 Ibid.
88 Quoted in footnotes, ibid.
89 Ibid.

48   *1958–1962: Iraqi Revolution*

90   Ibid. For a good account of Israel's relations with the Iraqi Kurds from 1965 onwards, see Kimche, David, *The Last Option: After Nasser, Arafat & Saddam Hussein: The Quest for Peace in the Middle East*, pp. 189–200.

91   See for instance: FO371/170429: 1963; 'FO 371/170448: 1963' (United Kingdom: The National Archives, n.d.); 'FO 317/170515: 1963' (United Kingdom: The National Archives, n.d.).

92   Gibson, op. cit., p. 84.

93   For Barzani's views of the USSR, Iran etc., see Barzanî, *Barzanî Û Bzutnewey Rizgarîxwazî Kurd: Bergî Sêyem, Beşî Duwem 1961–1975*, p. 209.

94   Crabb, Cecil Van Meter, *The Doctrines of American Foreign Policy: Their Meaning, Role, and Future* (Baton Rouge, LA: Louisiana State University Press, 1982), p. 153.

95   See ibid., pp. 153–192; Little, Douglas, 'The Cold War in the Middle East: Suez Crisis to Camp David Accords', in *The Cambridge History of the Cold War Volume 2: Crises and Détente*, ed. by Arne Westad and Melvyn Leffler (Cambridge: Cambridge University Press, 2010), pp. 305–326.

96   For a detailed account of US-USSR issues and the Truman Doctrine, see Crabb, op. cit., pp. 105–152; Little, *The Cold War in the Middle East: Suez Crisis to Camp David Accords*; Kaufman, *A Concise History of US Foreign Policy*, pp. 75–102.

97   Crabb, op. cit., p. 155.

98   Quoted in Crabb, op. cit., p. 179.

99   Ibid.

100 For more details, see Crabb, op. cit., pp. 153–193; Pauly, Robert J., 'US Foreign Policy During the Cold War'; Little, 'His Finest Hour? Eisenhower, Lebanon, and the 1958 Middle East Crisis'.

101 For more on Kennedy's policies and these issues see for instance: Costigliola, Frank, 'US Foreign Policy from Kennedy to Johnson', in *The Cambridge History of the Cold War Volume 2: Crises and Détente*, ed. Arne Westad and Melvyn Leffler (Cambridge: Cambridge University Press, 2010), pp. 112–133; Hartley, Anthony, 'John Kennedy's Foreign Policy', *Foreign Policy* (1971); Kaufman, op. cit., p. 94.

102 Shareef, Mohammed, *The United States, Iraq and the Kurds: Shock, Awe and Aftermath*, p. 138.

2 1963–1965: Seeking allies

Background

In early February 1963, Prime Minister Abd al-Karim Qasim, the man that had led the 1958 Revolution, was overthrown and murdered in a *coup d'état* carried out by the Ba'athists. This led to an interim pause of hostilities between the army and KDP before they resumed in June. The Kurdish Issue was a primary cause for the demise of Qasim's government. Before the coup, the Ba'athists and the Nasserites had promised Barzani autonomy for Kurdistan and even the right to self-determination if the Kurds ceased attacking the army and also issued a declaration supporting the coup upon its success. According to Jalal Talabani, a chief Kurdish negotiator and KDP leader at the time, the Ba'ath and the Nasserites had gone as far as promising the KDP and Barzani that the central government's role *would be as much as the Kurds' role in the Arab parts of Iraq*. However, once they succeeded, the coup plotters did not honour the pledge that they had made and were uncompromising, especially on the issue of the geographical borders of the would-be autonomous Kurdistan, particularly in relation to the oil-rich city of Kirkuk. This led to the resumption of the war.[1]

In November 1963, the Iraqi Ba'ath government itself was also ousted, by pro-Nasser Iraqi nationalists. The new government under President Abdul Salam Arif sought a rapprochement with Barzani. The KDP and Arif agreed a ceasefire to be effective from February 10, 1964. However, as Entessar has noted, because the constitution of 1964 'did not recognise the equality of Kurds and Arabs in Iraq'[2] and also because of disagreements about autonomy in Kurdistan, the ceasefire failed a year later, in April 1965. There was thus a resumption of what may be correctly called the Kurdish War.

Despite the use of chemical, phosphorous and napalm bombs in Kurdistan by the Iraqi army that was also able to call upon a force of some 50,000 combatants, the War again reached a stalemate with heavy losses for the state forces.[3] Hence, the government in Baghdad again sought to end the conflict peacefully. This new peace initiative, which became known as the Bazzaz Declaration, involved a 12-point programme announced by Premier Abd al-Rahman al-Bazzaz on July 12, 1966, promising autonomy for the Kurds, to which Barzani agreed.[4]

However, frictions had already developed both on the Kurds' side and in Baghdad. At the Kurds' end, these frictions appear to have been caused by what

50   *1963–1965: Seeking allies*

could be regarded as essentially a blend of ideological differences coupled with power rivalry between Mustafa Barzani, on the one hand, and Ibrahim Ahmad with Jalal Talabani, on the other.[5] At the same time, the hardliners in Baghdad were still in favour of a military solution as they saw it, despite the fact that the army had already tried and failed to achieve this. Further, the three successful coups in Baghdad since 1958 and also the polarisation of the Arab Iraqi society between nationalists, Ba'athists and communists, among others, testify to the divided nature of politics in Baghdad.

Also, before the pro-Nasser nationalists ousted the Ba'ath government in November, the Ba'athist elements that carried out the coup against Qasim suppressed communist leaders who objected to their move. Thereafter, communist leaders were given sanctuary in Kurdistan, which, according to Masoud Barzani, played well with the Socialist Bloc.[6] This also indicates the usefulness of the Iraqi Kurds for external powers, such as the USSR in this case. Similarly, it shows the complicated dynamics of Iraqi politics at the time, and it offers a good example illustrating why most of the actors concerned sought to maintain links with the Iraqi Kurds as an actor in the region and a major party within Iraq. This instrumentalisation meant that these links tended to be nurtured and employed in times of need, but the need of the other actors rather than that of the Kurds.

In Iran, by May 1964, the Shah was still weighing up whether to put his lot in with the Iraqi Kurds or the Iraqi government. According to the Shah himself, if Iran were to help Iraq in 'crushing'[7] the Kurds, this would be tantamount to helping Nasser and the new Arab federation, the UAR, while if Iran were to side with the Kurds, it would upset Turkey and also create problems for Iran itself by inspiring Kurdish nationalist aspirations in Iran. The Shah now admitted that Iran had provided a small amount of financial aid to the Iraqi Kurds and also that he saw that the Kurds could be weaponised against Nasser and the Arab Federation when needed. This was while the US wanted the Iranian government to essentially persuade the Iraqi government of the importance of serious negotiations to reach a deal with the Kurds. The US did, in fact, have prior knowledge that the new nationalist or pro-Nasser Iraqi government was contemplating the resumption of action against the Kurds.[8]

For his part, the Shah was also awaiting to see the result of recent visits by Iraqi Kurdish leaders to Cairo before deciding on whether to back the Kurds or not, while another reason for supporting them, was to pre-empt Russia's backing, as explained in Chapter 1, which he was dreading. In the words of the British ambassador to Iran, the Shah wanted 'to steal a march on the Russians' in this respect.[9] Adding to this complication, by June 1963 the Iraqis were complaining to the Iranians that Russia was supplying the Kurds via Iran. The Iranians thought that the Russians might be overflying Iranian territory at night for this purpose, which can only have exacerbated their concern about Russia's *Kurdish plans* and hence catalysed the decision to divert the Kurds away from the Soviets by portraying Iran as a source to which the Kurds could turn. In short, Iran was conflicted about how to balance its various interests vis-à-vis regional influence and the ongoing thrust of Kurdish nationalism; it was motivated to support

1963–1965: Seeking allies   51

Baghdad in blocking a Kurdish state in Iraq, it was motivated also to support that state itself in order to forestall what it saw as a nascent Russian patronage of a Kurdish state.[10] The reality, however, seems to have been that the Kurds were buying weapons on the black market, with some financial assistance from Russia. This was examined in Chapter 1.[11] There is no evidence thus far to indicate that Russia was directly supplying the Kurds with arms.

Meanwhile, Nasser does not seem to have had a dissimilar attitude towards the Iraqi Kurds as that of the Shah. The British ambassador in Cairo noted that Nasser was unlikely to give the Kurds his 'all-out encouragement',[12] for example, but could rather be expected to keep a line open to them in order to be able to influence Iraqi politics in Baghdad. That is the view argued here also as the rationale behind Nasser's friendship with the Iraqi Kurds. By November 1963, when the pro-Nasser Iraqi nationalists overtook power in Baghdad in a military putsch, Iran was also concerned that Iraq could fall into the hands of Nasser and thus other Arab states, which seemed to be happening, and was thus a further impetus for Iran to work against this and exploit the Kurds to be used as weapon as the Shah had in mind.

On the Russian front, after the Ba'athists took power in February 1963, followed by the resumption of hostilities with a particularly brutal campaign in Kurdistan, the Soviet Union made multiple attempts for the Kurdish Issue to be heard by various UN organs. In a letter to the UN Secretary General, dated July 9, 1963, it accused Iraq of 'brutally exterminating the peaceful population [...] and are reducing vast areas of Kurdistan to ruins'. It also accused 'the colonialist military pact of CENTO'[13] of being an accomplice to this and its members of meddling in Iraq and assisting it to this end. The Soviet letter requested an immediate end to this, arguing that CENTO's involvement in this constituted a threat to international peace and security, and warning that otherwise the Security Council may have to be convened on this issue. Following through on this, Moscow was also behind a request made by the Republic of Mongolia for 'Genocide in Kurdistan' to be put on the agenda of the 18th Session of the General Assembly.[14]

This Soviet move was a cause for concern among the Western Bloc countries, on this occasion spearheaded by the UK. The UK decided that the intention of the USSR was to internationalise the Kurdish Issue by having it heard by the UN, which was against the UK and US Cold War strategies of leveraging power through Baghdad, which now meant trying to win the favour of the new Ba'ath government there.

Led by the UK, CENTO members adopted the tactic of replying to the Russian letter to the UN Secretary General through CENTO and also individually, as member states, but not at the UN. This was in order to avoid the Kurdish Issue going to an international stage and in their attempt to prevent just that. This was despite the UK embassy in Baghdad confirming to its Foreign Office that the Soviet accusation was basically true and that the Iraqis were intending to drastically 'reduce' the Kurdish population by means of military force and repopulate the area with Arabs.[15] *The Washington Post* also reported

52   *1963–1965: Seeking allies*

on June 15, 1963, on 'Iraq Army Battles Kurds In War of Extermination', in which it stated that:

> Reliable sources reaching here [Beirut, Lebanon] said more than of Iraq's army is waging a war of extermination against the Kurds in the north, shelling and razing vil-lages [sic], shooting civilians and burning crops [...] The sources said Iraqi troops confiscated all vehicles and farm machinery, looted money and women's jewellery, pillaged churches, strung male villagers by their heels and whipped them. Two women who protested were executed.

As for the Ba'athists' sincerity regarding finding a lasting solution before the commencement of hostilities, the newspaper added that 'Diplomats here said the Iraqi government had avoided hard bargaining toward a set-tlment [sic] with the Kurds since the cease-fire and used the time to build up its northern forces'.[16]

The Soviet attempt to raise the matter internationally not only agitated CENTO but also risked antagonising the Arab world. The charges were thus subsequently withdrawn due to Arab pressure and its potential ramifications for USSR–Arab relations.[17] As well as heading off Russia's effort with the UN by having the issue discussed through CENTO instead, the UK and US furthered their support for the new regime with the provision of arms to Iraq, such as British Hawker Hunter bombers.

Parallel to the UN attempt, the Soviet media, primarily TASS, and commentators attacked Iraq in strong terms and accused it of treachery. On the one hand, the Ba'athists' assaults on the communists in Iraq and thus the nature of USSR's own relations with the Ba'ath in comparison to that of the latter with the Western world may help to explain the Soviets' attitude as presented here. On the other hand, the Kurds had given sanctuary to the communists, which could have had a positive influence on the Soviets regarding the Kurdish movement. Talabani confirms that one major problem between the KDP and the Ba'ath was the KDP's refusal to suppress the communists in Kurdistan and those that have taken sanctuary there. This account is consistent with that offered by a UK Foreign Office memo at that time.[18]

When it comes to the other superpower of the Cold War, the US, in July 1963, Mustafa Barzani wrote a letter to President Kennedy through the US consulate in Tabriz, Iran. Some three weeks after Barzani's letter to Kennedy, which received an oral acknowledgement, Barzani also sent another intermediary to the US consul in Tabriz asking the US to play a primary role in restarting negotiations and also reaching a ceasefire with the Ba'ath government. Essentially, Barzani seems to have wanted the US to play the role of intermediary. State Department officials consequently agreed to act as a 'post office' but nothing more than this and not what Barzani wanted.[19] Iran then recommended the US to join it as, or in some form of, an intermediary. However, just as in the case of acting as a post office, American diplomats dreaded that this could be detrimental to Iraqi–US relations as it may offend the Ba'ath government in Baghdad. This also

1963–1965: Seeking allies   53

contradicts the literature sources claiming that Kennedy pressed the Ba'ath regime to make peace with the Kurds.[20] Not at all, it would appear; on the contrary, the US held off from an intermediary involvement let alone pressing the Ba'athist regime. Also, the Kurds were prepared to announce a ceasefire and negotiate for a settlement, provided that international powers mediated this.[21] Manifestly, no power was willing to mediate a settlement between the two sites.

Multiple Kurdish emissaries thus failed to persuade the West, in general, to act as mediator or for the Kurds to be given international guarantees in future negotiations with Iraq assuring the implementation of the terms of any potential deal. In the second half of 1963, therefore, Barzani and the KDP were unsuccessful in their attempts to attract international attention and the mediation of the West in particular. Britain and the US also persuaded the Shah to refrain from openly declaring his support for the Kurdish movement. The Shah only hesitantly agreed. With this background or narrative skeleton for the present chapter established, we can now proceed to examine the issues in more detail.

After Qasim: the first Ba'ath regime, the Cold War and the hapless Kurds

The coup of February 1963 overthrew Abd al-Karim Qasim and brought the Ba'ath Party to power. The National Council that took over declared one of its aims to be resolution of 'the Arab-Kurdish problem'.[22] In the initial stages of the coup, the consensus from the US-DOD and the CIA was that if the coup were to succeed, then relations between Iraq and the US 'would be considerably improved'.[23] In addition to this, the CIA also believed that the internal Iraqi Kurd–Arab relations would also gradually improve.[24]

On February 8, 1963, the day of the Ba'ath coup, Robert W. Komer, Senior Staff of the National Security Council (NSC), wrote to Kennedy informing him that the coup appeared to have been successful and that it was 'almost certainly a net gain for our side'.[25] After the coup, the US sought to court the new Ba'ath government to, at minimum, remain in the non-aligned framework of the Cold War and thus minimise the influence over Iraq of America's two adversaries (the USSR and UAR). To give this approach substance, however, a new policy was needed, one that called for economic, military and technical assistance to Iraq. On the military front, by April 2, 1963, the US had already agreed to sell 12 helicopters costing up to $15 million to Iraq, and it was up to the Ba'ath regime to choose the kind it wanted.[26]

Inevitably, however, this new policy and the ongoing struggle between the Kurds and the Iraqi government was to have ramifications on the Iraqi–Kurdish status quo. The Iraqi army had not been able to overpower the Kurds since hostilities began in 1961, and Qasim's government had paid a high price for its failed campaign in Kurdistan. This was the primary cause for the downfall of the regime in which Qasim himself lost his life. The views of Harold H. Saunders of the NSC staff as expressed to the President's Special Assistant for National Security Affairs, McGeorge Bundy, on the US arms sale to Iraq on April 2, 1963,

54   *1963–1965: Seeking allies*

was indicative of US policy towards the Iraqi Kurds and the rationale behind it after the 1963 coup. This policy essentially entailed no change but was then to take a turn for the worse so far as the Kurds were concerned. Writing to Bundy, Saunders noted that the US had already turned down the Kurds' request for help and that:

> The Kurds may object to our military sales. [...] However, we think it's more important to be responsive to the new regime. Besides, we want [the] Kurds to negotiate a settlement with the new government. If that fails, our interests will be better served if the government can control the Kurds than if the Kurdish rebellion is successful enough to invite Soviet or Iranian meddling.[27]

The request to which Saunders alluded was yet another plea by the Kurds for US backing, this time delivered by Jalal Talabani from Mela Mustafa in March 1963. With Talabani, then head of the Kurdish delegation in Baghdad, negotiating with the Iraqi government, Barzani had once again offered the US friendship, requested assistance for the Kurds and asked for a US official to meet with him. The response given by an embassy officer, however, was along the lines of the already established policy, that the US considered the Kurdish Issue an internal Iraqi matter and was therefore unable to help. Moreover, a US official could not meet with Barzani.[28]

This illustrates the US policy in respect of the Iraqi Kurds in March 1963 under the first Ba'ath regime. It is to be noted here that while Saunders and Bundy were not from the State Department, they were both senior members of the Kennedy administration. Therefore, the policy in effect clearly went beyond the State Department. It seems that any related contemporary US diplomat or official already knew what answer to give to the Kurds, and this was precisely because this was the established institutionalised policy. The question here is not whether this was announced as official US policy as such but that there was a standard position adopted among US policymakers based on an assessment in respect of the Iraqi Kurds, and this was consistent across various governmental bodies. In fact, it *was* stated to be US policy, at least internally, in communications between the Department of State and the embassy.

Following Barzani's message to the US by Talabani and the embassy's response, the Department of State sent a telegram to its embassy in Iraq on April 5, 1963. This was, of course, after the embassy officer had already informed Talabani about US policy—in which the officer nonetheless reported the affair to the Department, which, in turn, endorsed the embassy's position, thus:

> United States policy remains unchanged; we consider [the Kurdish] problem strictly one between GOI and [the] Kurds. However, [the] consequences [of the] breakdown [of the] current negotiations [is] such that effort to persuade both sides of advantages [of an] equitable settlement through mutual compromise [is] warranted. You may, therefore, pass word to Talabani that

1963–1965: Seeking allies   55

Mulla Mustafa's message [was] transmitted [to the] USG, which fully endorses positions taken by [the] Embassy officer.[29]

The Department also instructed the embassy to convey that a solution to the 'Kurdish problem'[30] could and had to be found, emphasising that it would be advantageous for the Kurds were they to form an integral part of the Iraqi state and urging the Iraqi government to be forthcoming in meeting Kurdish aspirations to a certain degree. Additionally, it noted that US government 'understanding of and sympathy for legitimate Kurdish aspirations within [the] Iraqi state' would 'in no circumstances be allowed adversely to affect cordial USG relations with new Iraqi regime'.[31] The Kennedy administration, therefore, merely wanted a peaceful settlement for the Kurdish Issue in Iraq.

In other words, what can be inferred from these exchanges is that the US policy was to seek a rapprochement with the new Iraqi government by providing financial aid for the new regime's purchase of its military hardware and not providing any assistance to the Kurds to the extent even of declining Barzani's request just to meet an American official; yet, the US also urged a peaceful solution! The reasons for taking this line primarily were to avoid offending the Iraqis in Baghdad, of course, with the assumed ramifications for the wider region were the Iraqi Kurds to win a significant degree of autonomy. Despite the official line, however, there do appear to have been voices in the State Department preferring that the sale of arms to Iraq (12 helicopters and 40 light tanks, in this case) be made conditional on a quick agreement with the Kurds. This is evident by the memorandum of the Bureau of Near Eastern and South Asian Affairs of the State Department (NEA) to the then Under Secretary of State for Political Affairs Harriman W. Averell, on April 8, 1963, that 'asking Iraq for a quick agreement with the Kurds as a quid pro quo for the arms sale would defeat the purpose of the sale, which was to augment US influence with the new Iraqi regime'.[32] Nevertheless, there is no indication that this suggestion ever came to anything.

The point to emphasise here is that the US did have a developed view of the Iraqi Kurds at above-embassy level and its attitude was determined according to what was perceived as serving its own interests. Therefore, the fact that the US did not involve itself in the Kurds' cause does not imply that this was because it did not know who the Kurds were or that it lacked either the interest or the knowledge to become involved. On the contrary, keeping aloof and overtly so in respect of the Kurds' struggle within Iraq was a deliberate decision made by the US for its own interests, fully appreciative of the apparent contradiction that supporting Baghdad militarily held for this and in this matter concerned, rather, with the contradiction implied by putative support for the Kurds with respect to its primary relationship (i.e. Baghdad). The Americans knew very well the choice they were making, one organised by considerations of regional Cold War strategy, basically, rather than, say, democracy and UN-recognised rights of peoples to self-determination. The same analysis applied to the UK.

One reason for concern among American military and diplomatic circles in 1963 about a possible re-ignition of the Kurdish War, as discussed, was the usual

56 *1963–1965: Seeking allies*

fear of Soviet interference and presumably a potential Soviet sponsorship of a Kurdish state. In the words of John W. Bowling (NEA officer in charge of Iranian affairs), this comprised 'the possibility of an overland link-up with the Soviets, which would greatly facilitate the movement of supplies to the Kurds'.[33] The idea of this Kurdish land bridge was not particular to John W. Bowling, of course, but went back to the pre-1958 period, as initially developed by the Shah of Iran in the Eisenhower era. This was looked at in Chapter 1.

Such perpetual apprehension of a Soviet Kurdish client imperilling regional US allies of Iran and Turkey or potentially outflanking them or at least causing them internal instability, and thus presenting a vulnerable point for Soviet exploitation, seems to have been consistently lingering as far as the US and its regional allies were concerned. It was always in the background and the primary policy consideration. Accordingly, the course of the Cold War and the associated regional politics hugely directed the fate of the Kurds, including the Iraqi Kurds. The Iraqi Kurds were thus caught in the middle of the great power rivalries of the era, of the US versus the USSR interlinked with Turkey, Iran, Iraq, and Egypt or the UAR. None of these powers extended a sincere hand and nor yet wanting to keep away or otherwise inadvertently push the Kurds or allow them to drift into the opposing camp.

Before hostilities resume, the US did seek to prevent a resumption of hostilities between the Iraqi Kurds and the Ba'ath government after Qasim as its preference. To this end, the US embassy in Baghdad was instructed by the State Department to renew its démarche to the Iraqi government in May 1963 to continue the negotiations and avoid a resumption of hostilities—but the US did not push Iraq on this.[34] The Department, particularly through its embassy in Lebanon, was also urging the Kurds to do the same. However, the US desire for this Arab–Kurd peace was based on the idea that the Ba'ath government was anti-communist and thus the need to keep the Kurds away from the Soviets not only in Iraq but also in Iran too.

In addition to the USSR, the US also wanted to keep the pro-Nasserites as well as the Iranian-linked Shia of Iraq in check by stabilising the Ba'ath rule. Nasser's dislike of the Ba'ath may have been a major reason for his openness to maintaining his connection with the Kurds. In the US itself, meanwhile, Justice William Orville Douglas of the Supreme Court took up the Kurdish case in November 1963, which made it difficult, thereafter, for the State Department to outrightly reject visas for Kurdish representatives under Iraqi pressure.[35]

On July 19, 1963, Robert W. Komer of the NSC staff wrote to President Kennedy updating him on the Iraqi policy and the aid as intended to keep a divide between the new regime in Baghdad and the USSR. Along with the tanks that the US had agreed to sell to Iraq, Komer also informed Kennedy that they had agreed to sell '12 tank transporters, 500 big trucks, and 15 large choppers'.[36] These military sales were in line with and to materialise US Iraqi policy after the overthrow of Qasim. Here, however, the sale of offensive equipment was limited but this was not to save Kurdish lives, it was to avoid undesired impact on the Arab–Israeli front. Komer also confirmed that the UK had offered to sell Iraq 'some [Hawker] Hunters and ammo, etc'.[37]

1963–1965: Seeking allies   57

Crucially, in his memo to Kennedy, Komer also stated, 'As you know, we're giving Iraqis some ammo [*less than 1 line of source text not declassified*] for Kurd campaign', adding 'So are Syria and UAR apparently' (note original).[38] Regardless of the redacted information, this is the first indication that the US was directly supporting Iraq in its war with the Iraqi Kurds. The support may only have extended to 'some ammo', but nonetheless this was directly intended for the 'Kurd campaign'.

The rational for this commitment to the new Ba'ath regime was of course to drive a wedge between the USSR and Iraq, on one hand, and also Iraq and Nasser, on the other, as examined. It was essentially intended for bridge building with Iraq. As expressed earlier by Saunders, apparently it was also more in the US interest for Iraq to control the Kurds if negotiations failed than for the Kurds to be sufficiently successful as to invite Soviet intervention, in which case, presumably, Kurdistan would have been a Soviet base with serious consequences for the regional US allies of Iran and Turkey, and thus for the Cold War in the Middle East. Such appears to have been the mindset in the US. The US, therefore, was patently not a neutral player in the Iraqi–Kurdish war under the Ba'athists after Qasim.

The views of the Joint Chiefs of Staff to Secretary of Defense Robert McNamara on August 15, 1963, add further evidence regarding the explanation of this policy. Among the reasons for pursing a policy of appeasement towards Iraq, they believed, were the aim of eliminating the communist threat within Iraq with the implications of this (i.e. Soviet hegemony) as well as countering Nasser's power.[39]

With regards to the Kurds, therefore, not only the civilian part of the US government but also the military, while assisting Iraq, perceived a prolonged conflict between the Kurds and Baghdad as giving the Soviets an opportunity to meddle, and not only in Iraq but in Turkey and Iran too. In reference to this, the Joint Chiefs recommended to the US government to 'give favorable consideration to reasonable Iraqi requests for equipment and seek to use [the] resultant influence to urge moderation on the Iraqi Government [regarding the Kurds]'.[40] They also argued that, to circumvent USSR's intervention, 'a firm Iraqi military position' coupled with the accommodation of 'legitimate Kurdish grievances' was 'the most promising avenue for an early end to hostilities and advancement of internal stability in Iraq'.[41] This is further indication of the nature of the policy as contended in this section, and it also shows that although the US was in favour of a settlement for the Kurdish Issue within Iraq, it did not object to a military solution to be part of this *settlement*, or essentially for the Kurds to be subdued militarily and forced to submission, while some of their grievances addressed by the central government.

With the Ba'ath regime taking power in February 1963 and the corresponding adjustment in the US policy towards the Kurdish Issue and fate of Ba'ath–Kurdish negotiations, as seen, being a matter of both apprehension as well as interest for the US, it desired Iraq to dominate in the case of failure. Baghdad obviously could not be expected to remain oblivious and fail to take into account the US partiality

58 *1963–1965: Seeking allies*

in its approach to dealing with the Kurds. In other words, the US policy may be assumed as a contributing factor in the likely breakdown of talks and resumption of war, as in fact transpired, even if this policy was only intended to strengthen Baghdad's hand in forcing the peace; at best, this represents an American miscalculation.

However, no overall change in US policy regarding the Iraqi Kurds themselves occurred as compared to the Qasim-period policy. Adding to what has been established hitherto in this section, a circular airgram in March 1963 from the State Department on 'Interim Policy Guidelines for Dealing With Iraq'[42] approved by several Department officials provides further evidence of this:

> The United States should continue to regard the [Kurdish] problem as strictly an internal Iraqi matter in which there is no role for the United States *either directly or indirectly*. In discussion with Iraqis and others, United States officials should limit themselves to *expressions of hope* that the GOI and the Kurds will be able to come promptly to a mutually satisfactory agreement and *the United States is pursuing a strictly hands-off policy*. Our influence should be used with Iran and Turkey to assure a similar hands-off policy on their part.[43] (Emphases added.)

This Interim Policy Guidelines had earlier added that 'Failure to find a political solution soon would benefit only the Soviets and the Iraqi communists'. It is evident why the US under Kennedy viewed the issue as explicated. A number of sources from the UK government also verify the analysis presented here.[44] In short, it is clear that the Cold War and the pertaining regional politics essentially largely shaped the US approach towards the Iraqi Kurds and their desire for self-determination, and this was not, ultimately, one of neutrality but one of opposition and taking the side of the government in Baghdad.

Symbolic concern and not offending the Iraqis: the super-worried superpower

Evidence that the US was not only not ignorant of the Iraqi Kurds' cause and ambitions but actually closely weighing its local and regional interests in the matter is also observable from Mustafa Barzani's letter to Kennedy dated July 12, 1963. Barzani commenced the letter by stating that:

> The United States Diplomatic authorities are certainly informed and fully aware of the question of the Iraqi Kurds and our demands from former and present governments, which are entirely in harmony with the bill of human rights and the Charter of the United Nations.[45]

The letter also complained about successive Iraqi governments' policies towards the Iraqi Kurds and how the new Iraqi government after Qasim had reneged on all its promises 'made under oath' and that 'in a Hitlerian Fascist fashion' it had

1963–1965: Seeking allies   59

'adopted the policy of burnt lands' and 'committed outrages' that were 'a disgrace for mankind in the twentieth century'.[46] It is to be recalled here that Qasim was unseated from power and murdered by the Ba'athists in the February coup of 1963 and also that fighting between the Kurds and Baghdad under the Ba'ath Party government had flared up (again) in June 1963 after a short pause.[47] Barzani asked Kennedy and the US to use their influence to help the Iraqi Kurds 'acquire their rights, i.e., autonomy within the Republic of Iraq', adding that this request was being made 'in order to prevent bloodshed and eliminate the nightmare of cruelty which keeps down the Iraqi Kurds'.[48] Barzani was appealing here to the US to assist the Iraqi Kurds to better their status within Iraq rather than fostering an outright separate Kurdish state; that is, being realistic with the US policy, he was pushing for autonomy not independence.

Before Barzani's letter reached the White House, however, a reply was already proposed, first by the US ambassador in Tehran and then by the State Department. The ambassador, in forwarding the letter, rather frostily proposed to the Department to instruct the US consul in Tabriz, where the letter was received, 'not to indicate to Barzani's intermediary in any way that the letter has been forwarded'[49] and to 'reiterate orally the Department's position on the Kurdish problem'.[50] Meanwhile, in a memorandum dated August 6 sent from the Department's Acting Executive Secretary, John McKesson, to the President's Special Assistant for National Security Affairs, McGeorge Bundy, the Department also conveyed its belief that a reply from the President was not necessary because, in their view, 'a Presidential reply to Barzani might well damage United States relations with Iraq'.[51] Such details as this portray the nature and the rationale in the US dealings with the Kurds in Iraq in August 1963, and, more broadly, the instrumentalization of the Kurds in Iraq and the region generally for the end of the Cold War.

When blocking Barzani's plea from being made directly to Kennedy as damaging to US relations with Iraq, the Department instead proposed that an oral response be given to Barzani's intermediary by the Tabriz consul, and that this be:

> …along the lines of our standard guidance with respect to the Iraqi Kurds, i.e., that the United States sympathizes with legitimate Kurdish aspirations within the sovereign state of Iraq, but that our sympathy will not be permitted to prejudice the cordial relations now existing between the United States and Iraq.[52]

Contradicting the US ambassador in Tehran, the Department further proposed that if asked whether the letter had been forwarded or not, the consul in Tabriz should state that the letter had been forwarded to the Department and that the consul was replying on behalf of the Administration, as indicated. The Department believed that this would not 'damage United States-Iraqi relations' and, moreover, 'At the same time (…) would demonstrate, if only symbolically, United States' concern for and interest in the Kurds'.[53]

60   *1963–1965: Seeking allies*

In conjunction with what has already been shown, what this correspondence tells us about US policy and the Iraqi Kurds is, first, that the duplicity was entirely intentional and, second, that this response given to Barzani was an institutionalised response; it was systemic or, in the words of the Department a 'standard guidance'.[54] That is, this was not the result of semi or wholly independent schemes of US officials alone in some occasional or piecemeal fashion but a formalised policy in relation to the Iraqi Kurds' cause. That is, it was the policy of the USG and passed up and down as a 'chain decision' made by US officials for the way the US wanted to deal with the Iraqi Kurds and for the reasons given.

In addition to the existence of a US policy towards the Iraqi Kurds based on the calculations analysed, the documents cited here collectively show also that the Kurds had cordial relations with US diplomats in Iraq. This in itself also demonstrates that, like the other powers, the US wanted to maintain the bridge with the Iraqi Kurds—but essentially nothing more than this at this stage. This relationship was conducted on an informal level since US policymakers were afraid of offending the Iraqis, of course, as the US saw it, with the potential consequences for the Cold War in the region that such contacts carried or may have been perceived to have carried or at least were feared thus by the superpower.

Many of the documents consulted up until now, the result of meetings or exchanges between Kurdish emissaries and US diplomats, evidence both the existence of a relationship, whatever its scale, and also its nature. More importantly, with regard to the aim of this research, these documents also portray the impact that the Cold War and regional politics had on the struggle of the Iraqi Kurds. Indeed, it is proposed here, the Cold War and the associated regional politics were intertwined when it came to an issue like who was ruling Iraq, and the Iraqi Kurds were essentially in the middle of all these. This was the case up until the chronological point that has been covered thus far, or namely, from the Iraqi Revolution of 1958 to the Iraq under the first Ba'ath regime, after Qasim.

The rise of the pro-Nasserites in Iraq: heightened tensions between Iran and Egypt, and implications

As has been shown, the Soviet Union, Nasser, Iran, the US, Britain and also Turkey, among others, all had a stake in who and what prevailed in Iraq, although each for their own, and often quite different reasons. Apart from the Cold War rivalry in Iraq, the US was also apprehensive about Iraqi Kurds' relations and Iran's role in Iraq generally. The US was wary of the Shah derailing negotiations or a potential settlement between Baghdad and the Kurds. Indeed, the Shah had the ability to do so, but again, as motivated by self-interest rather than any *bona fide* sympathy for the Iraqi Kurds or their cause. As will be shown, it may be argued that Iran had a pivotal influence on the Iraqi Kurds' relations with Baghdad, and this was for a number of reasons, bilateral Iran-Iraq and regional.

In November 1963, the pro-Nasser nationalists overthrew the Ba'ath regime that had come to power after Qasim. It appears that this forced the Shah to overcome his dithering over whether or not to aid the Iraqi Kurds against

1963–1965: Seeking allies 61

Baghdad and taken steps to build closer relations with them. Iran's role in this context, therefore, cannot be overlooked. Indeed, it was Iran that was ultimately to decide the fate of the Kurdish liberation movement under Mustafa Barzani in 1975. The following sections present this Iranian influence on Iraqi–Kurdish affairs through US concerns on the matter once the Nasserites had come to power in late 1963 after the first Ba'ath regime.

The evidence for Iran's impact on the status of the Iraqi Kurds in terms of the trilateral Iraqi, Kurdish and American relations is copious, and similarly apparent are US apprehensions about Iran's role in Iraqi Kurds affairs with Baghdad in this era. After the start of the Baghdad–KDP negotiations in the aftermath of the overthrow of Qasim by the Ba'athists in February 1963, Robert W. Komer of the NSC staff wrote to the President's Special Assistant for National Security Affairs, McGeorge Bundy, regarding the potential for the negotiations to fail, thus:

> Some of our spies are beginning to get quite worried about [the] risk that [the] Kurdish problem may flare up again to bedevil [the] new Iraqi regime. [...] We're warning [the] Iranians especially to keep hands off, but if [the] Shah should decide that [the] new Iraq[i] regime is too cozy with Nasser, he may not take our advice.[55]

This indicates that for Iran, the Iraqi Kurds were a means through which to potentially weaken adversaries in Iraq or to meddle in and keep Iraq off balance in a manner desired by Iran. The Shah had his own reasons for this, and, given their landlocked geography, the Iraqi Kurds did not have many options. Both sides thus needed each other. A UK Foreign Office Research Department study on the Kurds and Iran's role in this history stated that 'The Iranian aim is to keep trouble firmly on the Iraqi side of the border'.[56] This, in short, was indeed the reason behind Iran's support for the Iraqi Kurds, broadly explaining Iran's aim in this matter until the Algiers Accord of March 1975.

In relation to Iran's exploitation of the Kurds, David Kimche basically also argues that Iran simply exploited the Kurds whenever necessary and betrayed them when the need was resolved or the aim was achieved.[57] Indeed, even while the first Ba'ath regime was still in power, a US Special Intelligence Estimate confirmed that Iran had 'an ambivalent attitude toward the Barzani movement' that it was 'concerned that Kurdish successes in Iraq' would 'breed unacceptable demands for political, social, and economic betterment among its own Kurdish population'. However, in continuance with the Estimate, the Shah remained 'deeply suspicious of Arab nationalism', especially 'the formation of a new UAR' threatening 'the appearance of Nasser on the banks of the Tigris'.[58]

Robert W. Komer's prediction of March 1963 regarding the likelihood that the Shah would interfere in GOI–Kurdish negotiations if he perceived that the Iraqi regime was 'too cozy with Nasser',[59] would be precisely the case later, as stipulated by the Shah himself in a letter to the US President Johnson on January 7, 1964. This letter confirms the reasons for Iran's interests in the Iraqi Kurds as contended, namely, here, in order to counteract a threat to Iran, and not based on

62 1963–1965: Seeking allies

any kind of compassion or a genuine sympathy per se. The threat to be countered for which the Kurds were to be utilised could broadly be referred to as Arab nationalism, primarily, and additionally, in the words of the Shah himself, 'Agents of international communism'.[60] As for the Arab nationalism, at this juncture it was spearheaded by President Gamal Abdel Nasser of Egypt.

The Shah conveyed to Johnson that if the GOI and the Kurds did not reach a deal, then they had 'reason to expect that the fighting [would] flare up again in the spring [of 1964]'.[61] The Shah also apprised the US President that 'The Kurdish question is still unsettled. Agents of international communism are making every endeavour to exploit the situation to their own advantage, and Cairo is anxious to play its dubious role in any development in this situation'. He conveyed that Nasser had been trying to mediate between the GOI and the Kurds, but, while this was good in itself, Nasser had malevolent intentions in this towards Iran. Nasser's malice towards Iran, according to the Shah, was fully revealed by the content of one of his messages to the Kurds. The Shah wrote that Nasser had 'said in effect, according to information, that it was a pity the Kurds were fighting the Arabs. He would have given them full support if their force[s] were directed against Iran'.[62]

Indeed, a letter written to Mela Mustafa by Jalal Talabani from Baghdad to Kurdistan in April 1963 indicates that the Kurds had been in close contact with Nasser, and also, indeed, that Talabani had met Nasser in Cairo to discuss the Kurdish Issue.[63] The Kurds, apparently, were open to the idea of Iraq joining a federation of Arab states, such as the UAR. This must have troubled the Shah even more when insofar as this involved Nasser and increased his apprehension of Arab nationalism. Talabani had already been received twice by Egypt as Barzani's representative by April 1963, and he is reported to have found the Egyptian leadership's views to be more enlightened than those of the Iraqis. At least Talabani, and presumably the Kurdish leadership in general, since he was representing Barzani in Cairo (and Baghdad), believed that the Kurds could perhaps fare better in a larger Arab federation with an enlightened leadership, Nasserites that is, than in Iraq.[64]

Before the Ba'athists were overthrown by the nationalists, it was also speculated that President Nasser might be tempted to arm the Kurds to cause the downfall of the Ba'ath regime if he so desired. It has to be recalled that the Kurds had been the primary factor in causing the demise of Qasim's regime. In other words, the speculation was that Nasser may have assisted the Kurds militarily had the Ba'ath regime not submitted to his authority through the pro-Nasserite nationalists of Iraq who overthrew the Ba'ath government in November 1963.[65]

The Shah then informed Johnson that he had an obligation to his country and people not to 'tolerate Egypt's subversive influence at our doorstep; nor fail to regard it seriously'.[66] It is worth recalling also that a ceasefire between the Kurds and the new nationalist Iraqi government was agreed upon on February 10, 1964, as mentioned earlier.[67] Indeed, a number of reasons may have increased the Shah's apprehensions by late 1964 and finally convinced him to side with the Kurds, albeit reluctantly. Among these, according to British archives, was that with a pro-Nasser nationalist government taking power after the Ba'athists, by

1963–1965: Seeking allies 63

late 1964, Arab unity had reached an extent such that officers from Egypt, Iraq, Syria, Yemen, Lebanon and even Kuwait were taking part in 'mountain warfare' courses under the auspices of the 'United Arab Command'[68] in Akrê in Kurdistan. These courses also included indoctrination by Egyptian lecturers. Furthermore, at least on one occasion a skirmish took place between this group and the Peshmerga when the former strayed into Kurdish-held territory. These are all despite Nasser having reassured the Kurds in August 1964 that Egyptian troops would not be used against Kurds in the case of a union between Iraq and UAR. It should be pointed out, however, that the logic on Barzani's side was that if this union did occur, then Egypt would be forced to assist Iraq in any future Arab–Kurdish hostilities because, from the Kurds' point of view, the pro-Nasserite nationalist Iraqi government was standing on such weak grounds already that it would have compelled Nasser to intervene to save it in the case of a renewal of the Kurdish War.[69]

This development came after the Shah's letter of January 1964 to Johnson, which also indicates the further weight added to the Shah's worries. Moreover, the presence of Syrian troops had already been publicly acknowledged by the Iraqi government by late 1963, and also acknowledged by the Kurds. Nader Entessar puts their number at 5,000.[70] President Nasser remained amicable towards the Kurds after the Ba'athists were unseated from power, but this was after the Iraqi army had suffered heavy losses in attempting and failing to advance in Kurdistan. Multiple sources, including British archives, indicate the army's losses after nationalists took power, and before the February 1964 ceasefire, to be in the hundreds. These went to an extent that the government in Baghdad had to fabricate victories and advances by the army in order to explain the high number of casualties to the families of dead soldiers.

Thus, according to the British embassy in Baghdad, the army was already stretched to its limits by the Kurdish War and therefore, since Nasser had no alternative to the nationalists if they were to be also ousted, he wanted the Kurdish Issue in Iraq to be resolved by peaceful means, or at least this consideration may have influenced his views. Essentially, with this being the case, it seems that for Nasser not only Iraq had failed to 'resolve' its Kurdish Issue by military means but a further continuation down this path risked a backlash and an overthrow of the pro-Nasserite government in Baghdad, like that of Qasim and the Ba'athists before it. Nasser appears to have been convinced that under the current circumstances there could not be a military solution to the Kurdish Issue. The strain of the Kurdish War on Arif's nationalist government, on the economy in particular, was such that the resignation of three ministers ensued, including that of the Minister of Finance precisely due to that burden.[71]

Meanwhile, in early June 1964, Mustafa Barzani made yet another attempt to advance the Kurdish case with one of the Cold War superpowers: the US. This time he sent Shawkat Akrawi and Luqman Barzani (Barzani's own son) to the US embassy in Cairo. The representatives met an embassy officer there and they conveyed Barzani's message that, *inter alia*, he wanted the pair to go to Washington 'to present the Kurdish case to officers in the Department'.[72] However, in

64   *1963–1965: Seeking allies*

response to the request, in a telegram to its embassy in Baghdad, which seemingly was personally concurred upon by the Secretary of State, Dean Rusk, the State Department replied that the representatives 'while not unwelcomed in Washington' but would 'not be able to advance Kurdish interests there'. In fact, the telegram stated, the 'delicate Kurdish-GOI situation might be irritated unnecessarily by conversations here with avowed Kurdish nationalists [i.e. by conversations with the Kurdish representatives in Washington]'.[73]

Also, and just as significantly, the Department stated that the Kurdish representatives might only find frustration when discovering that the Administration's position was parallel to that of its embassy in Baghdad. Additionally, the Department also relayed that its Baghdad embassy was capable of serving as a channel between the US government and the Iraqi Kurds and for the purposes of conveying 'subjects of concern to Iraqi Kurds and of making clear US positions'.[74] Thus, the US policy as it was at this stage (June 1964) was: (1) to refrain from escalating contacts with the Iraqi Kurds to anything above embassy, and desk level, for the reasons stated, and because it would be fruitless for the Kurds anyway and may even prove counterproductive; and (2) to keep US relations with the Iraqi Kurds merely on friendly terms.

Yet again, just like Iran and Turkey, which had earlier portrayed the Kurds to the Americans as Soviet agents, or at least to have the potential to be that if left unchecked, Iraq was also exploiting America's Cold War obsession. According to its Foreign Minister Naji Talib in a meeting with the US Secretary of State in New York, on December 10, 1964, the Kurdish Issue had preoccupied Iraq to the extent that it had little time or energy for much else, as it had 'fundamentally dominated the Iraqi scene'. Talib also told the Secretary that 'the Kurds were controlled by the Communists', and 'If a Kurdish state were established, it would be a Communist enclave which would split the Arab world, pierce the protective CENTO belt, and shatter the stability of Turkey and Iran'.[75] The US Secretary 'shared the Minister's concern about the dangers of Communist penetration of the Near East by means of a Kurdish independence movement' and categorically denied any direct or indirect US support for the Kurds. The denial came after the Minster stated that 'The Kurds are poor people and their land has been damaged by war. Where are they getting money from to buy staple foods, arms, and equipment? Who are these mysterious forces? What do they want?'[76] The Kurds were fighting for a nationalist cause, but it suited their adversaries to paint them as communists.

It appears that up to 1964, even though there was the opinion in the US that the Kurds might be turned into a client state by the USSR with drastic consequences for the regional Cold War struggle, still the US did not assist the state of Iraq to *decisively* eliminate Kurdish resistance. Indeed, from the evidence available, US material support to Iraq was limited.[77] The US did not necessarily want to antagonise or even harm the Kurds as if they were communists, but nor did it offer them any kind of support apart from sympathy. It could therefore be inferred that when it came to the Iraqi Kurds, the US policy in the early mid-1960s was similar to the attitude of the Shah and also Nasser, namely keeping relations with the

1963–1965: Seeking allies   65

Kurds in the balance, on friendly terms, lest the need arose to pit them against Baghdad in one way or another and especially not to give the USSR an opportunity to exploit their cause within the Cold War framework. The Kurds themselves, however, as Barzani put it, had few to no options available and would have accepted help even from the 'devil himself'.[78] Nonetheless, in the final analysis the US was prepared to sacrifice the Kurds in order to win Baghdad's favour, if that was what it took. At the same time, no one wanted to alienate and push them into the Soviet camp were Baghdad's allegiance to the West not already won and the Kurds no longer needed.

The overall picture seems to demonstrate that the Americans from early on were aware of the unfavourable circumstances of the Iraqi Kurds when the overall geopolitical nature of their region is considered and especially during the Cold War. The US perceived this as inevitably choosing between sponsoring or even encouraging a Kurdish entity in Iraqi Kurdistan or offending its Cold War allies: Iran and Turkey, but also Iraq. This would have been in addition to causing an Arab nationalist uproar both against the Iraqi Kurds and also against the US itself had it clearly sided with the Kurds. The US would not have traded all of these for the Kurds or their self-determination and it did not do so. Nevertheless, one other choice that the US could have pursued was to find a settlement to the Kurdish Issue within Iraq, as opposed to the Kurds breaking away, but it did not opt for this, either, in order to preclude the ramifications that the US thought would come with it. Nevertheless, one might argue, the US could have found a middle ground in this matter, something somewhat closer to justice, as it may be voiced.

A telegram from the State Department signed by Under Secretary of State George W. Ball on December 14, 1964, conveyed to the US embassy in Baghdad that the Department was 'persuaded that Kurdish participation in any scheme to overthrow Iraq government would not guarantee [the] establishment [of a] regime more sympathetic to Kurdish aspirations'.[79] The telegram also warned that if the Kurds were to take part in any plot involving Iran to overthrow the Iraqi government, they would only earn deep Arab suspicion along with resentment of Kurdish aspirations, and that that, in particular, may well end Nasser's favouring of a peaceful settlement between the GOI and Iraqi Kurds.[80]

The government in question here was Abd al-Salam Arif's nationalist government that had come to power in November 1963 after the Ba'athists were overthrown. Therefore, the above suggests to us that while, on the one hand, the US was not prepared to assist the Kurds in any way, on the other, it did not and was not viewing the (Iraqi) Kurds as such a communist risk as the Iraqis and other regional actors would have liked to portray. As evident, therefore, at these times certain US officials did have a small degree of sympathy for the Iraqi Kurds, which stood no chance in the face of broader US interests. While the US did not back the Kurds, it did not seek to mislead them either, not until the catastrophe of 1975 (see Chapter 4).

In fact, the cable from the Under Secretary to the US embassy in Baghdad stated that any Kurdish attempt to engage in a coup seemed that it would be 'bound [to] backfire and to worsen Kurdish position vis-à-vis GOI', precisely

66   *1963–1965: Seeking allies*

because the Kurds would expose themselves as willing collaborators of the Iranians in the Arab world.[81] This refers to the Shah's desire for the downfall of the contemporary pro-Nasser Iraqi government after the Ba'athists. The Kurds had reported to the US embassy Baghdad that Iran was urging them to renew the fighting. This was at the end of 1964.[82] This is a good indication of what could be described as personal sympathies by some US officials with regard to the Kurds in Iraq.

The views of the US ambassador in Baghdad add further evidence to this. When the Kurds reported to the Americans in December 1964 that Iran was urging them to resume the fighting with the GOI, the advice given by the US ambassador to Iraq, Robert C. Strong, in concurrence with that of the State Department, was to 'avoid appearing [to] act as agents of others or entangling themselves in [the] interests of others', meaning Iran.[83] Furthermore, certain US officials and communications also refer to the Kurds' struggle within Iraq as the 'Kurdish case', as opposed to terms such as the *Kurdish problem*. The term Kurdish *case* as opposed to *problem* suggests a degree of legitimacy in the eyes of some US diplomats. Such nomenclature is evident also in the use of *cause*. In the above telegram from the US ambassador to Baghdad back to the Department, the ambassador stated that 'we think [the] Kurds' cause will be severely damaged in Iraq if [the] Kurds appear to act as agents for [the] interests of others'.[84]

The US also did not take any significant measures to subdue the Iraqi Kurds, and therefore it did not view them as the communist threat that the Kurdish antagonists would have liked to portray them, as stated earlier. This in itself was also because the US had no interest as such in decisively backing the GOI to overpower the Kurds. Essentially, the US was ready to have the Iraqi government on its side if indeed the Iraqi government opted to work with the US, and the US was ready to sacrifice the Iraqi Kurds for the realisation of this relationship, if necessary. Essentially, Cold War interests trumped all in the related regional politics for the superpowers.

Iran's Kurdish trump card in Iraq, Israel and the Kurds

Two years into the era of the pro-Nasser nationalist government that took power from the Ba'athists in November of 1963, as early as April 1965, according to the Shah himself, Iran was helping the Kurds but apparently not encouraging them to resume hostilities. At this juncture, as the Shah told Secretary Rusk in Tehran, 'Iran considered that in its relations with Iraq it held a trump card in the Kurds, which it would not relinquish as long as a "truly national" government was not established in Iraq'.[85] Apparently, the Shah said 'We are not going to let the Iraqi Kurds down until a national government is established in Baghdad'.[86]

As has been noted, according to the CIA, in April 1965 the Shah's 'main external concern'[87] was the expansion of pro-Nasserites in the Persian Gulf area, and it was from this perspective that the Shah reluctantly came to embrace the Iraqi Kurds, in addition to the royalists in Yemen and also while cooperating on security matters with Israel.[88] Thus, the Shah was seeking to contain or counteract

1963–1965: Seeking allies   67

the rise of Nasserites or, broadly, that of Arab nationalism, and the Iraqi Kurds were instrumental in this insofar as it concerned Iraq. This implies that if Nasser could succeed in dominating Iraq, then the Shah would ensure that neither would this Nasserite Iraq be strong enough to pose a serious threat to Iran nor could it all be ruled by pan-Arabists alone (i.e. excluding non-Arabs, meaning the Kurds).

The Shah seems to have felt impelled to prevent the rise of an Arab super-structure or federal state ruled by Nasser and bordering Iran, with implications also for Iran's oil-rich Khuzestan region in addition to challenging Iran in the Gulf. Before this could happen, however, it would have only been natural for the Shah to want the Iraqi Kurds on his side with the ability to debilitate Iraq as well as create a buffer, 'Kurdish controlled' zone along Iraq's north-eastern border with Iran. The Kurds had the potential to tie down the Iraqi army at home, pre-venting it from adventures abroad and, indeed, this was what was to happened until the Algiers Accord of 1975.[89]

Concerning the Shah's worries about Arab nationalism, various American and British state archived sources portray him as a person somewhat obsessed with the risk to Iran of Arab unity.[90] Regardless of the extent to which this was a genuine feeling on the Shah's part or whether he was just exaggerating the risk in order to attain more US armaments, it was certainly the case that, by the late 1965, there were already a number of attacks on the Iranian frontier posts by Iraqi armed forces, including by fighter jets. In these attacks, at least two Iranian servicemen lost their lives. Nevertheless, there were no indications in terms of troop move-ments that either side wanted to take this to a full-scale war, and each side blamed the other. The Iraqis basically seem to have sought to intimidate Iran to back off from assisting the Kurds. It is important to stress, though, that these were not simply the actions of just any Iraqi government but of a 'pro-Nasserite' nationalist government, the Shah's nightmare.[91] And meanwhile, Iraq also launched a diplomatic offensive to pressure Iran to stop backing the Kurds and seal the border.

When Abd al-Rahman al-Bazzaz became the Iraqi Prime Minister in late 1965, his government initially appeared convinced that the only way to deal with the Kurdish Issue was for Iran to seal its border. The Iraqi attempts included asking Britain and the US to mediate between the two countries to that end. Even before Bazzaz became Prime Minister, the Iraqi government was already on that mission. For instance, in August 1965, the State Department instructed its embassy in Iran to ask Iran to change its policy towards the Iraqi Kurds, to cease assisting them as had been alleged by Iraq. Iraq was complaining both to the US and also to the UK that their arms were ending up in Kurdish hands, apparently provided by Iran. Furthermore, as early as September 1965, Iran was tying the Kurdish question in Iraq to other disputes that it had with Iraq, namely, the Shatt al-Arab question and Iraqi activities directed against Arabs living in Khuzestan, in addition to alleged maltreatment of the Iranian community living in Iraq. The Iraqis, of course, rejected and dismissed these accusations.[92]

By 1965, therefore, what Iran wanted was a comprehensive deal or package with Iraq, which included a resolution of all issues with Iraq, including the Iraqis

68   1963–1965: Seeking allies

toning down their 'Arabian' gulf rhetoric. However, neither side wanted to compromise, since the Iranian request was not acceptable to the Iraqis and the Shah had a valuable means of influencing developments in Iraq: his Kurdish card, as he saw it.[93] While Iran never admitted to supporting the Iraqi Kurds, by mid-1964 it had already established contacts with Mustafa Barzani.

Iran contacted Barzani for the first time in 1964. Before this, it had had contacts with a faction of the KDP politburo that had fallen out with Barzani, these being conducted through an Iranian liaison officer by the name of Isa Pejman. It seems that Iran's motivations for contacting Barzani were due to appreciation of Barzani as now the leader of the Iraqi Kurds and that by approaching him it would wield an even greater influence in the north of Iraq, and thus pressure Baghdad. This was significant because it denoted the high stakes involved here regarding the Kurds for Iran, as Barzani already had a pending death sentence in Iran due to his role in the ill-fated Kurdish Mahabad Republic of 1946 (Chapter 1). In the interests of establishing relations, therefore, Iran sent a General by the name of Pakravan to meet Barzani in Hacî Omeran, Iraqi Kurdistan, on July 20, 1964. This meeting was the result of an earlier visit by a SAVAK (Iranian secret police) representative to Barzani, who had asked Barzani whether he might like to visit Iran. In Hacî Omeran, General Pakravan had an imperial decree with him quashing Barzani's death sentence in Iran issued in 1947, so Barzani was able to visit Iran to meet with the Shah after this. The Shah had also sent his sympathy for the Kurdish revolution and indicated his willingness to help.[94]

Meanwhile, Iran was also abetting a breakaway politburo faction of the KDP through Isa Pejman. It not only had an influence on the Iraqi Kurds and thus Iraq, but it could also play a role between the two Kurdish factions, as it saw fit. Barzani was well aware that Iran had its own agenda, but he too needed Iran; although he pretended that he trusted Iran when dealing with the Iranians, in reality his view of the Shah was a mirror image of the Shah's view of the Kurds. Essentially, therefore, both sides wanted to exploit the other for their own benefit.[95] As argued, therefore, the Shah's willingness to quash Barzani's death sentence and to show a readiness to assist the cause of the Iraqi Kurds testifies to the high stakes involved for Iran. It also depicts Iran's role in the Iraqi Kurds' affairs, both with Iraq and also with external powers, for Iran's relations with the Kurds would change as the Iraqi Kurds' relations changed with other powers.

By 1965, Radio Israel was also taking an extraordinary interest in the fight between the Iraqi Kurds and Iraq by publicising Iraqi losses.[96] This is an indication of Israel's interests in the Iraqi Kurds. According to Mahmoud Othman, relations between Israel and the Kurds were established from 1963, even though David Kimche states these to have started from 1965. Indeed, what the Kurds hoped for the most was that Israel would be able and willing to use its influence with the US to advance the Kurdish cause and thus invoke a positive change in US policy towards them. However, even this relationship had to go through the Shah due to the landlocked geography of Iraqi Kurdistan. As Othman put it, 'the key of the matters was the Shah, be it for Israel or the US', since 'Iran was the geographical and the political key to the outside world'.[97] Turkey, in the meantime, with its Kurdish neuralgia, was not even talking to the Kurds.[98]

Concerning the actual situation in Kurdistan, the war resumed in July 1964; as the Peshmerga took more territory from the army while the ranks of Peshmerga themselves swelled, the Shah's pledge, which had been made earlier as a result of the contacts mentioned to help the Kurds, materialised. Masoud Barzani notes Iran's backing to comprise the stationing of an Iranian military representative (Ali Modarisi, an Iranian Kurd from Mahabad) with a wireless communication station in Kurdistan, sending 500 rifles, 8 mortars and munitions to Mustafa Barzani's Peshmerga. These were in addition to permitting Kurdish casualties to be treated in Iran's hospitals[99]; this aid is noted by Entessar to consist of 'large quantities of arms from the Iranian government'.[100]

US foreign policy and the Iraqi Kurds in a wider context: from Kennedy to Johnson

When Lyndon B. Johnson became president after Kennedy's assassination, he inherited a major issue in relation to international communism: Kennedy's Vietnam problem. On August 7, 1964, Congress passing the Tonkin Gulf Resolution, signed into law by Johnson on August 11, 1964, and thus escalating the war in Vietnam by early 1965. The Vietnam War dominated US public opinion and, alongside the civil rights issue, came to dominate American politics during Johnson's presidency.[101] Some 450,000 American troops were in Vietnam by 1966.[102] This is the broader global context in relation to the Cold War and the US, during the time covered in this chapter. Thus, when an issue such as the fate or justice of the cause of the Kurds is placed alongside the deep concern with containing communism worldwide, the former appears rather marginal, of little advantage or importance to America. Regardless of what was happening in Kurdistan, as long as the Soviets were not gaining from it, it was simply not sufficiently important or directly affecting American interests or perceived thus. Moreover, the Kurds did not have a state in the first place that could have been taken over by international communism, like Iraq or Lebanon, for instance. Therefore, as long as the Soviets stayed away, the US too could afford to overlook the Kurds' national aspirations, and notions such as liberty.

Regarding internal US politics, Joyce Kaufman has observed that 'In 1952 the United States elected Dwight Eisenhower president based in part on his pledge to "bring the boys home from Korea"'.[103] This shows the significance of the connection between domestic US politics and its foreign policy. For the US public, as a people on a remote land in the Middle East surrounded by hostiles who were already US allies (Iran and Turkey), the Kurds simply did not garner much attention. There is no indication of any public protest or support from any substantial number of influential figures for the Kurds in the US, apart from one US Supreme Court Associate, Justice William Orville Douglas. There may have been a few other figures supportive of the Iraqi Kurds, but nothing substantial.[104] There was, therefore, simply no real motivation for US policymakers to extend

70   *1963–1965: Seeking allies*

US idealisms of freedom and democracy, or any such thing, to the *case* or the *cause* and much less to the *problem* of the Iraqi Kurds.

Accordingly, as Frank Costigliola has noted regarding Latin Americans, 'the Kennedyites chose anti-Communist stability rather than risk radical change',[105] and this was also precisely applicable to the issue of the Iraqi Kurds; self-determination or any such right was out of the question in the context of the imperative to maintain whatever stability there was to keep the Soviets at bay. This is how the leading power of the Western world perceived the Kurdish Issue in Iraq in the period covered by this chapter.

Furthermore, the US simply had no interest in supporting Kurdish national aspirations given that these could have had negative consequences for Cold War US allies and thus the Cold War itself, if the Kurds were to be sponsored by the USSR or indeed by the US itself. On the contrary, it was motivated to maintain a discrete non-involvement. Pragmatism therefore, again, took precedence over idealism. This is how the US seems to have perceived the Kurdish Issue in Iraq under the Johnson administration, as under those of Kennedy and Truman before him.

Notes

1   For a detailed account of the Ba'ath ideology, their stance on the Kurdish issue and the development of the Ba'ath government of February 1963 as related to the Kurds, see Ghareeb, Edmund, *The Kurdish Question in Iraq*, pp. 44–69. Ghareeb's work for this period seems to have been influenced by Arab Iraqi sources but remains informative nevertheless. Also, see Entessar, Nader, *Kurdish Ethnonationalism*, pp. 64–66. For the promises made see Barzani, Mes'ud, *Barzanî Û Bzutnewey Rizgarîxwazî Kurd: Bergî Duwem 1958–1961*, p. 123; Selah reşîd, *Mam celal: dîdarî temen, le lawêtyewe bo koşkî komarî, beşî yekem* (Karo: Kurdistan; Iraq, 2017), pp. 210–217.
2   Entessar, op. cit., p. 67. Also, for more, see the same source, pp. 66–68.
3   Ibid., p. 67.
4   For more on these, see McDowall, David, *A Modern History of the Kurds* (London: I.B. Tauris, 2004), pp. 313–320; Ghareeb, op. cit., pp. 29–42; Entessar, op. cit., pp. 66–68.
5   McDowall, op. cit., pp. 313–320; Entessar, op. cit., pp. 66–68. Dr Mahmoud Othman considers this inter-Kurdish rivalry to be more due to the power struggle than ideological; Othman, in *Telephone Interview A*.
6   See Barzanî, Mes'ud, *Barzanî Û Bzutnewey Rizgarîxwazî Kurd: Bergî Sêyem, Beşî Yekem 1961–1975*, p. 110.
7   Quoted in 'FO 317/170456: E103134/2, Kurdish Problem in Iraq: Position as indicated by the Shah […]' (United Kingdom: The National Archives, 1963).
8   See FO 317/170456: EQ103134/8, Ambassadors talk […] the Shah, June 19, 1963.
9   Ibid.
10 The concern with Russian patronage was expressed by Iran's contemporary Minister of Foreign Affairs; see 'FO 317/170456: EQ103134/10, Iraqi Relations with Iran, June 29, 1963', and also 'FO 317/170456: EQ103134/8, Ambassadors talk […] the Shah, June 19, 1963.

1963–1965: Seeking allies   71

11 See Barzanî, *Barzanî Û Bzutnewey Rizgarîxwazî Kurd: Bergî Sêyem, Beşî Yekem 1961–1975*, p. 31.

12 'FO371/170429: E1015/25: Latest Kurdish Activities [...], February 6, 1963' (United Kingdom: The National Archives, n.d.).

13 'PR 6/10, FCO 51/191; Research Middle East: The Kurdish Problem in Iraq 1963–1971' (United Kingdom: The National Archives, n.d.).

14 FO 371/170448: 1963.

15 Ibid.

16 Washington Post, 'Iraq Army Battles Kurds In War of Extermination', Editorial, *Washington Post* (June 15, 1963).

17 See PR 6/10, FCO 51/191; Research Middle East: The Kurdish Problem in Iraq 1963–1971; FO 371/170448: 1963. Masoud Barzani also confirms the Arab pressure on Mongolia to back-down; see Barzanî, *Barzanî Û Bzutnewey Rizgarîxwazî Kurd: Bergî Sêyem, Beşî Yekem 1961–1975*, p. 125.

18 See FO371/170429: 1963. For Talabani's account see Selah reşîd, op. cit., p. 240.

19 FO 371/170448: 1963; FO 317/170515: 1963.

20 See Gibson, op. cit., p. 90.

21 See FO 371/170448: 1963; FO 317/170515: 1963; FO371/170429: 1963.

22 'Memorandum From Stephen O. Fuqua of the Bureau of International Security Affairs [...] Security Affairs (Sloan), frus1961-63v18/d153' (FRUS, February 8, 1963). Also, for an account of Ba'ath-Kurdish relations in this era, see Entessar, op. cit., pp. 64–66.

23 Ibid.

24 Ibid.

25 Ibid.

26 'Memorandum From Harold H. Saunders [...], frus1961-63v18/d204' (FRUS, April 2, 1963).

27 Ibid.

28 See footnotes of 'Telegram From the Department of State to the Embassy in Iraq, frus1961-63v18/d208' (FRUS, April 5, 1963).

29 Ibid.

30 Ibid.

31 Ibid.

32 'Circular Airgram From the Department of State to the Embassy in Iraq, frus1961-63v18/d216' (FRUS, April 18, 1963).

33 See 'Memorandum for the Record, frus1961-63v18/d251' (FRUS, May 16, 1963).

34 Ibid; FO 371/170450: 1963.

35 See FO 371/170450: 1963.

36 'Memorandum From Robert W. Komer of the National Security Council Staff to President Kennedy, frus1961-63v18/d293' (FRUS, July 10, 1963).

37 Ibid.

38 Ibid. The omitted text after 'ammo' here is an italicised insertion, '[*less than 1 line of source text not declassified*]'.

39 'Memorandum From the Joint Chiefs of Staff to Secretary of Defense McNamara, frus1961-63v18/d311' (FRUS, August 15, 1963).

40 Ibid.

41 Ibid.

42 'Circular Airgram From the Department of State to Certain Posts, frus1961-63v18/d174' (FRUS, March 2, 1963).

72 *1963–1965: Seeking allies*

43 Ibid.

44 See folder FO 371/170450: 1963.

45 The rest of an English version of the letter and the relevant attached airgram from US Tehran embassy to the State Department is accessible via 'Mullah Mustafa Barzani seeks Kennedy's aid [...]' (DDRS-Gale, July 30, 1963).

46 Mullah Mustafa Barzani seeks Kennedy's aid [...] (July 30, 1963).

47 For more on these see Entessar, op. cit., pp. 64–66.

48 Mullah Mustafa Barzani seeks Kennedy's aid [...] (July 30, 1963).

49 Ibid.

50 Ibid.

51 'Memorandum From the Department of State Acting Executive Secretary [...], frus1961-63v18/d307' (FRUS, August 6, 1963).

52 Ibid.

53 Ibid.

54 Ibid.

55 'Memorandum From Robert W. Komer of the National Security Council Staff to the President's Special Assistant for National Security Affairs (Bundy) frus1961-63v18/d173' (FRUS, March 1, 1963).

56 'PR 6/10, FCO 51/191; Research Middle East: The Kurdish Problem [...]' (United Kingdom: The National Archives, 1971), p. 17.

57 Kimche, David, *The Last Option: After Nasser, Arafat & Saddam Hussein: The Quest for Peace in the Middle East* (London: Weidenfeld and Nicolson, 1991), pp. 189–200.

58 'Special National Intelligence Estimate (SNIE) no. 30-3-63 [...]' (DDRS-Gale, May 15, 1963).

59 Memorandum From Robert W. Komer of the National Security Council Staff to the President's Special Assistant for National Security Affairs (Bundy) frus1961-63v18/d173.

60 The text of Shah's letter is accessible via: 'Letter From the Shah of Iran to President Johnson, frus1964-68v22/d2' (FRUS, January 7, 1964).

61 Ibid.

62 Ibid.

63 An electronic copy of the original, handwritten version of the letter (in Kurdish) was obtained from social media and is retained by the author. Jalal Talabani, 'Dear Beloved Sir [...] [trans. by author]' (April 6, 1963), p. 10. Also see Entessar, op. cit., p. 65.

64 These were the views of Talabani, see: Peter Mansfield, 'Kurds Sift Prospects in Arab State [...]', *The Washington Post* (June 5, 1963).

65 Ibid.

66 Letter From the Shah of Iran to President Johnson (January 7, 1964).

67 'Background Paper Prepared in the Department of State, frus1964-68v21/d3' (FRUS, April 6, 1964).

68 See 'FO 371/175754: 1964' (United Kingdom: The National Archives, n.d.); 'FO 317/170456: EQ101134/4, Kurds, May 18, 1963' (United Kingdom: The National Archives, n.d.); FO 371/170450: 1963.

69 See 'FO 371/175754: 1964' (United Kingdom: The National Archives, n.d.); 'FO 317/170456: EQ101134/4, Kurds, May 18, 1963' (United Kingdom: The National Archives, n.d.); FO 371/170450: 1963. Also Barzanî, *Barzanî Û Bzutnewey Rizgarîxwazî Kurd: Bergî Sêyem, Beşî Duwem 1961–1975*, p. 199.

1963–1965: Seeking allies 73

70 Entessar, op. cit., p. 66. The presence of Syrians troops is also confirmed by Masoud Barzani in addition to the aforementioned sources; see, for instance, Barzanî, *Barzanî Û Bzutnewey Rizgarîxwazî Kurd: Bergî Sêyem, Beşî Duwem 1961–1975*, p. 199.
71 See FO 371/175754: 1964; FO 317/170456: EQ101134/4, Kurds, May 18, 1963; FO 371/170450: 1963.
72 'Telegram From the Department of State to the Embassy in Iraq, frus1964-68v21/d165' (FRUS, June 5, 1964).
73 Ibid.
74 Ibid.
75 'Memorandum of Conversation, frus1964-68v21/d169' (FRUS, December 10, 1964).
76 Ibid.
77 Memorandum From Robert W. Komer of the National Security Council Staff to President Kennedy, frus1961-63v18/d293.
78 Quoted in Telegram From the Embassy in Iraq to the Department of State, frus1961-63v18/d49.
79 'Telegram From the Department of State to the Embassy in Iraq, frus1964-68v21/d17' (FRUS, December 14, 1964).
80 Ibid.
81 Ibid.
82 See ibid.
83 Ibid.
84 Ibid.
85 'Telegram From Secretary of State Rusk to the Department of State, frus1964-68v22/d75' (FRUS, April 8, 1965).
86 Quoted in ibid.
87 'Current Intelligence Memorandum, frus1964-68v22/d79' (FRUS, April 23, 1965).
88 Ibid.
89 For an account of the antagonism between Iranian and Arab nationalism and also the Iraqi Kurds' place in this, see, for example, Kimche, op. cit., pp. 189–200.
90 See, for example, #Memorandum on the Substance of Discussion at a Department of State-Joint Chiefs of Staff Meeting, frus1964-68v22/d80' (FRUS, April 23, 1965); 'FO 248/1617: 1965' (United Kingdom: The National Archives, n.d.).
91 See FO 248/1617: 1965. For more details on some of these issues also see Kimche, op. cit., pp. 189–200.
92 See folder FO 248/1617: 1965. Also see Kimche, op. cit., pp. 189–200.
93 FO 248/1617: 1965.
94 Barzanî, *Barzanî Û Bzutnewey Rizgarîxwazî Kurd: Bergî Sêyem, Beşî Yekem 1961–1975*, p. 176. Also see: PR 6/10, FCO 51/191; Research Middle East: The Kurdish Problem [...].
95 See Barzanî, *Barzanî Û Bzutnewey Rizgarîxwazî Kurd: Bergî Sêyem, Beşî Yekem 1961–1975*, pp. 176–178.
96 FO 248/1617: 1965.
97 Othman, in *Telephone Interview A*.
98 For more on this, see Barzanî, *Barzanî Û Bzutnewey Rizgarîxwazî Kurd: Bergî Sêyem, Beşî Duwem 1961–1975*, pp. 185–217; Kimche, op. cit., pp. 189–200; FO 248/1617: 1965.
99 For more on this relationship, see Barzanî, *Barzanî Û Bzutnewey Rizgarîxwazî Kurd: Bergî Sêyem, Beşî Yekem 1961–1975*, pp. 191–192.

74 *1963–1965: Seeking allies*

100 Entessar, op. cit., p. 67.
101 For more on this and Johnson's policies, see Costigliola, Frank, 'US Foreign Policy from Kennedy to Johnson', in *The Cambridge History of the Cold War Volume 2: Crises and Détente* ed. Arne Westad and Melvyn Leffler (Cambridge: Cambridge University Press, 2010); Crabb, Cecil Van Meter, *The Doctrines of American Foreign Policy: Their Meaning, Role, and Future* (Baton Rouge, LA: Louisiana State University Press, 1982), pp. 193–277; Kaufman, Joyce P., *A Concise History of US Foreign Policy* (Lanham, MD: Rowman& Littlefield, 2006), pp. 98–102. For an account of Soviet's policy between 1962 and 1975, see, Savranskaya, Svetlana and Taubman, William, 'Soviet Foreign Policy: 1962–1975', in *The Cambridge History of the Cold War Volume 2: Crises and Détente*, ed. by Arne Westad and Melvyn Leffler (Cambridge: Cambridge University Press, 2010), pp. 134–157.
102 Kaufman, op. cit., p. 100.
103 Ibid., p. 100.
104 See FO 371/170450: 1963. For more on Justice Douglas and Kurds see 'US Supreme Court Justice's travels through Kurdistan' (Kurdistan Iraq Tours, 2016).
105 Costigliola, op. cit., p. 122.

3 1965–1971: Politics and struggle

Background

By 1965, following the coup in late 1963 when the Ba'ath regime was overthrown and a pro-Nasser nationalist government came to power, fighting had resumed between the nationalist government and the KDP. In the face of Iraq's failure to curtail Iran's backing for the Kurdish movement in Iraq, this became intense and continued until Abd al-Rahman Arif became the president of Iraq, replacing his brother Abd al-Salam Arif who died in an air crash in April 1966. The new president declared that under his presidency the Kurds would be granted self-rule. This and the failure of the Iraqi military campaign in Kurdistan led to the Bazzaz Declaration of June 29, 1966, a 12-point peace plan offered by Prime Minister Abd al-Rahman al-Bazzaz that was also accepted by Barzani.

The Bazzaz Declaration essentially promised autonomy for Kurdistan and stipulated what was to be offered, including a freely elected Kurdish legislative assembly.[1] However, this plan was overtaken by events in Baghdad again, as, in July 1968, the nationalists' government was itself overthrown by the Ba'ath Party, before the Kurdish Issue could be resolved. The Kurdish War continued, notwithstanding the Declaration, and not only was the Iraqi army unable to subdue the Kurds, but its preoccupation in Kurdistan prevented it from making an effective contribution to the Arab–Israeli War of 1967.[2]

Returning to power for the second time since 1963, the Ba'athists initially vowed to implement the Bazzaz Declaration. It transpired, however, that this acceptance was partly a manoeuvre intended just to consolidate their own grip on power, bringing the Kurds on board, given the military stalemate. Voices in Baghdad were soon accusing the Kurds of being agents for imperialists and receiving outside support from the CIA and from Iran. In January 1969, the Ba'ath government reinitiated the war, dispatching some 60,000 troops to Kurdistan and escalating the bombing of Kurdish villages that had been recommenced in November 1968 to a more discriminative bombing campaign by late 1969.

A number of factors again led the government to return to negotiations, however, and the Ba'ath government and Kurdish leadership agreed on an autonomy plan in an accord signed on March 11, 1970. Again, the peace was problematic and the resolution unfulfilled. Some provisions of the plan never materialised and hostilities flared up again, albeit short of full-scale war.[3]

76   *1965–1971: Politics and struggle*

Cold War victims?

In 1965, Barzani made another attempt to acquire US backing, this time with a change of approach. On April 12, Shamsaddin Mofti and Masoud Barzani (Mela Mustafa Barzani's son) met with a US embassy officer in Tehran. The two carried an entreaty from Mustafa Barzani to the US administration in which Barzani asked for American financial and military aid, including heavy American armaments and conveyed his willingness to receive American officials in 'their area', expressing, moreover, his desire for Iraqi Kurdistan to be regarded as 'another state of the union'.[4] Barzani's desperate plea even went so far as to indicate that a direct arrangement should be made for Iraqi Kurdistan's oil resources to be handled by an American company. In other words, Barzani therefore was suggesting a Kurdish oil-rich entity sponsored by and beneficial to the US. Regarding Iran, the Shah's distrust of the Iraqi Kurds was reciprocated by Barzani's representatives, who told the embassy that the Kurdish leader desired direct channels of communication with the US government rather than through the Iranians whom he 'did not trust to report his views accurately'.[5] The Kurdish leadership was clearly aware that Iran's interest overlapped theirs and that this was the reason for Iran's friendly attitude towards the Iraqi Kurds' national liberation movement.

The response given to Barzani's representatives, firstly by the embassy officer and then in a telegram from the State Department two days later, emphasised that US policy towards the GOI–Iraqi Kurds had not changed. In other words, the US was still treating this as an internal Iraqi matter, implying that the US would not become involved and support the Kurds beyond offering goodwill, at most. Thus, the Department instructed the embassy to courteously continue to refuse to be drawn into dialogue with Barzani's representatives and requested that SAVAK be promptly informed of the visit.[6]

Mustafa Barzani had already explored several channels in his attempt to change the US position, including the US embassies in Cairo, Iran and Baghdad as discussed, but now, on a different occasion, he extended also an arm into the US itself by sending a representative there. This representative was Ismet Sherif Vanli. Vanli appears from US sources to have travelled independently, with no special or diplomatic privileges, but nevertheless an individual with a mission. An exchange of messages between the US ambassador, Robert C. Strong, in Baghdad and the State Department, in which the ambassador was reporting and seeking clarifications on his meetings with the Foreign Minister of Iraq Naji Talib suggests that Vanli, 'the Kurdish representative', was endeavouring to establish a permanent representation in Washington, albeit largely an unwelcomed and lone one.[7] Unsurprisingly, this did not go down well with the GOI, whose Foreign Minister at this time, Naji Talib, in a meeting with Strong pressed for the expulsion of Vanli and also for the US to pressure the Shah to refrain from aiding the Iraqi Kurds.

The pressure must have reached an unbearable point on the US ambassador in Baghdad, for in a telegram requesting thoughts on the matter from the

1965–1971: Politics and struggle   77

Department, he commented that he had 'about run out of arguments on [the] Kurds-Iran-Iraq triangle except possibly pointing out Arab interference in Khuzistan cannot be ignored by Shah'.[8] Submitting to the Iraqi pressure, the ambassador also proposed to the Department that Vanli's US visa be terminated, he be deported from the US and that he, the ambassador, be authorised to tell Mustafa Barzani to instruct Vanli to leave the US.[9]

In response, the Department concurred with the ambassador's proposal, gave him the green light to ask Barzani to have Vanli leave the US and also stated that it was looking into deportation regulations for Vanli, rather cold-heartedly, 'including possible bearing registration as foreign agent on deportation proceedings'.[10] The Department also commented on a meeting between the Deputy Assistant Secretary of State for Near East and South Asian Affairs, John D. Jernegan, and the Iraqi ambassador to Washington, Nair al-Hani, in which Jernegan 'reiterated that our reply to Kurdish petitions is always the same, we regard their problem [as] an internal affair of Iraq'.[11]

We see further evidence of the effect of the Cold War and the regional political framework on the Iraqi Kurds when it came to how the US treated their petitioning. This basic approach was adopted at least from 1958 and the reasons behind it had not changed, as analysed. The US policy towards the Iraqi Kurds, as established, was not an *ad hoc* policy but lasting and institutionalised. While the US had sympathy for the Kurds, it was up to Iraq to choose how it wanted to *resolve* its Kurdish question. The US merely wished for a peaceful settlement, if possible, but most of all to keep the Soviets away from Iraq and to avoid offending Cold War US allies Iran and Turkey by favourably looking upon the Kurdish Issue within Iraq. The US was particularly sensitive to Turkey, Iran and even Iraqi Arabs' sensitivities precisely because it needed these actors on its side against the perceived Cold War communist threat of the USSR. The stability of these states was more important for the US than any Kurdish rights, as much as the US was concerned, as the next section explains.

Regional stability, the US, Iran and the Kurds

As touched upon in the previous section, in August 1965 the State Department succumbed to Iraqi demands for the US to intervene to stop the flow of arms for the Iraqi Kurds. This was after the *chargé d'affaires* of the US Iraq embassy, J. Wesley Adams, had been summoned by the Iraqi Undersecretary for Foreign Affairs, Kadhm Khalaf, 'to request "in the strongest terms" that the United States intervene with the Iranians to obtain cessation of the flow of arms from Iran to the Kurds'.[12] The State Department accordingly instructed its embassy in Iran to covey US concerns regarding this to the Iranians.

Consequently, in pursing this, the *chargé d'affaires* of the US Iran embassy, Martin F. Herz, met with Iran's Foreign Minister Abbas Aram. However, Aram insisted that Iran was not helping the Kurds. What is more revealing here are the Department's notations to its Iran embassy in the cable, seemingly authorised by Rusk himself; in conveying that 'Our consistent policy has been [that] Kurdish

78 *1965–1971: Politics and struggle*

insurrection [is a] matter concerning only Iraq and [the] flow of arms and men across [the] border to bring pressure to bear against [the] Iraqi government [is] incompatible [with] our goal [for] area stability'. It stated that a Kurdish victory in Iraq could 'have only most ominous import for stability if not integrity [of] Iran and Turkey'.[13] The US was thus linking the Iraqi Kurds' struggle to 'area stability' and the integrity of neighbouring countries with Kurdish populations. There was no reference to notions like self-determination or liberty.

Concerning regional politics, the forthcoming British withdrawal from Aden and the Gulf were already an additional concern for the Shah by 1965; it further elevated his apprehensions, as he believed that the area could be a weak spot for outside 'predatory' powers (i.e. communists and Nasser). Therefore, as early as 1965, the Shah was of the opinion that Iran remained the 'single constructive free world power capable of protecting commerce and peace in [the] Gulf area'.[14] In other words, the Shah wanted Iran to fill the gap that would be left by Britain, accordingly forestalling communists and Nasserites' expansions into the Gulf.

The Shah's fears of Arab aims seem to have compelled him to seek to take pre-emptive measures, for it is clear from his Thanksgiving Day conversation with the US Iran ambassador, Armin H. Meyer, in November 1965, that he considered all major Arab powers to pose threats to Iran. The Shah construed that Nasserites could take over Kuwait and other Gulf principalities and that the Iraqis and Syrians all had the same aim, which was an Arab move on Iran's Khuzestan region. These perceived risk factors also help to explain the Shah's avarice for Western military hardware, which, he complained to the US ambassador, was being denied to him, such as naval destroyers that America had apparently provided to the Turks but not Iran.[15]

The Shah's worry and somewhat paranoia about Arab nationalism helps to comprehend his amicable relationship with the Iraqi Kurds. The Shah seems to have calculated that if Arab nationalism, Nasserism in particular, were to be triumphant in the Gulf and the Arabian Peninsula, then at least the Kurdish War could preoccupy Iraq. Similarly, the Shah would rather have had Kurdish Peshmerga across a long stretch of Iraq's frontier with Iran than Arab troops. In the face of Arabs to the south and given their landlocked geography, the Kurds would have been dependent on Iran in any case, so the Kurdish risk to Iran was much smaller than that from the Arabs. Moreover, by embracing the Iraqi Kurds, the Shah could also keep the pressure on Baghdad, and thus encourage the likelihood of Baghdad seeking a compromise with Iran rather than taking a hard-line approach. At worst, Iran could contain Iraq through the Kurds, while at best it could even compel Iraq to meet its desires for exchanging the Kurds. As will be seen in the next chapter, the latter outcome was ultimately the case; Iran got what it wanted in the end.

Different aims and motivations

An airgram from the US Iraq embassy to the State Department sent by ambassador Robert C. Strong on October 30, 1965 reflected on who was involved and how they

1965–1971: Politics and struggle   79

had a stake in the Iraqi Kurds' status. The ambassador offered his own 'Analysis of the Kurdish Problem'[16] to the Department. He also reiterated US policy on this and, as well as weighing the pros and cons of the issue, essentially noted that everyone had a stake in the issue but for different reasons and with various purposes.

Pursuant to the ambassador's assessment, in 1965, while the USSR, the US and Nasser were advocating for a peaceful solution, Iran, Israel 'and perhaps the British'[17] appeared to be favouring a continuation of the conflict, due to its debilitating effects on Iraq in which each had a different motivation. This both shows the multi-faceted nature of the Kurds' cause, in general, and the Iraqi Kurds, in particular, and also confirms that Iran was a major player in terms of the Kurds' relations with other powers, including the central authority in Iraq, which affected all the balances between the Kurds and all the other actors. For the US, it seemed that a Russian or a communist takeover of the Kurds' struggle seemed to have been unlikely at the time the ambassador was speaking (1965). Indeed, as examined, US policy in the Middle East generally during the Cold War and in the context of the Kurds in particular revolved around containing the USSR and what it saw as international communism. Therefore, given that the Kurds were not communists and neither could they have been an effective tool to equate to Iran, Turkey or even Iraq, when it came to containing regional communism, since the Kurds were not a sovereign state actor, they did not merit any particular attention.

As the Iraqi Kurds did not predominantly lean towards communism and thus substantiate a major communist threat, this meant for the US, as the ambassador clearly put it, that 'the consequences do not, at least for the time being, warrant a major initiative by the United States'.[18] Therefore, as seen by the US, the Kurds were neither likely to be a major communist actor at that time nor would they be able to force a military solution upon Iraq or establish their own separate entity that could be of use or otherwise to the US. This was especially so given the uncompromising opposition such a Kurdish entity would have faced from Iran and Turkey, which considered any potential Kurdish entity in Iraq as an existential threat to, what they considered to be, their own territorial integrity.

Therefore, as seen by the US, the Iraqi Kurds did not have a particular place in US policy priorities for the region or even in the Cold War itself. Iran and Turkey were already US regional allies whose tasks in the Cold War were to contain the Soviets from moving southwards to the Middle East. On the one hand, it would have been unthinkable for the US to offend these regional power pillars by assisting the Iraqi Kurds, presumably leading to destabilisation of these countries through their own Kurds. Yet, on the other, had the US been forthcoming towards the Iraqi Kurds and thus offended the Iraqi government, it would also have had ramifications on US–Iraq relations insofar as it would have either driven Iraq deeper into Nasser's arms with an uproar in Arab anti-Americanism, or else forced Iraq into the Soviet camp or even a combination of the two.

Just as the US did not want to offend Turkey and Iran for any kind of Kurdish rights, so also were the above scenarios quite undesirable; losing Iraq to communism during the Cold War divide was simply unthinkable. Even against this unfavourable situation of the Kurds and backdrop, the Iraqi Defence Minister

80 1965–1971: Politics and struggle

Abd al-Aziz al-Uqayli claimed in 1966 that the Iraqi Kurds were seeking to establish 'a second Israel'[19] in the Middle East and that 'the West and the East' were both 'supporting the rebels [Kurds] to create a new Israeli state in the north of the homeland as they had done in 1948 when they created Israel'; thus, he said 'It is as if history is repeating itself'.[20] This is indicative of the hostility to the potential Kurdish state sponsored by the US. The opposition did not just come from Iraq. As Ofra Bengio has noted, 'An Arab commentator had warned earlier that if such a thing should happen, "the Arabs will face within two decades their second *nakba* [catastrophe] after Palestine"'.[21]

The ambassador's view was that 'For the immediate future, neither the Kurds nor the GOI' appeared able to 'force a military solution' and that 'even a negotiated solution' was 'not likely to be permanent'. Indeed, he stated, 'The Kurdish problem is long-term'.[22] It is this view that underpins the analysis presented in this chapter. The ambassador also added a second dimension, confirming a point made in this book, when stating that

> a high degree of autonomy or independence for the Iraqi Kurds would be disruptive of area stability and inimical to our interests in the long run. Neither is the continuation of the fighting in United States interests, although the consequences do not, at least for the time being, warrant a major initiative by the United States. That the communists and Soviets will gain control of a large-scale insurrection seems unlikely, as is Kurdish ability to establish an autonomous or separatist regime.[23]

The US stance in the mid-1960s was that a continuation of the conflict was not in US interest because it would have invited third parties to join in, namely, the Soviets, at least indirectly.

In fact, a high degree of autonomy won by the Iraqi Kurds would have opened the gates for many possibilities in the US view. In addition to the potential for a Kurdish entity to become a Soviet satellite, Iraqi Kurds might have been presumed to assist the Kurds of Iran and Turkey and thus destabilise these US allies, in one way or another. Hence the ambassador's statement that 'The central conclusion from the standpoint of the United States is that a high degree of autonomy or independence for the Iraqi Kurds would be disruptive of area stability and inimical to our interests in the long run'.[24] So far as the US was concerned, therefore, an Iraqi Kurdish autonomous entity would clash with its own interests and even the threat of such was a cause of concern. It must be made clear here that this analysis is how the Kurdish Issue was seen by the US, and not whether this policy was right or wrong.

The government of Abd al-Rahman al-Bazzaz and the Kurdish Issue

Abd al-Rahman al-Bazzaz, who became the Prime Minister of Iraq on September 21, 1965, was, according to Bazzaz himself in a private conversation with an

1965–1971: Politics and struggle   81

unnamed US Secretary, 'willing [to] look at [the] Kurdish peoples as [a] nation'.[25] Nevertheless, for progress to be made, he wanted the US and the UK to put pressure on the Shah to stop aiding the Kurds, while at the same time also 'predicting'[26] that there would never be a Kurdish state encompassing all the Kurds. As before, the response given to Bazzaz's request was that the US had limited influence on other countries, including, in this case, Iran. The US, Bazzaz was told, could not simply ask other countries to do what it wanted. Bazzaz was also seeking a rapprochement with the US, but while accusing the Shah of 'encouraging disturbances [in] northern Iraq [Kurdistan] for purely destructive reasons' and recognising that the 'Shah's problem' was his 'attitude towards Nasser'.[27]

Bazzaz raised the issue of Iran's backing for the Kurds in his meeting with various US officials, including Vice President Humphrey, having earlier raised it with Department officials. However, the VP did not comment on the Kurdish Issue here, 'saying he was uninformed [of the] details'.[28] In a different meeting, 'Bazzaz raised Kurdish problem in [an] economic sense as [a] drain on Iraq's finances'.[29] This all shows the importance of the Kurdish Issue for Iraq, or rather its effects on Iraq in the absence of a lasting settlement.

Bazzaz's démarche to the US to pressure the Shah to abandon the Kurds appears to have had some success. According to the US ambassador to Iran Armin H. Meyer, who met the Shah in January of 1966, there were at least two long-lasting issues between Iran and Iraq—the question of the Shatt and Iran's aid to the Iraqi Kurds—and the ambassador conveyed to the Shah that the US did not want him to abet the Iraqi Kurds. However, US officials seem to have simply expressed their disapproval of the Shah's Iraqi–Kurd policy rather than exert any kind of real pressure. This deduction is based on the ambassador's account of the Shah's view:

> [The] Shah indicated he has no intention antagonizing his Kurds by actions against Iraq's Kurds. He described Kurds as [the] "purest Aryan" segment of [the] Persian race. [The] Shah's point was that [the] problem of [the] Kurds in Iraq is an internal Iraqi problem, not solvable by "butchering" Kurds and not exportable to Iran.[30]

This indicates that while the ambassador may have expressed disapproval of the Shah's backing for the Iraqi Kurds, the Shah had come up with his own reasons to counter the ambassador's point. According to the Shah, if he were to take action against the Kurds of Iraq, it would antagonise the Kurds of Iran. In other words, the Shah was essentially implying that he was reluctant to take action against the Iraqi Kurds as this would be counter-productive at home. However, it is to be recalled here that twenty years earlier the Shah's forces had smashed the Kurdish Mehabad Republic and hanged its founders, as mentioned (see Chapter 1). The Shah did not have a *bona fide* interest in the Iraqi Kurds winning autonomy from Iraq, but only really wanted to exploit the Iraqi Kurds for Iran's own interests, and what he told the ambassador was only for him to find a way for refusing the

82   1965–1971: Politics and struggle

ambassador's request, as ultimately in 1975 the Shah would sell out both the Iraqi Kurdish movement and everything that they had fought for.

The two issues mentioned, as confirmed by the US ambassador to Iran, therefore, were the most outstanding issues between Iran and Iraq at this juncture, or in early 1966, and had the potential to decide the Kurds' fate in Iraq. The Shah also considered both of these matters unresolved, but he did not see any urgency to resolve them. He remarked that Iran had waited for decades to resolve the Shatt question and that it could 'afford to wait few more years'.[31]

Human rights: not applicable to the Kurds?

In January 1966, Mustafa Barzani appealed again to the US president. In a letter to Johnson, he first explained the origins of the Kurdish Issue and how the Iraqi Government was intent on the destruction of the Kurds' lives and property in a scorched earth campaign, having failed to declare a victory over the Kurds on the ground. Then, Barzani tried to challenge the established US policy by stating that:

> if the Iraqi government defends itself by stating that the Kurdish case is an internal problem it will be false, because the Kurdish nation form a language, customs and possessions and because the League of Nations recognised the rights of the Kurdish people [...] in a special agreement on the rights of Southern Kurdistan in Iraq.[32]

Barzani's letter appealed to the US leader by evoking US values, stating that the Kurdish demands corresponded 'with the traditions of your country concerning the freedom of peoples and your government's positions on human rights'.[33] He asked Johnson to prevent the supply of arms to the Iraqi government, to support the Kurds in their war with Iraq and for the President to use his 'great influence and effort' to solve the issue.[34] Barzani ended his letter by stating, 'I ask this for the sake of peace and the basic constitutional rights of my people'.[35]

However, the letter was not forwarded until March and then in the same cable with a US Iranian embassy request and recommendation that it to be authorised to give Barzani the same reply as had been given previously, in 1965, outlining US policy vis-à-vis the Iraqi Kurds (Chapter 2). The embassy relayed to the Department that they saw 'no advantage in a written response or acknowledgement of Barzani's letter'.[36] A fortnight later, on March 23, 1966, the Department concurred on the response proposed by its Tehran embassy. Barzani's appeal, with the response given demonstrating—again—that the policy remained unchanged. This also confirms the pragmatic nature of the policy, in which *US values* had no place and for which US diplomats worked on the basis of seeing advantages. Unfortunate for the Kurds, this advantage was not perceived at these times.

Again, also we see that there was an institutionalised US policy towards the Iraqi Kurds, at Departmental as opposed to field diplomat level, devised against the backdrop of the Cold War and its regional politics. While US field diplomats

1965–1971: Politics and struggle   83

did play a part in the formation of this policy, in this case by proposing the action to be taken, or the lack thereof, the ultimate decision was made back in the US, above embassy level. This also raises interesting questions of how policy is formulated and the manner in which diplomats' views and proposals contribute to policy making, but this goes beyond the scope of this book.[37]

Throughout the next two years until the Ba'ath coup of 1968, and in fact beyond, the Kurdish Issue in Iraq and GOI–Kurdish settlement was one of the key issues in meetings between US and Iraqi officials. Iraqi officials relentlessly requested the US to put pressure on Iran to cease assisting the Kurds, even though a ceasefire with the KDP was reached in June 1966. The Iraqis were also aware that Iran had ambitions in the Shatt.[38] However, as had been the case earlier, there was no indication to show that the US brought any kind of significant pressure on Iran to stop backing the Iraqi Kurds, even though the US was aware of the Shah's relations with them. In the words of the US ambassador to Iraq, reporting of his conversation with Iraqi Prime Minister Naji Talib on August 18, 1966, 'Iran gave limited help to Kurds for limited objective[s]'.[39] The ambassador's opinion also confirms that the Shah has had his own objectives in aiding the Iraqi Kurds.

The recommendations of the Country Director for Israel and Arab–Israel Affairs, Alfred L. Atherton, to the Assistant Secretary of State for Near Eastern and South Asian Affairs, Raymond A. Hare, in 1966 succinctly described the reasons why the US was taking the posture that it had with the Iraqi Kurds in the 1960s. They were an 'attempt to offset Soviet influence in the Kurdish area by maintaining *a friendly though correct* relationship with the main body of the Kurds [Barzani], who constitute a sizeable proportion of the population and hold strategic Iraqi territory' (emphasis added).[40]

In February 1967, Barzani sent yet another letter to Johnson, urging the US president to use his influence for a final and just settlement for the Kurdish Issue within Iraq. Barzani and Iraq had reached an agreement in June 1966 with the Bazzaz Declaration, which was largely the result of a crushing defeat for the Iraqi army in Kurdistan on March 12–13, 1966, in the Battle of Mount Handren, where Peshmerga forces had ambushed a large army column. The Iraqi army catastrophically suffered somewhere between one and two thousand casualties as well as the loss of large quantities of arms to the Kurds. Handren shook the Iraqi army's morale.[41] Towards the end of 1966, Barzani sent a memorandum to the Iraqi President complaining that the government had not implemented the Bazzaz agreement or acted in good faith. Barzani's messenger, Mahmoud Othman, also delivered a copy of this memo to the State Department, 'at the desk level, where Kurds and Kurdish emissaries are received'[42] together with another letter from Barzani to Johnson.

This time the letter was forwarded to the President's Special Assistant, although again not without a recommendation from the Executive Secretary of the State Department stating that because Barzani 'has technically still not submitted to the Iraqi Government',[43] the Department recommended that no written acknowledgement be sent to Barzani and that, as usual, an officer at Desk level should

84   *1965–1971: Politics and struggle*

orally acknowledge receipt of the letter on behalf of the President and reassure the Kurds of [the] United States Government's concern on a humanitarian basis as evidenced by the continuing flow of surplus foods to the destitute Kurds in Iraq. Such a reply would be consistent with our previous handling of messages from Barzani.[44]

Indeed, the US had been running a programme of providing surplus US food to Kurdish refugees in Kurdistan affected by the war since 1964. This also tells us that the US was well aware of the humanitarian costs of the conflict. However, there is no sign to suggest that the US at any point insisted on cessation of hostilities. The US was worried that even a presidential reply to Barzani would offend the Iraqis, let alone demanding cessation of hostilities.

Concerning Barzani's letter of 1966, in May 1967 the White House eventually deemed it unnecessary to reply or to take any action.[45] This also shows that this decision on how to deal with the Iraqi Kurds came directly from the top, regardless of the nature of the decision. Certainly, it appears that the US increasingly took the Iraqi Kurdish Issue at a higher and more senior level towards the end of the 1960s. This may have been in part due to the notion that, as laid out by an Intelligence Note from the Director of the Bureau of Intelligence of the State Department, Thomas Hughes, to the Secretary of State, Dean Rusk, if Iran and Israel were successful in persuading the Kurds to renew hostilities with the Iraqi army, and if this was exposed by the Arabs, then 'Arab radical propaganda would no doubt claim that this [was] a new "plot" against the Arabs instigated by the US'.[46] This is not to say that there was a change in US policy, but US officials do seem to have observed the Iraqi Kurds with an increasing interest. Iranian and Israeli aid along with this concern about renewed Iraqi–Kurdish hostilities in the latter parts of 1967 began to develop as before, but for different reasons.

Tahir Yahya, the new Iraqi Prime Minister, who took office in July 10, 1967, was seen as pro-Nasser by the Shah. The Shah naturally, therefore, wanted him replaced by someone he thought might be more amicable. One way of doing this was to persuade Barzani to renew the fighting with the GOI to generate more internal friction and political instability in Baghdad, thus leading to the toppling of the Yahya government. Also, the Shah could exploit the Kurds as a bargaining tool for concessions from Iraq in the Shatt, which was what the Shah had wanted in 1965 (Chapter 2).[47]

According to the same Intelligence Note, regarding Israel, before its war with Arab countries in June 1967, it had urged Barzani for 'some Kurdish action'[48] to tie down the Iraqi army and thus prevent it from joining the impending conflict. This was unsuccessful, but the bulk of the army had already been deployed in Kurdistan in any case. On the Kurdish side, according to Thomas Hughes, the GOI was defaulting on its promises given, leading to more militant and younger Kurds after the June 1967 War to call for action, especially at a time when Arab armies had just been badly defeated in the war with Israel.[49] Also, just before the Arab–Israeli War, the Iraqi Government had for a second time requested Barzani

1965–1971: Politics and struggle 85

to send a force of some 3,000 Peshmerga to join Iraqi troops in Jordan against Israel, but Barzani refused. The latter was, of course, when the ceasefire between the GOI and the KDP was still in place.[50]

On the way to totalitarianism: the return of the Ba'athists in July 1968 and their search for a bogeyman

The inability of the nationalist government to solve internal problems, the Kurdish Issue included, was the excuse given by the right wing of the Ba'ath Party for the coup of July 17, 1968.[51] From its onset, the Ba'athists reached out to Mustafa Barzani in an apparent effort to secure a settlement, but this was only a tactical move to facilitate their seizure of power, as with the preceding governments. According to the State Department's Director of Intelligence and Research in 1969, 'This initial effort [to make peace with Barzani] by the Ba'athists was soon nullified by a Ba'ath decision to support the "progressive" rival Kurdish group of Jalal Talabani in a rather crude divide-and-rule campaign designed to undermine Barzani'.[52] The Iraqi armed forces had been unable to overpower the Kurds since hostilities in Republican Iraq started, in 1961, so the government now wanted to drive a wedge in between them. The government wanted to capitalise on the inter-Kurdish rivalry involving the breakaway faction of the KDP led by Talabani and Ibrahim Ahmad, on the one hand, and Barzani, on the other. From November 1968, also, Iraq's military campaign in Kurdistan was resumed.[53]

Soon after retaking power from the Nationalists in July 1968, the Ba'athists embarked on a demagoguery policy, aiming to consolidate their own grip on power, to justify their actions, minimise threats, having been overthrown in 1963, and to also rally public support. They expelled a number of Americans from the country and even detained one with his wife on espionage charges for several weeks. He was said to have been a technician with the Iraq Petroleum Company (IPC). Their release was only secured under considerable American diplomatic pressure through third-party channels. The exact number of Americans working or living in Iraq that were expelled or detained is unknown, but it seems to have numbered at least in the dozens. Among those detained included American wives of Iraqi citizens as well as the American wife of a British UN official. Government propaganda painted the US and Israel as 'the relentless foe of Iraqi and Arab aspirations'.[54]

The Ba'athists sought to escalate tensions with Israel by accusing it (and the US) of seeking to bring down the government. On January 17, 1969, a number of Iraqi citizens were convicted by a revolutionary tribunal in Baghdad on charges of spying for Israel, and of the fourteen that were hanged on January 27, nine were Jews. According to one of the convicts, as claimed by the Baghdad Radio, the 'Israeli spy group' was apparently linked to another clandestine Iraqi group, consisting of various individuals, that was plotting to bring down the new Ba'ath government and reignite the Kurdish conflict in order to preoccupy the Iraqi army so that it could not face the Israelis. This group had been accused of aiming to

86   1965–1971: Politics and struggle

make peace with Israel if it succeeded in establishing a government consisting of Kurds and Arabs and allegedly was to be supported by CENTO members. Therefore, this group was meant to have been a pro-Israel, pro-Western organisation that would also be at peace with the Kurds. Regardless of the truth or otherwise of such allegations, these events serve to depict the wider picture and the political context of the developments that followed.[55]

The Ba'athists, it is evident, were still furious over their 1963 overthrow. They seem to have turned on anyone that they considered an obstacle. The new regime engaged in arbitrary arrests, the execution of prominent figures and replacement of military commanders. Coup rumours also played into their hands. In this way, the regime tied the alleged internal threats to the external threats, which Iraq was supposedly facing. The cycle of violence would provide the Ba'athists the excuse they needed to consolidate their power. The new President, Ahmed Hassan al-Bakr, told a mass meeting in Baghdad that while Iraq was facing the Israeli enemy on the front, the US and Israeli agents were striking from behind. This fear-mongering seems to have been intended to rally the public to the Party en route to absolute power.[56] One figurehead of the Ba'ath Party at this time was Saddam Hussein.

Strikingly, the US was aware of these developments and the anti-Americanism, so one would expect that the rise of such a government in Baghdad would have at least led to a review of US policy towards the Iraqi Kurds. This was not to be the case, however, until 1972. In relation to Israel, meanwhile, as the Director of Intelligence and Research of the State Department recognised, by escalating tensions with Israel, Iraq seemed to be almost wishing for an Israeli strike. This would have proved its point to the Iraqi people that Israel and the US were seeking to weaken the country and thus allow the Party to justify a new level of totalitarianism and further strengthen its power. An Israeli attack, that is, would have given the Ba'ath an excuse to be harsher on its perceived adversaries within Iraq. The Iraqi action seems to have been successful in somewhat provoking Israel. For instance, the Israeli premier Levi Eshkol denounced the (mentioned) executions and told the Israeli Parliament that nothing 'apart from Israel and her strength'[57] stood between the Jewish communities (presumably in Iraq and elsewhere) and annihilation.

Meanwhile, in March and April 1969, tensions between Iran and Iraq flared up over the Shatt. It is beyond the aim of this research to determine the blame for this new escalation, but the events seem consistent with the Ba'athists' brinkmanship to exploit external issues in order to garner favour at home and hence cement their powerbase. A diplomatic war of words between Iran and Iraq had led to Iraq declaring that it would search Iranian vessels in the Shatt. This prompted a response from Iran, most importantly in the form of denouncing the 1937 Treaty on April 19, 1969, which delineated the pertaining border, in addition to a large troop movement to the Shatt area and Khuzestan. Iraq took other measures to irritate Iran, such as giving an Iraqi diplomatic passport to the Shah's foe, General Teymur Bakhtiar, as well as mistreating and expelling Iranian citizens from Iraq as part of the larger Ba'ath campaign. Bakhtiar was a former head of the Iranian

1965–1971: Politics and struggle 87

intelligence service who had fallen out with the Shah and was exiled in 1961. After Iran abrogated the 1937 Treaty, Bakhtiar was said to have sent messages of support to the Iraqi President Ahmed Hassan al-Bakr, and a message allegedly from Bakhtiar was publicised by the Iraqi press urging the people of Iran to rise up against the Shah.[58]

The Deputy Chief of Mission of America's Iranian embassy was of the view that while it was Iraq that had initiated this new crisis, it was Iran that escalated it to the level of a risk of armed conflict. Against that, he also noted that Iran may not have really intended to go as far as an actual military engagement over the Shatt at the time, but merely wanted to exploit the opportunity to denounce the Treaty of 1937 and hence give the Iraqis the signal that the issue was yet to be resolved as far as Iran was concerned. This was in addition to Iran simply displaying its military prowess to the Gulf States and monarchies, and thereby aiming to strengthen Iran's leadership in the Gulf.[59]

Meanwhile, in April 1969, Barzani was visited by two distinguished American Assyrians from the US in order to 'to ascertain the condition of Assyrians in Kurdish territory'.[60] The men's journey to Kurdistan had been facilitated by the Iranian government, including helicopter transportation, which clearly also indicates Iran's close relationship with the Iraqi Kurds, albeit fluctuating. According to one of the American Assyrians, Sam Andrews, they held long talks with Mela Mustafa every evening during April 20–23, in which Barzani simply told them that Iran's support for the Kurds was directly proportional to tension between Iran and Iraq, and that at times it became 'a mere trickle'.[61] Barzani's statement and the account given by the visitor further supports the analysis developed here, that the Shah's backing of the Iraqi Kurds was intended to influence Iraqi politics for the Shah rather than a genuine sympathy for the Kurds, and at any one time, therefore, it was determined by the dynamics of that influence.

Also, according to the same individuals, who had also reportedly met Israelis while in Iran, Israel was providing arms to the Kurds while Iran was providing them with other necessities. Israel's involvement here and Iran's stratagem may not have been anything new, but this nevertheless confirms other reports and, just as importantly, shows the drastic effect of regional politics on the status of the Iraqi Kurds. The Kurds were essentially used by all parties involved for the advancement of their own interests and with scant regard to the Kurds themselves. These individuals then called on the State Department on May 29, where they met with the relevant desk officials. They conveyed that Barzani had wanted them to inform US officials that the Kurds were pondering upon attacking Kirkuk oil installations because its revenue was being used to found Iraq's war on the Kurds. They also cited Barzani as having said that 'he would like to see Kurdistan become the 51st state'. The two also carried a letter from the Kurdish leader to the Secretary of State, Williams Roger, which was to be delivered in the coming week in the presence of Shafiq Qazzaz who was representing the Kurds in Washington.[62]

As mentioned, given the Ba'ath Party's anti-Americanism and the fact that Iraq had broken off diplomatic relations with the US after the June 1967 Arab–Israeli

88   *1965–1971: Politics and struggle*

war, one might have expected an inclination towards the Iraqi Kurds from the US, but these internal developments and also the regional tensions provoked by the Ba'athists failed to cause a rethink in US policy at this point. In terms of stability, too, one could think that it was only logical for the US to move towards a rapprochement with the Iraqi Kurds since, as implicitly expressed, the State Department's view was that the new Ba'ath regime was basically rather paranoid.[63] The section below assesses why and how the character of the second Ba'ath government did not prompt some sort of realignment of US relations with the Iraqi Kurds, especially as they now enjoyed close relations with both Iran and Israel.

On June 13, 1969, the Assyrian notables that were mentioned, with others, returned to the State Department with Shafiq Qazzaz 'Representative of the Kurdish Revolution in the USA',[64] as a Department memo described him, in order to essentially plea for US assistance for their peoples in Iraq. Among the group were the two Assyrians that had travelled to Kurdistan in April to see Barzani and ascertain conditions (as discussed).[65] They carried with them a letter from Barzani, as stated, to the Secretary of State William Rogers. As in previous meetings in the State Department, US backing for the Iraqi Kurds was requested in a cordial conversation, but and again the result was unhelpful, as the group was informed by one of the State Department's Country Directors that while the US was 'sympathetic toward the sufferings of the Kurds and the Assyrians', they did not, however, 'support an independent Kurdish/Assyrian state' and they were 'not prepared to support this objective *either overtly or covertly*' (emphasis added). The best organised diplomatic move in the US by the Kurds to date was met by the most forthright response yet, a plain rebuff, in fact. This is despite Shafiq Qazzaz, being realistic, conveying that what the Kurds wanted was not independence but 'limited autonomy and cultural integrity'.[66]

Shafiq Qazzaz then told the Department officials that they (the Kurds) might feel impelled to attack IPC oil installations, around Kirkuk, to prevent the Iraqi government from gaining revenues it would employ to fund the purchase of weapons for use on the Kurds. This indication to the Americans of Kurdish intentions to disrupt the flow of oil certainly appears as a sign, a warning, perhaps, that the Kurds had the potential to disrupt the flow from Kirkuk's oilfields and demonstrate to the Americans that the Kurds occupied a strategic location.

According to Qazzaz, the Kurds had also made an unsuccessful appeal to the UN Secretary General U Thant to have their issue heard by the Human Rights Commission.[67] In a sign of what must have been utter frustration with the US, Qazzaz also told the Department officials that 'if the Kurds succeeded in gaining limited autonomy or independence, they would not forget who had refused them aid when they needed it'.[68]

Barzani's letter had conveyed the usual appeal, perhaps more forcibly expressed, for the US to help the Iraqi Kurds. After explaining that a racial war had been imposed on the Kurds and the Assyrians 'by the dictators in Baghdad, who seized power through bloody military coups' and that the people of Kurdistan were deprived of basic needs such as health and education, in appealing for US help, he stated that:

> Any serious step you [Rogers] may take towards this end will ensure for your country the generous gratitude and support of our people, as well as prove the best application of the policy of the United States, whose objective is to serve humanity and stand by small nations subjected to distress and suffering.[69]

Barzani also wrote that he had authorised the representatives to speak on his behalf and expressed his hope that 'the delegation will enjoy the favor of an audience with you [William Rogers]'.[70] State Department officials assured the delegation that the letter would be forwarded to the Secretary. What should also be noted here, of course, was that from January 1969, and hence during this meeting too, the US had a new President, Richard Nixon. Indeed, in his letter Barzani also notes this by stating that 'we hope that President Richard Nixon's administration may usher in more propitious times for our cause, and that this appeal may meet a receptive ear on your part and gain the necessary sympathy and support'. What is also unfortunate to mention here is that as the group was leaving their meeting with the Department officials, one of the Assyrian guests, excluding the two that were named and had tried in vain to press their case, took one of the Department officials aside and informed him that 'he really wouldn't look with favor upon an independent Kurdish state because he knew that the Muslim Kurds at that point would immediately turn on the Christian Assyrians'.[71]

Despite the totalitarian and violent nature of the Ba'ath regime, of which it was fully aware, the US not only refused to look at the Kurds' request favourably but, in fact, surprisingly it even refused to offer any support to a group of Iraqi émigré coup plotters planning to overthrow the regime with forces inside Iraq through 1968–1969. Barzani and Kurdistan were supposed to have been the pivot in this endeavour. According to one of the individuals involved, Loutfi Obeidi, Saudi Arabia was also understood to have put some money into the operation, which was destined for Barzani. However, he believed that the money did not reach Barzani but was pocketed by junior Iranian officials.[72]

The question that arises here, then, concerns why the US did not even take any steps towards bringing the Ba'ath regime to an end. This was a regime that had made an enemy of almost every player in Iraq and also many others outside Iraq, including the US. This is a question directly linked to the US–Iraqi Kurd relations, since Iraqi Kurdistan was supposed to be the base in the coup attempt mentioned as its launching pad. The US position of not proactively seeking the downfall of the new Iraqi regime is clear; this is confirmed by a telegram from William Rogers to the US Lebanese embassy, which concluded that

> In summary, [the] USG [is] unable to become involved in plotting against current Iraqi regime nor in making advance commitments. Should [the potential] new government prove to be moderate and friendly, however,

90 *1965–1971: Politics and struggle*

we would be prepared to consider prompt resumption of diplomatic relations and would certainly be disposed to cooperate within the limits of existing legislation and our overall policy.[73]

The reason that the US did not assist the coup planners, which also included the Kurds, to overthrow the Ba'athists is not evidential. It may have been simply that the US did not see the likelihood of a replacement government as being sympathetic to the US or much different from the past governments. Too many actors had a stake in Iraq to herald the rise of a new government that could provide internal stability as well as being pro-Western. According to this view, therefore, the US would not gain any advantage from entangling itself in this affair. Essentially, nothing good was likely to come out of it for the US, while the risk of failure was also considerable. Had the coup failed and its plotters been arrested, the Ba'athists would have been even further alienated, presented with apparently good reason for further repressive policies and possibly even pushed into the Soviet camp. Any US involvement in a coup attempt would have come with considerable risks and no certain advantage for the US.

Another consideration complicating this scenario, however, involves an actor that may have benefitted from all this, Iran. The Shah was now stating that it needed the capacity for 'over-kill',[74] meaning the threat of overpowering force as a deterrent, so that anyone considering attacking Iran 'would think twice or even three times', as the Shah put it in a meeting with Secretary Rogers.[75] The Shah was demanding this capacity since, in his view:

many of them [the Arab counties] were now in the hands of unprincipled bandits who either for their own purposes or in the misbegotten belief that Communism was a wave of the future were disposed to cooperate with the USSR.[76]

Thus, when the Shah was challenged by Rogers suggesting that Iran was already much stronger than Iraq and that it would be madness for Iraq to attack Iran, the Shah replied, 'those fellows in Iraq are mad,'[77] adding that Iraq had amassed all its troops but one division on the border with Iran. Further to make this case for Iran to be given an overkill capacity, the Shah also complained to the US in October 1969 that the USSR was backtracking on its decisions on the sale of arms to Iran and was instead equipping Iraq.[78] What this narrative undoubtedly does show is that the wider context of the Cold War and superpower rivalry continued to have a profound effect on the situation of the Iraqi Kurds.

Soviet pressure, KDP–Ba'ath negotiations, and Iran's objections

After the Iraqi army had failed to succeed in Kurdistan, another round of negotiations, initiated from Baghdad, started between the Ba'ath government and Barzani in December 1969. According to Nader Entessar, this was due to President al-Baker being convinced that the Kurdish Issue could not be resolved

1965–1971: Politics and struggle 91

through military means.[79] However, there was also another side to this which was the Soviets' desire for the issue to be resolved. Accordingly, on December 8, 1969, a Soviet representative, Yevgeny Primakov, travelled to Kurdistan to meet the Kurdish leadership with a letter from the Soviet leadership. The letter stated that Moscow desired the apparently golden opportunity that had arisen to resolve the Kurdish Issue to be utilised and that the Soviet leadership would exert all of its influence to press Baghdad to accept a lasting solution.[80] Thenceforth and in early 1970, the Soviet embassy staff in Baghdad were to play a mediating role between the Ba'ath government and the KDP. Ultimately, when Saddam Hussein visited Kurdistan in January 1970, he told Barzani that he had gone there to reach a solution with him and not merely a ceasefire, as with the previous Iraqi governments. Saddam asked Barzani to help him strengthen his own position in Baghdad, stating that in return he would resolve the Kurdish Issue based on the 'principle of autonomy'.[81] The USSR thus seems to have played a significant role in Ba'ath–Kurdish negotiations at this time, and Masoud Barzani confirms that the USSR did indeed pressure the Ba'ath to reach a settlement.[82] And indeed, on March 11, 1970, an accord was reached.

According to Israel's Foreign Ministry, the Soviets had put intense pressure on Iraq to make a deal with the Kurds. The Soviets were said to have put their arms supplies and energy cooperation on the line with the Iraqi government. The Director General of Israel's Foreign Ministry apparently voiced the opinion that, in the end, the 'Iraqi negotiators had literally asked [the] Kurds to state their terms for agreement and then signed [it] without further discussion'.[83] The State Department believed, initially at least, that this was an exaggeration of the Soviet role,[84] but the analysis of Soviet pressure was later confirmed by the observation of the Deputy Chief Representative of IPC in Baghdad, Mike Gardiner, when he explained, in July 1972, that the Ba'ath in fact had surrendered to Soviet pressure in an unwelcome deal with the Kurds.[85]

Having become aware of the potential for a KDP–Ba'ath agreement, the Shah had sent a letter to Barzani promising Iran's assistance in every way as long as Barzani did not sign the initiative into an agreement with Iraq, on the basis that this would strengthen the USSR's hegemony. Iran's endeavour to prevent an agreement between the KDP and the Ba'ath extended to inviting and warmly receiving Barzani in Tehran, where the Shah then promised him—on behalf of Iran but also of the US—that whatever Barzani required the Shah would provide, as long as he did not sign the agreement. Were the need to arise, apparently, Iran would practically commit to defending Barzani and the Kurdish movement. When Barzani returned to Kurdistan, the Shah sent repeated letters making the same offer, or request, or warning. According to Masoud Barzani, 'the last letter was even of a threatening nature'.[86]

Asadollah Alam, the Minister of Iran's Royal Court at the time, also confirms this, reporting the Shah's worrying about the issue even when on a holiday in Switzerland.[87] For his part, the Shah was still advocating a coup to overthrow the Ba'ath. The Kurdish leadership was not convinced by the Shah though, and went ahead with the negotiations that led to Saddam Hussein himself visiting Barzani,

92   1965–1971: Politics and struggle

and again staying overnight in order to reach a deal and sign the final agreement, on March 10, 1970.[88] Following this, the General Secretary of the Central Committee of the Communist Party of the Soviet Union Leonid Brezhnev himself sent a congratulatory letter to Barzani via the Soviet embassy, while in Baghdad the agreement led to mass public celebrations.[89] What must be emphasised here, as is evident, is the fact that the Kurds indeed were not a tool in the Shah's hands, but when they had to they did not hesitate to seek allies in their struggle against Baghdad, and of course this included Iran.

After the agreement was signed, a number of hostile actions perpetrated by radical anti-Kurdish Ba'athists occurred. The most significant of these was a failed assassination attempt on Mustafa Barzani's life at his headquarters in Hacî Omeran in Kurdistan in September 1971, along with an attempt on his son, Idris' life, in Baghdad. The KDP's intelligence agency, *Parastn*, had already warned that such actions were impending, and, as tensions and distrust heightened, the Soviets sent an envoy to Hacî Omeran led by a member of the Central Committee of the Communist Party and other Soviet diplomats. The envoy conveyed a letter to Barzani from the Soviet leadership stating that the assassination attempt was work of imperialists and conservative forces and that it was important that the Kurds and the Ba'ath honour the settlement. The Ba'ath was said to have been given the same message.[90] The Soviet envoy orally advised Barzani that a re-ignition of hostilities would not be in the Kurds' interest, and reportedly acknowledging that certain elements of the Ba'ath leadership were unwise, ignorant and did not wish for a peaceful settlement of the Kurdish Issue.[91] Indeed, the Kurdish leadership seems to have kept to the agreement, despite the hostile acts committed against them.

In 1983, Saddam Hussein admitted that he had been aware of the plot to assassinate Barzani back in 1971 and was upset that it failed. An assassination *was* carried out though, of the *Şingal* mayor, which the Ba'ath blamed on the KDP but Masoud Barzani states to have been the work of 'a foreign power'—Iran, it would appear—seeking to derail the peace process. Several other failed assassination attempts were also made and evidence was produced to the Ba'ath by the Kurds that at least some high-ranking military and security personnel in Baghdad were behind them. SAVAK, through mercenaries, also tried to derail the March 11 Accord by killing a number of Iraqi officials in Kurdistan and carrying out sabotage acts, such as blowing up a train on the *Kifrî-Qeretepe* railway, again to sabotage the peace process.[92]

In response to SAVAK's acts of sabotage, the Ba'ath government arrested and brutally executed innocent KDP members. This included murdering a Kurdish man accused of the train bombing by having his eyes gouged out in public, including in front of his family.[93] For SAVAK, the rationale behind these savage acts was that the Iraqi government would blame the Kurds, and this would then lead to renewal of hostilities and ultimately the collapse of the Accord.[94] Iran was therefore strongly against the Kurds' Accord with Baghdad and it negatively changed its relations with the Kurds until the signing of the Soviet–Iraqi Treaty of Friendship and Cooperation in 1972. Iran then perceived this treaty to be a serious

1965–1971: Politics and struggle   93

threat to it; thus, it restarted its relations with the Iraqi Kurds with a new vigour in order to counter that threat (see Chapter 4).[95]

The British withdrawal and heightened regional tensions: implications for the Iraqi Kurds

The British withdrawal of late 1971 from the Gulf was a milestone in the international relations of the Middle East during the Cold War, particularly for those of the Gulf region. At least, this is what one discerns from US archives pertaining to that era and the area, as will here be explicated. This development had the potential to reshuffle regional politics, and, as seen, the Iraqi Kurds' political status was deeply affected by the wider context and their relations with all of the principal states mentioned in this work were dependent on those states' relations with Baghdad.

Indeed, regional and international politics, such as the Cold War and, in its simplest form, Persian versus Arab nationalism, had profound regional implications generally. American attempts to counteract the spread of communism through principled positions like that expressed in the Eisenhower Doctrine indicated the effect of the Cold War in the region, while the establishment of CENTO to help contain the Soviet Union was another manifestation of that, as was the Iranian–Iraqi disputes and the Shah's unease with Nasser. A significant point to note here, though, is that even within this generally zero-sum political context, none of these actors' existence as political entities, states essentially, was decided by any of these dynamics. Why, therefore, should this political setting have such as profound effect on the status of the Iraqi Kurds? The answer, simply, was that while regional states were caught in the struggle between greater powers for influence and dominance, nevertheless, they were still sovereign states and enjoyed _de jure_ rights under international law. No state actor in the international community recognised the (Iraqi) Kurds as a sovereign actor and accorded them these rights; their power was _de facto_ and thus officially unacknowledged and regard for them practically malleable, meaning that state actors felt free to do as they wished.

For instance, the contemporary Iran versus Iraq dispute as an expression of a longstanding Arab–Persian power rivalry did not have an existential effect on Syria or Jordan in terms of these states as political entities, regardless of into whose camp these actors fell. Equally, the Cold War struggle did not imply that states such as Jordan or Kuwait would somehow lose their sovereignty were a strongly pro- or anti-Soviet or Western government to take power. While the Cold War and associated regional issues did have significant effects on those countries, these struggles did not go as far as determining the very existence of these states as _de jure_ political entities. Because the Kurds were not recognised as a state actor, they were unable to control an officially sanctioned geopolitical entity whose sovereignty could be protected by a claim to international law as construed or honoured by the international community. The right to self-determination was simply not extended to the Kurds, even though they did have that right under

94 *1965–1971: Politics and struggle*

international law, like any other people.[96] The question here, therefore, concerns not whether it was morally right for the Kurds to be treated in this way or that, but how the international community perceived them at the time: essentially, as an actor with no sovereignty. Thus, they were basically given no say in their own future; the future was decided for them.

The reality of functioning of the international system in this case may be regarded as closer to respecting power than justice. Iraq itself is a good example of a territory that, despite a number of coups and recurrent political turmoil, continued to exist as a sovereign state whose minimal sovereign rights were respected. There was a limit to the implications of regional and international politics on a state already recognised by the international community as sovereign—whereas for the Kurds, of course, there was almost no boundary that might delimit this effect. This analysis is not related to the question of the legitimacy of the Kurdish claim but rather to the pertinent fact of the matter, that the international setting was one in which *free will* was not accorded to the Kurds.[97]

The scheduled British withdrawal was a matter of anxiety and rigorous consideration for the Shah, the US and Iraq, too. Essentially, as much as it concerned Iran and the other Arab states, the UAR and Iraq, for instance, it appeared to be old matters with new dimensions: namely tensions between Arab and Persian nationalism and thus the question of who would fill the gap and replace Britain as the principal power in the Persian Gulf. For Iran, this entailed not only precluding Arab nationalists from dominating the Gulf but also reaffirming Iran's claim over the Islands of Tunbs and Abu Musa. It was important for the Shah to ensure that a hostile power did not take over the Trucial Sheikhdom once the British had departed. Antagonist powers hostile to Iranian regional hegemony could have been Iraq under the Ba'athists, the UAR under Nasser or local 'reactionaries' as opposed to the conservative regimes.[98] A consequence of the British withdrawal, therefore, was heighted regional tensions.

In the late 1960s and early 1970s generally, Iraq was reaching out to the Gulf states and Shaykhdoms, which must have further antagonised the Shah, if not confirming his apprehension of a hostile Arab takeover of the Gulf in the post-British era. In the last few years of the 1960s, for instance, as a sign of Iraq's intentions and increased activity in the Gulf, Saddam Hussein, VP at the time, and other Iraqi officials made numerous trips to the Gulf Shaykhdoms and states, such as Kuwait. According to the US intelligence at the time, Iraq was seeking to expand its presence in the Gulf through visits by its officials, such as Saddam, to the area, which were reciprocated in Baghdad, and also through developing Iraq's economic ties to these regions, such as with the opening of a branch of Iraq's Rafidain Bank in Bahrain. Like the Shah, the Ba'athists in Baghdad appear to have had their own strategy for the Gulf in view of the scheduled British withdrawal.[99]

The Shah's view in March 1970 was that hostility could come about in the Gulf either as a result of '(a) weakness of moderate riparian [Gulf] states and/or (b) miscalculation on [the] part of radical [A]rabs' unless there was a 'strong and credible [I]ran deterrent'.[100] Considered in the broader context, what the Shah was

1965–1971: Politics and struggle   95

implying was that in the case of the latter, radical or revolutionary local Arab elements would take over these Shaykhdoms, while in the case of the former, the British withdrawal would lead to hostilities between Iran and Arab states as each or any tried to establish authority in the Gulf. As seen from Iran, therefore, the likelihood of its having to face hostile Arab actors meant that it needed a credible deterrence. To this end, the Shah demanded an increase in US military credit. According to a telegram sent from the US embassy in Iran, he also told the Soviet ambassador that Iran had no intention of attacking Iraq but 'If Iraq created trouble in the Gulf Iran "would punish Iraq very badly"'.[101] This was another reason for why the Iraqi Kurds were needed by Iran more than ever to distract Iraq from the Gulf. This also helps to explain why the Shah tried so hard with Barzani to prevent a settlement with Iraq.

Without an Iranian–Iraqi agreement, a Kurdish–Iraqi settlement would have only meant that Iran would have had to directly face Iraq in the Gulf to thwart its ambitions, and Iran would have lost its Kurdish card. In the absence of the British, however, Iraq was now backed by the USSR in the Gulf. An agreement between the Iraqi Kurds and Baghdad leading to a settlement would have also meant that Iraq would have had its hands free to divert forces from Kurdistan to the Gulf, or elsewhere, as desired. It is to be recalled that since 1961, in fact, the bulk of the Iraqi army had been pinned down in Kurdistan—which in itself had created deep problems for successive Iraqi governments. According to the Shah, a Kurdish–Iraqi agreement in 1970 would have freed some 20,000 Iraqi troops for deployment in the Gulf.[102] Asadollah Alam confirms the Shah's worries of an agreement between the Kurds and Baghdad that would have freed up Iraqi troops.[103]

Indeed, it could be argued that the Iraqi and Soviet attempt to reach a settlement with the Kurds, even if temporary, was also influenced by these states' desires to strengthen their respective positions in the Gulf by freeing Iraq's hands from its Kurdish Issue, just as the Shah feared. The Soviets would thereby be able to dominate the Gulf through their client (Iraq) and Iraq could challenge Iran. This would have only served to increase the USSR's influence in the region. Certainly, we may conclude that the fact that the USSR pressured Iraq to reach the March 1970 Accord with the Kurds shows the Soviets' desire for Iraq to play a role in the Gulf after Britain's withdrawal, which has been beneficial for the USSR's hegemony as explained.

What can be deduced from all this for the Kurds, therefore, is that the Russian pressure, alluded to earlier, on the Ba'athists to offer the autonomy promised in the Accord of March 11, 1970, came in the context of other regional factors related to the British withdrawal. Indeed, as Iran's posturing suggests, Iraq *was* increasing its activity in the Gulf in the late 1960s, which indicates another Ba'athist motivation to want to free up its military by *shelving* its Kurdish problem in the north to fill the gap in the Gulf left after Britain's withdrawal. It may be worth noting here too that the government of Iraq was under pressure from the Soviets to pay back overdue loans.[104] This may also have played a part in the Ba'athists' acceptance of the Soviet push for an agreement with the Kurds.

96 1965–1971: Politics and struggle

It should further be emphasised here that for nine years, between 1961 and 1970, Iraqi troops had not been able to access the border with Iran along much of the Kurdistan or *northern* front, which was solidly in the hands of the Peshmerga (see map, Figure 3.1). Effectively, therefore, this was a buffer zone between the Persian rulers of Iran and the Arab world or Iraq, one that the latter had repeatedly tried and failed to capture. Implicitly, if the Iraqi Kurds and Iraqi government in Baghdad were to come to a lasting settlement that would have allowed Iraq's military forces to reach the border with Iran from the north, and if these two countries were to go to war with each other, then, in the absence of the *Kurdish buffer zone*, Iran would have a longer front to defend. In other words, and

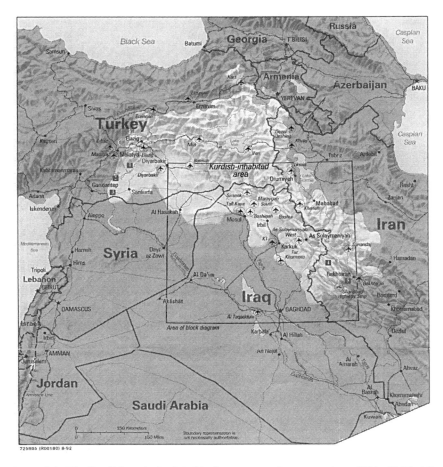

Figure 3.1 The Kurdish majority inhabited area as contiguous territory (CIA, 1992). The Pershmerga controlled most of the rural Kurdish area in Iraq as shown, including the Iran–Iraq border. Courtesy of the University of Texas Libraries, The University of Texas at Austin.[105]

1965–1971: Politics and struggle 97

simply, if Iraq were to secure internal harmony and a war were to start between Iran and Iraq, then this war would not only be along the entire length of the shared border of Arab Iraq with Iran but also of Iran with the border with Iraqi Kurdistan.

In September 1971, a Special National Intelligence Estimate stated that if Iraq were to attempt to invade Iran, it would do so from the southern Abadan–Khorramshahr region in the south or possibly on the Kermanshah region, the centre of the border, since the border with Iran in the Kurdish north was out of bounds for Iraqi troops and had been so for several years, notwithstanding Iraq's vigorous efforts to change this.[106] If the March Accord of 1970 had led to a solution of the Kurdish Issue with Iraq, in such an event, moreover, the Iraqi Kurds would also have sided with Baghdad rather than fighting against it with Iran, at least in theory, depending on what Iraq could offer them. Iraq would have played its *Kurdish card* and, to make things worse, it could have turned the tables on Iran by supporting Iran's Kurds against Tehran.

In his March 18, 1970 meeting with the US ambassador in Iran Douglas MacArthur, the Shah said that the March Accord would 'improve' the Iraq government's 'capacity for mischief in the Gulf and, for present at least, strengthen its overall position'. According to the ambassador, the Shah had hoped that the Accord would not last long but only time would tell. In March 1970, the Shah was again advancing his idea of the USSR's 'Grand Design'[107] for the Middle East that he had believed, or at least professed, prior to the 1958 Iraqi Revolution. According to the Shah this Soviet strategy included the USSR dominating the Middle East via Iraq and with the long-term objective of a Soviet-sponsored Kurdish state stretching all the way from Iraqi Kurdistan through to the borders of the Soviet Union, thus incorporating the Kurdistan of Iran and Turkey. The Shah believed that ultimately this would give the Soviets a land bridge to the Middle East.[108]

This was the same argument that the Shah and Turkey had presented in the early years of the Cold War, as discussed in Chapter 1. Regarding the 1970 Accord, the Shah therefore 'wanted top level USG to know that [the] agreement between [the] Kurds and [the] Iraq[i] Govt [sic] was [a] very grave development greatly increasing [the] threat to [the] gulf area and Arabian Peninsula'.[109] It is important to underscore that the sources referred to here are the minutes of actual meetings between the US ambassador to Iran and the Shah himself. The ambassador then forwarded the contents of these meetings to the Secretary of State as a matter of priority. It is quite clear that there was a direct link being made at the highest levels between the Gulf and what was happening in Kurdistan and Iran's objection to a potential Iraqi Kurdish–Iraqi government settlement.

The Shah's worries about these developments were such that he put immense pressure on the US ambassador in Tehran for the US to increase its military sales credit to the country so as to appear as a credible deterring force in the Gulf.[110] Most importantly here, it was Iran that ultimately played a pivotal role between the US and the Iraqi Kurds in the years after the Accord up until 1975, framing the

98   *1965–1971: Politics and struggle*

struggle in Iraqi Kurdistan as a Cold War issue. Iran was the maker and the breaker of this relationship (Chapter 4).

Against this backdrop and that of the actual situation for the Kurds, Iran, Israel and the US, British governmental archives, in addition to US sources, provide conclusive evidence to back up the assertion made here: that Iranian assistance for the Iraqi Kurds was given to weaken its adversary Iraq and also to pre-empt any Soviet assistance for the Kurds.[111] Israel's support for the Kurds was similarly based on weakening or preoccupying Iraq. For Israel, too, if the Iraqi army was to be pinned down in Kurdistan (i.e. at home), Iraq would not be able to participate significantly in Arab–Israel hostilities.[112] As mentioned, this was indeed the case in the 1967 war. The interests of both parties here lay with the Iraqi Kurds simply absorbing the Iraqi state's energies.

While Israel and Iran both had a stake in continuance of the Kurdish War, the US had not sought to support the Iraqi Kurds and thereby undermine the government in Baghdad up until this point in time (1971), either implicitly or explicitly. The US had neither made any promises to the Kurds and thereby misled them to expect US support nor exploited them to exert pressure on Iraq. On the contrary, the US saw its primary interests—those dictated by Cold War considerations—as best served by a strong Iraqi state, which precluded helping the Kurds and thus resulted in repeated rebuttals of their supplications.

According to the CIA, on March 4, 1970, just days before the autonomy Declaration of March 11, 1970, SAVAK invited Idris Barzani (Mustafa Barzani's son and a high-ranking Kurdish leader) and other Kurdish figures 'for discussions concerning the future of the Kurdish Revolution'[113] and also to meet representatives from the government of Israel. In Tehran, the Kurdish delegation met the Israelis, who 'pushed hard' for a 'resumption of hostilities in Northern Iraq and promised the Kurds that they would supply anti-aircraft weapons and light artillery'.[114] In addition, the Kurds asked for armoured vehicles, and the Israelis promised these too, including 'tanks with crews', as long as the Kurds first captured at least two Iraqi tanks to be used as a cover. Idris responded that they (the Kurds) preferred entirely Kurdish crews for the tanks; the Israelis 'readily consented to this request' too, implying that Israel would have accepted training Kurdish tank crews.[115]

On March 6, Idris Barzani also met with the head of SAVAK, General Nematollah Nasseri, who told Barzani that 'Iran was fully behind the Israeli plan to renew the fighting in northern Iraq, and Idriss [sic] should carefully note what the Israelis were suggesting'.[116] Nasseri also discussed Iran's concerns over the negotiations between Barzani—the father—and the Iraqi government, in addition to discussing 'Iranian plans for further aid' for the Iraqi Kurds.[117] In terms of financial assistance, as reported by the CIA, Israeli and Iranian support to the Kurdish movement under Barzani totalled some $3,360,000 during the month prior to the meeting (i.e. in February 1970).[118] However, Iran and Israel's attempts to persuade Mustafa Barzani into reigniting the conflict were ineffective. The Declaration of March 11, 1970 was made despite Iran and Israel's strong contrary desires. The concern conveyed to the Kurds by the head of

1965–1971: Politics and struggle   99

SAVAK is consistent with other sources reporting on the Shah's worries on this matter, as cited.

While the Shah was involving himself in the implications of the end of hostilities in Iraqi Kurdistan, the superpower behind Iran at this time, the US, did not believe that the settlement would last. Indeed, only three days after the Accord, the State Department sought to comfort the Shah to this effect. A cable, seemingly from Secretary Rogers to the US Tehran ambassador, conveyed the message thus:

> [We] [d]oubt therefore that [the] Iraqi government will feel free for long to make [a] significant shift in its attention and resources away from [the] Kurds to Iran and [the] Persian Gulf area. Furthermore, any easement on this score might well see troops being redeployed in Jordan and Syria rather than southern Iraq.[119]

The above was in response to the Shah's views to the US ambassador in Tehran, Douglas II MacArthur, on March 12 that he 'believed his worst fears of Soviet influence on Iraq had been confirmed with the formation of an autonomous Iraq-Kurdish province'.[120]

The Department's assessment regarding the impermanency of the agreement was to be proven accurate, as will be presented in the next chapter. Indeed, the Department's expectation was already materialising by the autumn of the same year (1970), when the Kurds wanted the acceleration of the implementation of the Accord and also 'freedom for political parties'.[121] And once again, the Kurdish movement under Barzani had given sanctuary to communist leaders feeling the Ba'ath Party rule. This leads to a question: seemingly, what the Kurds wanted was a multiparty political system (i.e. a democratic Iraq) and the US (the Nixon administration) was aware of this, yet the US was still disinclined to view the Iraqi Kurds' cause favourably by assisting them as a democratic force let alone supporting their secession—and this despite the fact that US officials were aware not only of the Kurds' expressed desire for a free, multiparty political system but also of the Ba'ath government's adamant opposition to this.[122] The advocacy of pluralism and claim to liberal democracy and similar such values, therefore, had no effect on the US approach.

In fact, by the end of October 1970, the US was also fully aware that the Iraqi government had postponed a census scheduled for October 25, 1970, that was meant to determine the Kurdish majority areas that would be included in the territory designated for *Kurdish autonomy*, as stipulated by the March Agreement—and the US was also aware that this postponement was jeopardising the settlement.[123] Instead, it stuck to its policy of 'non-intervention', while all the time gathering intricate information on the state of affairs between the parties.[124]

One should be quite clear here that the US knew perfectly well the nature of the Iraqi regime, as a totalitarian government, that is, since this was precisely what the Assistant Secretary of State Joseph J. Sisco asked the Belgian ambassador to Iraq in a question: whether the government of Iraq was a totalitarian government or not. The latter replied in the affirmative, with the exception of the Kurds and their

100 *1965–1971: Politics and struggle*

newspaper, *al-Ta'akhi*, which were permitted: 'this is [the] only form of freedom permitted in Iraq today', the Belgian ambassador replied.[125]

The freedom granted the Kurds and their newspaper cannot have been due to the Ba'athists' somehow believing in freedom for the Kurds as good, of course, since they did not allow it even for their own people (Iraqi Arabs); rather, it was a necessary measure for the Accord. In fact, the relaxation on this matter is a further indication that the government must have been under pressure from outside (i.e. from the USSR) to work with the Kurds, as indicated. The Ba'ath government was not acting in good faith though; it simply needed to buy time, as events would ultimately prove. The US was also aware that Soviet influence on Iraq was increasing—another consideration that failed to lead to a rethink in US policy vis-à-vis the Iraqi Kurds during the period covered by this chapter, up to 1971. Meanwhile, Saddam Hussein al-Tikriti, as the US embassy in Lebanon called him, and who was Assistance Secretary General of the Ba'ath Party and Vice Chairman of the Revolutionary Command Council, was en route to attaining absolute power in Baghdad.[126]

Notes

1 Entessar, Nader, *Kurdish Ethnonationalism* (Boulder, CO: Lynn Rienner Publishers, 1992), pp. 66–68.
2 McDowall, David, *A Modern History of the Kurds* (London: I.B. Tauris, 2004), pp. 313–320.
3 See, for example, Ibid., pp. 323–339; Entessar, *Kurdish Politics in the Middle East*, pp. 66–77. For inter-Kurdish issues, also see McDowall, op. cit., pp. 323–339. For the details of the 1970 Accord, see the views of one of the participation members of the Kurdish delegation, Muhsîn Dzeyî – Nwênerî Pêşûy Mes'ud Barzanî – Beşî Duwem and also Aziz, 'Mhemmed 'Ezîz – Beşî Sêyem', in *Pencemor*.
4 Quoted in 'Telegram From the Embassy in Iran to the Department of State, frus1964-68v21/d172' (FRUS, May 6, 1965).
5 Ibid.
6 See ibid., footnotes.
7 See 'Telegram From the Department of State to the Embassy in Iraq, frus1964-68v21/d174' (FRUS, May 6, 1965).
8 'Telegram From the Embassy in Iraq to the Department of State, frus1964-68v21/d173' (FRUS, April 30, 1965).
9 See Telegram From the Department of State [...] Iraq, frus1964-68v21/d174.
10 Ibid.
11 Ibid.
12 See footnotes of 'Telegram From the Department of State to the Embassy in Iran, frus1964-68v21/d175' (FRUS, August 11, 1965).
13 Ibid. Also see FO 248/1617: 1965.
14 'Telegram From the Embassy in Iran to the Department of State, frus1964-68v22/d108' (FRUS, November 25, 1965).
15 Ibid.
16 'Airgram From the Embassy in Iraq to the Department of State, frus1964-68v21/d177' (FRUS, October 30, 1965).

1965–1971: Politics and struggle 101

17 Ibid.
18 Ibid.
19 Quoted in Bengio, Ofra, 'Surprising Ties between Israel and the Kurds', *Middle East Quarterly,* 21 (2014).
20 Quoted in ibid. The named Minister was later sentenced to death by the Ba'ath regime, see 'Airgram 295 From the Embassy in Lebanon to the Department of State, frus1969-76ve04/d270' (FRUS, July 2, 1970).
21 Bengio, op. cit.
22 Airgram From the Embassy in Iraq, frus1964-68v21/d177.
23 Ibid.
24 Airgram From the Embassy in Iraq [...] (October 30, 1965).
25 'Telegram From the Department of State to the Embassy in Iraq, frus1964-68v21/d176' (FRUS, October 26, 1965). And also see FO 248/1617.
26 Ibid. And also see FO 248/1617.
27 Telegram From the Department of State to the Embassy in Iraq, frus1964-68v21/d176; FO 248/1617.
28 Telegram From the Department of State to the Embassy in Iraq, frus1964-68v21/d176; FO 248/1617.
29 Telegram From the Department of State to the Embassy in Iraq, frus1964-68v21/d176.
30 'Telegram From the Embassy in Iran to the Department of State, frus1964-68v21/d179' (FRUS, January 20, 1966).
31 Ibid.
32 An English version of Barzani's letter is accessible via: Herz Martin, 'Iran-Iraq: Letter to President Johnson [...]' (DNSA, March 12, 1966).
33 Ibid.
34 Ibid.
35 Ibid.
36 Ibid.
37 See, for example, Mitchell, David, *Making Foreign Policy: Presidential Management of the Decision-Making Process* (Aldershot: Ashgate Publishing Limited, 2005); Eugene, Wittkopf, *et al.*, *American Foreign Policy: Pattern and Process* (Belmont, CA: Thomson/Wadsworth, 2008); Jentleson, Bruce W., *American Foreign Policy: The Dynamics of Choice in the 21st Century* (New York, NY: Norton, 2004); Crabb, Cecil Van Meter, *The Doctrines of American Foreign Policy: Their Meaning, Role, and Future* (Baton Rouge, LA: Louisiana State University Press, 1982).
38 See, for example, 'Telegram From the Embassy in Iraq to the Department of State, frus1964-68v21/d180' (FRUS, May 17, 1966); 'Telegram From the Department of State to the Embassy in Iraq, frus1964-68v21/d184' (FRUS, October 8, 1966).
39 'Telegram From the Embassy in Iraq to the Department of State, frus1964-68v21/d183' (FRUS, August 19, 1966).
40 'Memorandum From the Country Director for Israel and Arab-Israel Affairs (Atherton) to the Assistant Secretary of State for Near Eastern and South Asian Affairs (Hare), frus1964-68v21/d185' (FRUS, November 1, 1966).
41 See, for instance, O'Ballance, Edgar, *The Kurdish Struggle, 1920–94* (Basingstoke: Macmillan, 1995), p. 83.
42 'Memorandum From the Executive Secretary of the Department of State (Read) to the President's Special Assistant (Rostow), frus1964-68v21/d189' (FRUS, February 16, 1967).

102   *1965–1971: Politics and struggle*

43 Herz Martin, 'Iran-Iraq: Letter to President Johnson'.
44 Ibid.
45 Ibid.
46 'Intelligence Note From the Director of the Bureau of Intelligence and Research (Hughes) to Secretary of State Rusk, frus1964-68v21/d197' (FRUS, September 1, 1967).
47 See FO 248/1617: 1965.
48 Intelligence Note […] (September 1, 1967).
49 Ibid.; Osgood, Kenneth, *Eisenhower and Regime Change in Iraq: The United States and the Iraqi Revolution of 1958* (London: Routledge, 2009).
50 See Osgood, op. cit.; Barzanî, Mes'ud, *Barzanî Û Bzutnewey Rizgarîxwazî Kurd: Bergî Sêyem, Beşî Yekem 1961–1975*, pp. 239–240.
51 See 'Memorandum From John W. Foster of the National Security Council Staff to the President's Special Assistant (Rostow), frus1964-68v21/d200' (FRUS, July 22, 1968); Memorandum From John W. Foster of the National Security Council Staff to the President's Special Assistant (Rostow), frus1964-68v21/d199' (FRUS, July 17, 1968).
52 'Research Memorandum RNA–6 From the Director of the Bureau of Intelligence and Research (Hughes) to Secretary of State Rogers, frus1969-76ve04/d251' (FRUS, February 14, 1969).
53 See 'FCO 17/408, Iraq: Political Affairs- Internal Kurdish Affairs, EQ1/4: 1966–68' (United Kingdom: The National Archives, n.d.); Entessar, *Kurdish Politics in the Middle East*, pp. 68–77.
54 Research Memorandum RNA–6 From the Director of the Bureau of Intelligence and Research (Hughes) to Secretary of State Rogers, frus1969-76ve04/d251.
55 'FCO 17/408, Iraq: Political Affairs – Internal Kurdish Affairs', EQ1/4: 1966–1968. Also, see Observer, 'Iraq Under Fire at Home and Abroad', Editorial, *The Observer* (May 25, 1969).
56 FCO 17/408. For more on the Ba'ath and their ideology see Ghareeb, Edmund, *The Kurdish Question in Iraq* (New York, NY: Syracuse University Press, 1981), pp. 44–69.
57 Quoted in Research Memorandum RNA–6 From the Director of the Bureau of Intelligence and Research (Hughes) to Secretary of State Rogers, frus1969-76ve04/d251.
58 See 'Airgram 386 From the Embassy in Lebanon to the Department of State, frus1969-76ve04/d261' (FRUS, September 22, 1969). For background information, also see Kimche, David, *The Last Option: After Nasser, Arafat & Saddam Hussein: The Quest for Peace in the Middle East* (London: Weidenfeld and Nicolson, 1991), pp. 189–200.
59 'Telegram 1925 From the Embassy in Iran to the Department of State, frus1969-76ve04/d17' (FRUS, May 19, 1969).
60 'Memorandum of Conversation, frus1969-76ve04/d258' (FRUS, May 29, 1969).
61 Ibid.
62 Ibid.
63 See, for example, Research Memorandum RNA–6 From the Director of the Bureau of Intelligence and Research (Hughes) to Secretary of State Rogers, frus1969-76ve04/d251.
64 'Memorandum of Conversation, June 13, 1969' (June 13, 1969).
65 Among these were William Yonan, President of Assyrian American Federation, Sam Andrews, Secretary of Assyrian-American Federation and Zaya Malek Isma'il,

1965–1971: Politics and struggle   103

Representative of Assyrians in Syria. The latter two were the individuals that had visited Barzani in Kurdistan in April of the same year (i.e. 1969), see ibid.

66 Ibid.
67 Ibid.
68 Ibid.
69 Ibid.
70 Ibid.
71 Ibid.
72 Loutfi Obeidi was an Iraqi Émigré and businessman; this data is extracted from a documented exchange between Obeidi and Talcott W. Seelye (Country Director, NEA/ARN), ibid.
73 'Telegram 204979 From the Department of State to the Embassy in Lebanon, frus1969-76ve04/d264' (FRUS, December 10, 1969).
74 Quoted in 'Memorandum of Conversation, frus1969-76ve04/d33' (FRUS, October 22, 1969).
75 Quoted in ibid.
76 Quoted in ibid.
77 Quoted in ibid. For more on the Shah's desires for US arms, see Kimche, op. cit., pp. 189–200.
78 Memorandum of Conversation, frus1969-76ve04/d33 [...].
79 Entessar, *Kurdish Ethnonationalism*, p. 70.
80 Barzanî, *Barzanî Û Bzutnewey Rizgarîxwazî Kurd: Bergî Sêyem, Beşî Duwem 1961–1975*, pp. 23–40. Mahmoud Othman also notes the mediating role that the Soviets played in this: Othman, in *Telephone Interview B*.
81 Barzanî, *Barzanî Û Bzutnewey Rizgarîxwazî Kurd: Bergî Sêyem, Beşî Duwem 1961–1975*, pp. 23–35.
82 Ibid., pp. 85–90.
83 'Telegram 54598 From the Department of State to the Embassy in Israel, frus1969-76ve04/d269' (FRUS, April 14, 1970).
84 Ibid.
85 See Airgram 295 From the Embassy in Lebanon to the Department of State, frus1969-76ve04/d270.
86 Barzanî, *Barzanî Û Bzutnewey Rizgarîxwazî Kurd: Bergî Sêyem, Beşî Duwem 1961–1975*, p. 36.
87 Alam, Asadollah, *The Shah and I: The Confidential Diary of Iran's Royal Court, 1968–77* (London: I.B. Tauris, 1991), p. 129.
88 For the details of the 1970 Accord, see the views of two of the participating members of the Kurdish delegation, in 'Muhsîn Dzeyî – Nwêneri Pêşûy Mes'ud Barzani – Beşî Sêyem', in *Pencemor*; 'Mhemmed 'Ezîz – Beşî Sêyem', in *Pencemor*.
89 A copy of the letter and its Kurdish translation is available from Barzanî, *Barzanî Û Bzutnewey Rizgarîxwazî Kurd: Bergî Sêyem, Beşî Duwem 1961–1975*, pp. 277–278.
90 A Kurdish (translated) version of the letter is available from ibid, p. 73.
91 Ibid., pp. 73–74.
92 As reported by Masoud Barzani, see ibid., pp. 73–83.
93 Ibid., pp. 85–90.
94 Ibid., pp. 105–106.
95 Othman, in *Telephone Interview B*; 'Muhsîn Dzeyî – Nwêneri Pêşûy Mes'ud Barzani – Beşî Sêyem', in *Pencemor*. For more on the terms of the 1970 agreement see the latter source. Mahmoud Othman was the head of the negotiating Kurdish delegation

104 *1965–1971: Politics and struggle*

to Baghdad that led up to the Accord and Dizaei was also a member of the same delegation.

96 For more on the Kurds and the right of self-determination in international law, see Ali, Hawraman, 'Self Determination for the Kurds?', *Coventry University Law Journal,* 16 (2011).

97 On the nature of the international system, see e.g. Bull, Hedley, *The Anarchical Society: A Study of Order in World Politics*, 3rd ed. (New York, NY: Columbia University Press, 2002); Mearsheimer, John J., *The Tragedy of Great Power Politics* (New York, NY & London: Norton, 2001); Morgenthau, Hans and Thompson, Kenneth W., *Politics among Nations: The Struggle for Power and Peace* (New York, NY: Knopf, 1985). Also, Ali, op. cit.

98 See, for example, 'Memorandum from the Country Director for Saudi Arabia, Kuwait, Yemen and Aden (Brewer) to the Country Director for Iran (Miklos), frus1969-76ve04/d51' (FRUS, February 27, 1970); Kimche, op. cit., pp. 189–200.

99 See, for example, 'Intelligence Note RNAN Prepared in the Bureau of Intelligence and Research, frus1969-76ve04/d271' (FRUS, July 16, 1970). Kimche, op. cit., pp. 189–200.

100 'Telegram 1019 From the Embassy in Iran to the Department of State, frus1969-76ve04/d55' (FRUS, March 19, 1970).

101 Quoted in ibid.

102 'Telegram 928 From the Embassy in Iran to the Department of State, frus1969-76ve04/d53' (FRUS, March 12, 1970).

103 See Alam, op. cit., p. 129.

104 See Airgram 295.

105 CIA, 'kurdish_lands_92.jpg' (University of Texas at Austin, 1992).

106 'Special National Intelligence Estimate 34–70, frus1969-76ve04/d86' (FRUS, September 3, 1970).

107 Telegram 1019 From the Embassy in Iran to the Department of State, frus1969-76ve04/d55.

108 See ibid. and Telegram 928 From the Embassy in Iran to the Department of State, frus1969-76ve04/d53.

109 Ibid.

110 Ibid.; Telegram 928 From the Embassy in Iran to the Department of State, frus1969-76ve04/d53. Also, Kimche, op. cit., pp. 189–200. For US arms policy towards Iran during the Shah, see McGlinchey, Stephen, *US Arms Policies Towards the Shah's Iran* (London: Routledge, 2014).

111 See, for example, PR 6/10, FCO 51/191; Research Middle East: The Kurdish Problem in Iraq 1963–1971; 'Central Intelligence Agency Information Cable TDCS DB-315/01044-70, frus1969-76ve04/d267' (FRUS, March 9, 1970); Special National Intelligence Estimate 34–70, frus1969-76ve04/d86' (September 3, 1970).

112 For Israel's interest in the Iraqi Kurds and a history of this, see Kimche, op. cit., pp. 189–200; Bengio, op. cit.

113 Central Intelligence Agency Information Cable TDCS DB-315/01044-70, frus1969-76ve04/d267.

114 Ibid.

115 Ibid.

116 Ibid.

117 Ibid.

118 Ibid.

1965–1971: Politics and struggle   105

119 'Telegram 37806 From the Department of State to the Embassy in Iran, frus1969-76ve04/d268' (FRUS, March 14, 1970).

120 See the footnotes of ibid.

121 'Central Intelligence Agency Information Cable IN 143628, frus1969-76ve04/d273' (FRUS, August 10, 1970).

122 Ibid. This source also reports that the Kurds' *al-Ta'akhi* newspaper's appraisal of Secretary Roger's peace Arab–Israel proposal and President Nasser's acceptance of a peaceful solution for the Palestinian issue was now another source of contention between Baghdad and the Kurds, as the government had asked the newspaper to attack the peace proposals, but the newspaper did otherwise.

123 'Telegram 9048 From the Embassy in Lebanon to the Department of State, frus1969-76ve04/d278' (FRUS, October 16, 1970).

124 See, for example, the following document, which asks the US ambassador to Iran (Douglas Macarthur) to enquire about the views of the Israeli Mission in Iran when they meet regarding the 'deteriorating situation between Barzani and the GOI: Charles W. McCaskill, 'Meeting with Meir Ezri, Head of the Israeli Mission [Biographic Sketch Not Attached]' (DNSA, December 19, 1970).

125 'Telegram 67409 From the Department of State to the Embassies in Jordan, Lebanon, Belgium, Saudi Arabia, Kuwait, the United Kingdom, Iran, the Soviet Union, and the Interests Section in Cairo, frus1969-76ve04/d286' (FRUS, April 21, 1971).

126 Ibid.

4 1971–1975: Hope and betrayal

Background

As described in the previous chapter, the Ba'ath government and Kurdish leadership had agreed on an autonomy plan in the Accord of March 11, 1970, but some provisions of the plan never materialised and hostile acts, including an attempt to assassinate Barzani, soon remerged, although short of a full-scale war. On March 11, 1974, however, four years to the day after the Accord was signed, the Iraqi government unilaterally announced a different autonomy plan and gave Barzani or the KDP a fortnight in which to accept it. Prior to this, Iran and Israel had informed Barzani of their unwavering support in the case of war and also arranged for covert US involvement. In the early 1970s, though, Iraq and the USSR further strengthened their bilateral relations, culminating in the 1972 Iraqi–Soviet Treaty of Friendship and Cooperation.

In addition to the gap that was left by Britain's withdrawal in the Gulf, the upgrade in Iraq–Soviet relations after 1972 was an additional motivation for Iran to back the Iraqi Kurds in order to contain Iraq or to even work for the downfall of the Ba'ath regime. The Soviets initially wanted the Ba'athists to establish a national unity government, to include the ICP and also the Kurds. The Ba'athists went along with this idea to share power but only to neutralise internal threats to their power and to secure Soviet backing. The Soviets had made it very clear to the Ba'ath that their continued support was conditional on the ICP taking part in the government, and it was the Soviets, similarly, that wanted the Ba'ath to bring the KDP into the new power-sharing arrangement. Alvandi sees this as due to the Soviets wanting to have a strong client in Iraq, a view with which this book acquiesces.[1]

Related to this implied Soviet design of a strong, united and somewhat pluralistic Iraq, the Soviet Union sent a delegation to Barzani's headquarters in Kurdistan following the 1970 Accord, led by the VP of the Central Committee of the Communist Party of the Soviet Union, Rumanystev. The delegation had as its purpose the aim of both pressuring Barzani and also reassuring him of Soviet support if he joined the National Front Government. However, the Shah responded by intensifying his efforts to prevent Barzani from joining. SAVAK conveyed messages to the Americans that if Barzani or the KDP were to join a national government in Iraq this would instigate a further Soviet domination of the Gulf.

1971–1975: Hope and betrayal 107

In 1971 and early 1972, the Iraqi Kurds repeatedly requested US backing, and, as previously, all requests were turned down.[2] Not convinced by Iran and Israel, the Kurdish leadership, however, insisted the US join in backing the Kurds if they were to reject the Soviet demand. The Kurdish leadership's insistence on the involvement of the US was desired to gain the insurance of a *superpower guarantee*, so that they would not be summarily abandoned by the Shah, since the Kurdish leadership did not trust him. In fact, so much was at stake for the Shah, that it was at his behest that the US agreed to receive a Kurdish delegation in Washington. This occurred on July 30, 1972, with Idris Barzani and Mahmoud Othman representing the Kurds.[3] Mahmoud Othman has been interviewed for this work, while Idris Barzani is deceased. Plainly, this concession comprised a major revision of a long-standing policy of non-intervention in Kurdistan by the US, albeit a covert one. The upshot was the US, Iran and Israel all providing weapons, munitions, and financial aid to the Kurdish Peshmerga under Barzani—although each did so for their own, different objectives. Declassified US documents, the presence of Israel's military personnel in Kurdistan, and meetings between Kurds and high-ranking Israeli officials all point to a significant Israeli involvement in this affair, which is examined in this chapter.

Meanwhile, when the Iraqi ultimatum expired, Baghdad sent troops, newly armed with latest USSR weaponry, to attack the Peshmerga in an offensive intended to dislodge the Kurds from their mountain strongholds. As previously, the Iraqi state forces were unsuccessful. On March 6, 1975, however, Iraq and Iran signed the Algiers Accord, upon which Iran sealed its Kurdish (northern Iraqi) border and gave the Kurds three options: to surrender to the Iraqis, to surrender the Iranians, or to keep fighting the Iraqi army, with the Iranian border sealed on them, now fully backed by the USSR. Suddenly undercut by the US, Iran and Israel and shocked, the Kurdish leadership took a majority decision to abandon the armed struggle for a more suitable time, rather than risk a complete annihilation of its fighting force. The Kurdish national liberation movement was thus betrayed, primarily by Iran and then by the US and Israel. Over 100,000 Kurds fled to Iran, joining additional refugees there. According to the Red Cross, the war had also cost Iraq the lives of 7,000 of its troops and some 10,000 casualties.[4]

The Iraqi government then declared the Turkish and Iranian borders prohibited security zones, extending into the country by up to 30 km. The inhabitants of the territories now made into security zones, some 600,000 or more people were relocated to collective settlements, and anyone caught in the zones was summarily executed. The Kurds' September Revolution or *Şorrşî Eylul*, which had proven formidable since 1961, was thus decisively crushed. The Iraqi government also depopulated and then Arabised a number of Kurdish inhabited areas, in particular around the fault lines where Kurdish land met Arab Iraq, such as oil-rich Kirkuk. It expelled Kurds from their homes and their properties were given to Arabs, among other such measures, like giving financial rewards to Arab men who took Kurdish wives. This ultimately became known as the Arabisation Campaign.

108 *1971–1975: Hope and betrayal*

A report by the Human Rights Watch described the displacement of Kurds and other non-Arabs in Kurdish areas thus:

> Since the 1930s, but particularly from the 1970s onwards, successive Iraqi administrations have forcibly displaced hundreds of thousands of ethnic Kurds, Turkomans (a Turkish-speaking Iraqi minority), and Assyrians from northern Iraq, and repopulated the area with Arabs moved from central and southern Iraq [...]. The methods used by the Iraqi government to effect the forced displacements of the 1970s and 1980s involved first and foremost military force and intimidation: entire Kurdish villages were completely depopulated and bulldozed by Iraqi forces. But the Iraqi government followed up the brutality with legal decrees aimed at consolidating the displacement. First, the property deeds of the displaced Kurds were invalidated by legal decree, most frequently without compensation or with nominal compensation. The Iraqi government nationalized the agricultural lands, making them the property of the Iraqi state.[5]

The Kurds and the US: a missed opportunity to overthrow the Ba'ath regime

In July 1971, Barzani sent another deputation to the US embassy in Lebanon. This time, too, as before, Barzani offered a covert relationship with the US and requested that either a US government representative go to his headquarters in *Hacî Omeran*, some 3 km from the Iranian border in Iraqi Kurdistan, or else a Kurdish representative be permitted to travel to Washington on his behalf to meet with US officials. As well as desiring a relationship with the US, Barzani wanted the US to know that he was 'ready to consult with the US in every political matter, to implement US policy, and to sweep anti-US elements [i.e. communists] from his area of influence'.[6]

Specifically, Barzani wanted a mutual friendship with the US in order to counter the Ba'athists and for the US government to understand that 'Kurdish justice will not be satisfied until Iraq is governed by a democratic regime representing both Arabs and Kurds and protecting the principles of Kurdish Society by according the Kurdish community its national rights of autonomy'. Also 'Barzani's dream is cooperation with the United States'.[7] Barzani's desire to cooperate with the US as opposed to the USSR is also confirmed by Jalal Talabani. Indeed, the Kurds' *Şorşî Eylul*, an armed struggle for self-determination that had started in September 1961, had the motto of 'Democracy for Iraq and autonomy for Kurdistan'.[8] Besides the Kurds wanting a democratic system in Kurdistan, the rationale on the side of the Kurdish leadership was that only a fully functioning democratic system in Iraq could assure respect for Kurdish rights in the country.[9]

Barzani this time wanted the US to assist him, and also other non-Kurdish actors seeking sanctuary in Kurdistan in areas under Peshmerga's control, in

1971–1975: Hope and betrayal   109

overthrowing the Ba'ath government, as Barzani's representative Zayid Uthman explicitly stated to the embassy officer. Because the Ba'athists had now tightened their grip on power, an internal coup was not a viable option, so the plan was to launch a revolt from Kurdistan with other non-Kurdish anti-Ba'ath elements. Uthman also wanted the US to know that the Kurds had never trusted the Ba'ath regime to honour the March Agreement, that 'circumstances [had] forced them to sign', and he conveyed that Iran had provided support in the past but only on the proviso of controlling Kurdish affairs and in a very heavy-handed manner.[10]

Uthman had also visited Saudi's King Faisal on the same matter; the King had endorsed the revolt idea in principle but asked for more information. The response given to Barzani's representative, however, was unforthcoming, as the US again communicated its policy of non-intervention in the affairs of other countries.[11] Essentially, Barzani wanted the US backing on the grounds that, as reported to Washington, the Ba'ath regime was 'mistreating the Iraqi people' and the 'government that would emerge from such an uprising would be pro-American'.[12]

As alluded to earlier and is acknowledged by various sources, including British archives, the Kurds' desire for a democratic parliamentary Iraq went back to before the 1970s. This was one of the Kurds' principal demands in the 1967 negotiations, for instance, which essentially amounted to a claim for a constitutional, parliamentary and pluralistic democracy, when the central government had instead sought to capitalise on inter-Kurdish rivalry between Barzani and Talabani's splinter group.[13] Both USINTS (representing the USG) in Baghdad and the KDP newspaper *al-Ta'akhi* confirm this, with a number of *al-Ta'akhi*'s editorials early in 1973 calling for the establishment of a national assembly that would be empowered to approve a permanent constitution, hold elections and adopt legislative powers, as recognised by internal US documentation.[14] Indeed, the major decisions made by the Kurdish leadership of the KDP were determined either by consensus or majority vote.[15]

Following this path, the Kurdish leadership also submitted a proposal in May 1973 calling for a high degree of autonomy for Kurdistan with a legislating assembly and an executive body and also the establishment of a national (Iraqi) constitutional court; the Kurdistan legislature was to have been freely and directly elected by the people.[16] So far as the Kurds were concerned, indeed, short of Kurdish statehood, only a democratic Iraq could guarantee their rights.

The US line of 'non-intervention', meanwhile, was again confirmed by the State Department when, in early November 1971, Barzani sent out yet another feeler for assistance from the US to its embassy in Lebanon. The emissary conveying news of the likelihood of a widespread popular uprising against the Ba'ath regime was informed that the US was following a policy of non-intervention that applied to Iraqi politics as a whole, not just the Kurds. The emissary asked the embassy for the State Department's confirmation, which was provided, with the Department adding that 'a meeting between Barzani and US officials would only nurture false hopes of US assistance'.[17]

Associated to the Cold War, at this point, the US was aware that the Ba'athists were not communists, that the communists had no chance of taking an effective

110 *1971–1975: Hope and betrayal*

part in the government let alone hijacking power and that, moreover, with their Arab nationalism tendencies, they would be most unlikely to capitulate to Soviet influence. The US, therefore, did not fear Iraq becoming a full USSR client—in fact, the Department expressed, there was also 'little likelihood' that Iraq would be able to 'expand its influence very much in the Arab world'.[18] On the other hand, were the US to assist the anti-Ba'ath forces and usher a new democratic pro-US government as envisaged by Barzani, it is unlikely that this would have led to a government sufficiently well established as to resolve its territorial disputes with Iran. A US-friendly government in Iraq would have left the US in a difficult position with the Shah. The US priority thus far had been Iran, so sponsoring a pro-US government in Iraq would have ultimately created a dilemma for the US over which of two uncompromising, opposed allies to support. This is assuming that any attempt to overthrow the Ba'ath would have resulted in a democratic pro-US government, which was an unrealistic expectation in the first place. Taking these factors into account, therefore, it is clear why the US view was that its regional approach could coexist with the Ba'ath regime.[19]

It is understandable that the chances of a 'pro-American' government coming to power were so slim that this did not seem to have been worthy of a serious consideration by the US. Since 1958, Iraq had seen the rules of Qasim, the nationalists and the Ba'athists (now for the second time), and none of these had resulted in a government that was really pro-Western or that enjoyed lasting stability, so there was no real prospect of a US-friendly government gaining power being established without the nationalists, Ba'athists and the ICP, let alone one that would be democratic. While Barzani's proposal may have appeared interesting, US officials must have been aware that the chances of its success were so slim as to be unworthy of serious consideration; there was no point in replacing one government with a similar one or uncertainties.

Furthermore, Iraq had severed diplomatic relations with the US after the 1967 war, so it could hardly suddenly become pro-American. One may also consider that the internal instability in Iraq was also indirectly beneficial for the US, as one consequence of this was Iraq not being able to participate effectively in Arab–Israel hostilities or to pose a threat to US regional allies, such as Iran or in the Gulf. Nevertheless, it is not unreasonable to suggest that there was a chance of overthrowing the hostile Ba'ath government, provided that anti-Ba'ath elements came together backed by the US. This is because the Ba'ath had not yet taken absolute power and eliminated all other non-Ba'athist factions, as is evident by what is covered in this chapter.

The strengthening of relations between the Soviets and the Ba'ath government post 1970: a closer look

The US was aware that the Soviet Union's influence was increasing in Iraq in the early 1970s, of course. Indeed, the Soviets had signed and were carrying out multimillion-dollar projects in Iraq, ranging from the energy sector to agriculture and defence and to an extent, it would appear, that the Soviets were seeking to

1971–1975: Hope and betrayal 111

make a client of Iraq under the Ba'ath.[20] However, despite warning by figures such as Lebanese journalist Edward Saab that the Iraqi regime, having strengthened its roots at home, was about to embark on a mission of expanding its influence in the Gulf and eastwards into the Arab world, US regional diplomats and the State Department were not convinced that the Ba'athists could exert a significant impact beyond Iraq's borders. The US embassy in Lebanon took any possible Iraqi ambitions beyond its borders as conditional upon its internal stability—which was where this concerned the Kurds. US diplomats were not convinced that the March 1970 agreement between Barzani and Baghdad would last for long, and thus fully expected that Iraq would have little time for adventures abroad—especially now that anti-Ba'ath Arab elements had joined the Kurds' camp in wishing the downfall of the Iraqi regime (as indicated by Barzani's plan).[21] Iraq's perceived need for internal stability to realise any possible external ambitions, therefore, may also have had an effect on the US decision not to look upon Barzani's proposal any more favourably than it had his previous entreaties.

Additionally, frictions between the Soviets and Barzani are reported to have grown. According to informants of the US embassy in Lebanon, Barzani was aware of the growing ties between the Iraqi and Soviet governments and correspondingly, in the US perception, was 'no longer disposed to pay much attention to Soviet advice'.[22] This implies that Barzani had lost faith in the Soviets' sincerity as a mediator between Baghdad and Kurdistan and the Americans knew it. Masoud Barzani confirms that the Iraqi Kurds knew that the Soviets were only interested in a settlement to serve their own interests and were unconcerned about any possibility of the Kurds having to be the ones paying for this. The Soviets simply tried to convince the Kurds to commit to the March Accord, even after the failed assassination attempts—including one on Mela Mustafa himself. The Soviets knew that at least some of these acts were the works of high-ranking Ba'ath figures, but all that was important for them was to ensure that the Kurds remained committed to the March Accord, regardless. The USSR had indeed initially put pressure on the Ba'ath also to reach a deal, but as relations with the Ba'ath strengthened, the Kurds were simply gradually sidelined.[23]

As the Soviets and the Ba'ath developed closer ties, the former armed Iraq with their latest advanced weaponry, such as TU22 bombers, MIG25 aircraft and T60 tanks, among others. The Soviets' desire for the ICP to form an alliance with the Ba'ath duly occurred in June 1973. Soviet diplomats also went to Kurdistan to ask Barzani to participate in this apparently coalition government, but when Barzani asked for a guarantee from the USSR that the Ba'ath would honour all agreements, it declined. The Ba'ath–ICP partnership must have been a great political triumph for the Ba'ath, for this now weakened the anti-Ba'ath front and strengthened the government's base both among the Iraqi public and also politically. Soviet designs and relations with the Ba'ath government, meanwhile, point to larger ambitions in the country and, indeed, in the region. Naturally, this had repercussions; Iran was particularly unsettled and looked to the US.

112   *1971–1975: Hope and betrayal*

Implications of the Soviet–Iraqi rapprochement

Throughout 1971 and early 1972, and in fact going back to the years prior to this, SAVAK, and ultimately the Shah, alarmed by the rising influence of both the Ba'ath and the USSR in Iraq, petitioned the US to help Barzani lead an anti-Ba'ath initiative aimed at disposing the Ba'ath government.[24] In February 1972, after Saddam Hussein's visit to Moscow, a Soviet delegation visited Barzani's headquarters asking Barzani to join the National Front Government in Baghdad that was supposed to be led by the Ba'ath Party, and to include the KDP and the ICP, as mentioned earlier. The Soviets gave Barzani a number of assurances, including that the Soviets would station a liaison mission with Barzani with communication equipment and that Barzani would be invited to Russia with Soviet guarantees for his safety (Barzani was extremely distrustful of the Ba'athists, and especially so since their attempt on his life).[25]

In Iran, as mentioned, the perception was that if the so-called national government that the Soviets wanted were successful and the Kurdish Issue resolved, then Iraqi troops would be freed up for the Gulf. According to a memorandum from Harold Saunders of the National Security Council Staff to the President's Deputy Assistant for National Security Affairs, Alexander Haig, 'al-Barzani had asked SAVAK to inform [the] USG that if the present trend continued, Iraq would assume a status similar to that of the East European satellites'.[26] Forthcoming events were to reveal this as a fair assessment.

One other such request by SAVAK urging US backing for the Kurds reached Kissinger via Saunders in March 1972. In this, Saunders stated that '[s]imilar approaches' had been made 'over the last ten years' and 'turned down', that the British had 'also avoided involvement', the Israelis were 'probably paying Barzani a sizeable monthly subsidy' and King Hussein when visiting 'may support US involvement'. He also confirmed that the 'purpose of any move the Iranians supported now would be to try again to overthrow the Iraqi Ba'thist government and to reduce chances of Soviet entrenchment [sic] in Iraq'.

However, Saunders recommended that he 'tell [the] CIA we concur in their judgment that we should not involve ourselves'. This was because, as Saunders put it:

> any assistance that may be needed by Barzani is fully within the capability of Iran or Israel to provide. There is nothing absolutely needed from us except that they want to involve us. Another factor is that the odds are against the Kurds succeeding. Also, our involving ourselves for the first time at this point could be regarded by the Soviets as a move directed against them. My instinct is to remain out of this as we have in the past, but I felt that you ought to be aware because of the Soviet angle.[27]

Kissinger approved the recommendation. For his part, Barzani appears to have foreseen the growing capabilities of Iraq as backed by the USSR.[28] The Ba'ath government in Baghdad had never implemented the 1970 Accord fully, apart

1971–1975: Hope and betrayal   113

from a construction programme of social facilities (building schools, hospitals, etc.), whose purpose was to drain support for Barzani's national liberation movement. According to informants of the US embassy in Lebanon, moreover, Barzani was convinced that the Soviets were at least aware of the assassination attempt on him, if not behind it, along with, of course, the Ba'athists in Baghdad. Evidently, therefore, Barzani did not only distrust the Ba'ath but was also suspicious of the Soviets.[29]

Although he distrusted Iran also, Barzani sought to acquire its backing and ultimately US backing through Iran as a counterweight to the developing Soviet–Iraqi axis, in addition to seeing the US as trustworthy. As Saunders had noted, it surely was within the capabilities of Iran and Israel to back Barzani without the US, but it was precisely the guarantee that would come with the superpower's commitment that Iran sought and to also convince Barzani to remain close to Iran and not join the Soviet plan of a so-called unitary government in Iraq led by the Ba'ath. These, together with Barzani's insistence, may explain why Iran seems to have genuinely wanted to involve the US in this matter.

With the USSR pressing Barzani to join the National Front and Saddam Hussein's visit to Moscow in February 1972 resulting in the Soviet–Iraqi Treaty of Friendship and Cooperation, the Kurdish leadership must have discerned a developing danger. Iran, meanwhile, was pressing Barzani not to join the National Front. Barzani, therefore, was effectively caught in a dilemma in which he trusted neither side. And as well as having this choice, there was also the option of a renewal of hostilities were both to be rejected. By the end of March 1972, Iran, making every effort to stop Barzani from joining the National Front Government, had already asked Idris Barzani to 'send them a list of requirements of their current military and material needs'. Kurdish sources again confirm that the Kurds did not trust Iran, and thus this explains their desire not to rely on Iran.[30]

As the subject (title) of a memorandum from the Director of the CIA to the President's Assistant for National Security Affairs, Kissinger, to Secretary Rogers, and to Secretary Laird of Defence put it, Barzani sought to 'Recruit International Support for [the] Kurdish Position in Their Drive To Combat Closer Soviet-Iraqi Relations and Resulting Pressure on the Kurds'.[31] Barzani also sent an emissary to Jordan to see an unidentified Jordanian figure to explain and convey the nature of the perilous situation that was arising as a result of the Iraq–Soviet alliance.[32] Consequently, Jordan also conveyed to the Americans that the Iraqi Kurds were pressed by the potentially perilous implications of the Soviet–Iraqi friendship and that the West, therefore, ought to reconsider its position. The Kurdish leadership no longer thought about this as a Kurdish issue alone but it considered the Ba'ath (backed by the USSR) to be a countrywide problem and that Kurds and Arabs needed to work together to overcome this.[33]

In May 1972, King Hussein of Jordan sent his secretary to visit Barzani with a letter stating that, among other things, the purpose of the visit was to offer, as it was expressed, 'complete support and unconditional inclination in anything that you are trying for'.[34] The King also asked to see Barzani the following month when he visited Tehran, and the substance of the letter was also orally conveyed

114 *1971–1975: Hope and betrayal*

to Barzani by the emissary. More importantly, the King's secretary stated that the King had put a feeler out to the US Administration (regarding the Iraqi Kurds) and received a positive response. The King and Barzani finally met. As reported by Masoud Barzani, all that is known about this meeting is that the King had played an important role in convincing the Nixon administration to assist the Kurds. Therefore, it was not only Iran and Israel that pushed for this to happen; Jordan was also involved in the plan that Barzani was to propose. Indeed, US documents point to the involvement of Jordan even so that some of these documents are heavily excised when it comes to the identity of the actor—but that much can be ascertained (Jordan).[35]

What Barzani wanted was assistance on all fronts—political, military and financial—albeit covertly, with the aim being to unseat the Ba'ath regime for a constitutional government comprised of both Kurds and Arabs. This government was initially to be based in Kurdistan until the Iraqi army was enlisted. The KDP had already won over the support of a number of prominent Iraqi figures who would join the new government. Reportedly, support among elements of the army had already been ensured, too.[36] From another American memorandum—passed from the CIA to Kissinger—we also learn that the Kurds reported further information on the developing relations between the Soviet Union and Iraq, including in the military sector, weapons to be acquired and the forthcoming date for the signing of the Treaty of Friendship as well as the nature of the Treaty.[37] The fact that Kurdish intelligence already knew these details in advance, according to the Americans, also lends credibility to the rest of the story as reported by the Kurds.

In early April 1972, Barzani sent one last representative to the US. Carrying a letter to the Secretary of State, the representative, Zayd Uthman, explained the pressure being brought on Barzani by the USSR and the Ba'ath, which he could no longer withstand, and that neither could he rely on the Shah's assistance, which 'blows hot and col[d] in his support of the Kurdish national liberation movement'. Continuing, Uthman asserted that 'Barzani cannot commit himself to an all-out struggle against the Ba'ath regime in Baghdad on the basis of such unpredictable support'.[38] King Hussein, he added, had not been able to offer any material assistance, but the Kurds trusted him nonetheless; this was, of course, before the King's secretary met Barzani in May and offered strong support.

Uthman requested an answer be given to him for this 'final appeal' by April 6, as the Soviets and the Ba'ath were pressing Barzani for an answer within the next calendar month. Barzani's representative also stated that if a reply for this final appeal were not positive, then Barzani would be obliged to join the National Front even though he did not trust the Ba'athists, since only the US had the capacity to turn the Soviet tide in Iraq. The purpose of this assistance would initially be to establish what he called a 'liberation' government in Kurdistan as a stepping stone that would subsequently topple the Ba'athists in Baghdad.[39]

When Nixon and Kissinger visited Iran on May 30–31, 1972, after the Moscow Summit, the Shah raised the question of the Kurds with them and the possibility of the Soviets establishing a coalition of the KDP and communists with the Ba'athists.[40] The Shah once again referenced Cold War motivations telling Nixon that 'the Kurdish problem instead of being a thorn in the side could become an asset to the Communists'.[41] When Kissinger asked what could be done, the Shah replied that 'Turkey needs strengthening [...] Iran can help with the Kurds'.[42] Prior to Nixon and Kissinger's visits to Iran in May, unidentified sources had proposed to Kissinger that he and Rogers should meet Barzani while in Tehran, but this was rejected on the grounds of Kissinger not having sufficient time. The unidentified source (not declassified) is likely to be the Shah himself, King Hussein or else Israel.[43]

It seems that the Shah had an in-depth talk with Nixon and his companions while in Tehran regarding the developments in Iraq, for on June 5, 1972, and following on from their discussions in Tehran, the Shah sent a message to Kissinger requesting that the Kurdish representatives who would be travelling to the US be personally received by him; the Shah even wrote that he 'expects'[44] Kissinger to share with him his views on the meeting, as well as expressing the view that 'the Kurds should be protected from Communist influence and prevented from following the same policies as those of the Iraqi government'.[45] In forwarding the memorandum, however, Saunders added his views, stating, among other things, 'The balance is fairly fine on the question of whether we should support the Kurds'.[46] According to Saunders, the argument to support the Kurds was to 'permit or encourage them to remain a source of instability in Iraq', to thwart USSR efforts for a stable united Iraqi government, and also, since Iran, Israel and Jordan were US allies, to have the Iraqi army tied down.[47]

Indeed, as we have seen, internal instability in Iraq was not necessarily unwelcomed by the US, for the reasons stated here, again, by Saunders. The Kurds' ability to preoccupy the Iraqi army and the geopolitical significance of this was also confirmed by Anwar Sadat of Egypt and Egypt's contemporary Chief of Staff, who, according to Kurdish sources, said that whenever Egypt asked for Iraq's participation in an Arab–Israel war before 1973, the response was that it was busy fighting the Kurds and so was unable to participate.[48] In addition to this regional complexity, the belief was that domestic instability in Iraq would also weaken Iraq's potential meddling in the Gulf, as examined.[49]

During the 1973 war, Israel unsuccessfully enquired of the Kurds if they could launch an offensive on the Iraqi army; this was rejected by the US and the Shah on the grounds that the Kurds were not properly equipped to attack the Iraqi army beyond their mountain strongholds. The American ambassador to Iran considered this to be 'a reckless undertaking'[50] while the Shah had 'no desire to have the Kurds branded as mere henchmen of Israel and the USA'.[51] Indeed, had the Kurds launched such an offensive in 1973 as Israel requested, they would surely have appeared as pawns of Israel and thus would have lost whatever sympathy there may have been for them in the Arab world. Nonetheless, they requested advice and then based on that they rejected the Israeli request. The Kurds too had an aim of their own.

Saunders' memorandum to Kissinger reveals a number of other points. First, in stating that 'US policy for some time has been to avoid involvement in Kurdish affairs', Saunders again confirmed the view expressed here, as explained in

116   *1971–1975: Hope and betrayal*

relation to the Cold War and regional politics.[52] Second, he voiced the assessment that 'If the battle turned against the Kurds, we would have neither the assets nor the interest to provide decisive support'.[53] Even if the US were to intercede on the Kurds' behalf, apparently it would necessarily not be a decisive commitment—the gap between the Kurds' hopes and even the likely maximum support of the US was really quite wide, it would seem. Finally, Saunders counselled that 'One would have to consider the implications of supporting the Kurds in the context of the Moscow summit talks', arguing that 'Since the Soviets have made an effort recently to persuade the Kurds to join the Ba'ath Party in a national unity government in Baghdad, support for the Kurds would be a direct counter-Soviet move'.[54] This seems to be a clear warning about the significant consequences of taking an action in the context of consideration about Russian intentions and the signal that such a move would send. Saunders' views, therefore, further support the present argument in respect of the Americans assessing their strategy regarding the Iraqi Kurds in the regional context as it pertained to the Cold War.

On the visit of the Kurdish emissaries scheduled to travel to Washington, ultimately, Saunders recommended to Kissinger that he not personally meet them; rather, Saunders himself should be tasked with that. He proposed this because, he stated, 'My own feeling is that it would be better not to involve you personally at this stage since that comes so close to involving the President at least by implication'.[55] Ultimately, moreover, not involving Kissinger and Nixon gave room for plausible deniability on the part of the Administration in this affair as looked at in the next section.

Iraqi Kurds: a stumbling block for the Ba'athists and the Soviets?

Subsequent to the Shah persuading Nixon and Kissinger during their Tehran visit to grant the Kurds a proper hearing of their proposal and the Shah's telegram asking Kissinger to personally meet the Kurdish representatives in Washington, a reply was given to the Shah that the CIA Director, Richard Helms, and Deputy Assistant to the President for National Security Affairs, Alexander Haig, would meet the visiting Kurds.[56] It is recalled here that in the recent months prior to this, SAVAK and the Shah together with Barzani had intensified their efforts to obtain US backing. This was in conjunction with other actors, as mentioned in the last section. The name of at least one of those actors remains classified in the US archives, but as evidence of the involvement of King Hussein of Jordan is available, in light of Israel's involvement in this affair and the sensitivity of this matter, one must assume the unnamed other actor to be, indeed, Israel.[57]

Under pressure to respond to the Soviet scheme of the KDP joining the coalition government, as explained, Barzani agreed to the meeting, which was arranged for July 30, 1972. The meeting took place in Washington, between Dr Mahmoud Othman and Idris Barzani, on the Kurds' side, and Richard Helms and Richard Kennedy of the NSC staff. This was the highest-level meeting between the US and the Kurds.[58] In the words of Kennedy, the Kurdish visitors gave their hosts 'an excellent presentation' in which they explained the state of affairs and why it was important for the US to back the Kurds.[59] They then requested that the US assist them in all spheres. Politically they asked for US recognition of their objective for autonomy and maintenance of ongoing but covert direct contact, and militarily they requested that the US provide sufficient armaments at least for them to keep the Iraqi army at bay in Kurdistan—or, scaling up, that they be given the offensive capabilities to engage the main part of the Iraqi army with a view to causing a reaction in Baghdad that would result in the toppling of the Ba'ath regime in coordination with other anti-Ba'ath non-Kurdish elements in Iraq (the Barzani plan, in other words).

The Kurdish representatives warned that the Kurdish leadership believed that without outside support for the Kurds, the Soviets would overcome the last non-Soviet fortress in Iraq (i.e. Kurdistan). Once the Soviets had a tight grip over all of Iraq, they stated, this would have dire consequences for the region and the Kurds would not be able to 'resist this combination of Soviet and Iraqi pressure for much more than six months without significant foreign assistance', warning that 'If such aid is not forthcoming, the Kurds believe that within six months they will either have to reach a political compromise with the Iraqi central government or fight to a sure defeat'. Finally, they conveyed Barzani's wish for 'increased foreign assistance not just to defend his area from the Soviets and Iraqis, but preferably to make Kurdistan a positive element on the side of the United States and its friends and allies in the Middle East, notably Turkey, Iran, Israel, Saudi Arabia, Jordan, and the Persian Gulf states'.[60]

Thus, the Kurds did indeed make an attractive case, culminating with recognition of the full regional and Cold War ramifications of what was being proposed. Helms responded that the US would consider it once they had details of the aid that the Kurds needed, that Kissinger had authorised conveyance of US sympathy for the Kurdish movement and also that such contact or potential aid from the US must be kept absolutely secret—failure to honour which would sour 'this new relationship'. Also, any assistance from the US was to be provided through proxy countries.[61]

After the above meeting, Helms and Kennedy favoured support for the Kurdish movement for a variety of reasons, among which were the growing aggressiveness of the Ba'ath regime and the belief that if the regime were to eliminate the Kurds, either by forcing them into the government with the Ba'ath (and ICP) or by military means, Iraq would then turn its attention to its neighbours. In a memorandum to Kissinger, his Deputy Assistant for National Security Affairs also recalled that during the 1960s, the Kurds had tied down two-thirds of the Iraqi army and thus effectively paralysed it from manoeuvres abroad, conditions that caused a number of military coups. The rational, therefore, was now to agree to what Barzani had in mind: to push the army to a limit that would cause it to turn on the Ba'ath government in coordination with the other anti-Ba'ath non-Kurds, as before.[62]

The most important point to draw from the above correspondences between the Nixon administration officials is that the primary reason to back the Kurds was not for the Kurds as such but to paralyse Iraq in order to secure US regional allies

118   *1971–1975: Hope and betrayal*

and prevent Soviet expansion. The Nixon administration wanted to exploit the Kurdish need for American support for the advancement of its own interest and that of its allies. There were, therefore, motivating elements here both of the Cold War and of protecting the security of US allies in the region through debilitating the Iraqi army. Indeed, giving or winning freedom for the Kurds was not part of the thinking of US officials.

Haig and the other two named US officials were all convinced that Soviet influence on Iraq had reached a level that needed to be countered; Iraq could put the entire region at risk if it eliminated the Kurdish movement. Haig thought that the alternative to US support for the Kurds would be for Barzani to join the National Front, in which case the Ba'athists would gradually erode the Kurds' resistance. What Haig and others were suggesting to Kissinger was that essentially the Kurds could be a stumbling block for the Ba'athists and the Soviets in Iraq. As perceived by the US and Iran, therefore, the Kurds were a means of containing both Iraq itself and the USSR's regional desire through Iraq.[63] The idea that internal instability in Iraq was not necessarily against US interests, considered already, here receives further confirmation.

Haig also forwarded a proposal for action from Helms and Kennedy after the two had listened to the Kurds' needs. The proposal stated that while the Kurds had asked for some $60 million a year in order to raise and maintain an army and to fund a local government, in order to finance 25,000 Peshmerga, Barzani only needed $18 million. They also recommended that the US not involve itself with the Kurds' plan for a local government, as that would surpass a covert operation. Essentially, they argued that the aim was to keep the Iraqi army off balance, as has been explained in this section. Also on the military sphere, they suggested that an estimated total of $2 million worth of ordnance, which was in the CIA stocks, could be delivered. This comprised of light weapons, weapons that the Kurds were most familiar with and which were not attributable or else used also by Iran and Iraq's armies. It was recommended that heavy weapons, such as anti-aircraft and tanks, should not be supplied. Iran was speculated to be ready to pay half of the $18 million while the US would pay $3 million and unidentified sources would pay the rest.[64]

However, there were a number of issues to be cautious about, which concerned Russia, Turkey and the Kurds themselves. First, assistance for the Kurds, it was recommended, must not be in such a manner and quantity as to draw in the Soviets on the side of the Iraqi regime, as this could lead to a major international confrontation; for instance, the Soviets could deploy their pilots to help the Iraqi regime. Here, the Soviets' recent investments in Iraq in all sectors were noted, as well as their role in the nationalisation of the IPC. Second, there was a concern about the Turks, whom Haig stated were 'acutely sensitive to any manifestations of Kurdish nationalism on their borders'. Despite the risks that Iraq as a Soviet client posed to all its neighbours, Turkey still considered Kurdish nationalism as the more challenging threat, even though, as Haig noted, the Kurds in Turkey had 'been vigorously suppressed' and 'were now called "Mountain Turks"'.[65] Haig's 'mountain Turks' comment, it may be noted, shows clearly that US policymakers

1971–1975: Hope and betrayal 119

were well aware of who the Kurds were, their desires and how they were treated by the *parent state*, in this case Turkey, an important Cold War ally and NATO member. Similarly, the treatment of the Iraqi Kurds by the US was, beyond any reasonable doubt, based on decisions made quite consciously. Finally, there was a worry about Kurdish factionalism and an ideological divide. Haig and Kennedy suspected that some Leftist-Marxist Kurds, still under Barzani's leadership, might leak the secret support to the Soviet Union.[66]

Ultimately, Alexander Haig, Kissinger's assistant, proposed two courses of action to initiate the operation. These were:

(1) To go directly to the President (Nixon) who would authorise this policy and then direct Helms (CIA Director) and the Office of Management and Budgetary of the State Department (OMB) accordingly; or

(2) To inform the leading figures of the 40 Committee but 'avoid any paper and tell them that the President wants this done',[67] the task would then be handed over to the CIA and OBM for execution, with the insurance of plausible deniability were any information regarding the operation to leak.

Haig suggested the latter course, and Kissinger also subsequently opted for it.[68] Back in Kurdistan, by July 1972, sporadic apparently spontaneous skirmishes between the Peshmerga and Iraqi army were breaking out.[69] On implementing the operation, by October, according to Kissinger himself, Iran had received 111 (imperial) tonnes of arms and ammunition from the US destined for Iraqi Kurdistan, in addition to another 71 tonnes from an unidentified (not declassified) country, presumably Israel or Jordan. Either or both of these countries could have been involved, since the weapons were 'captured Fedayeen ordnance'[70] (having been captured from the 'Fedayeen', these weapons, largely of Soviet origin, were not attributable to the donor itself). Barzani had also received a monthly cash subsidy for his Peshmerga from July 1972. Regarding this course of action, Kissinger also indicated to Nixon that the rationale behind it was that the Kurds would continue to pin down two-thirds of the Iraqi army 'and deprive the Bathists [sic] of a secure base from which to launch sabotage and assassination teams against Iran'.[71]

The US also continued to bolster Iran's military capabilities on the Shah's insistence. The Shah was either concerned about a brewing war with Iraq or at least wanted Iran to be a credible deterrence, when it came to Iraq. For its part, the US appeared keen to preserve Iran's military superiority over Iraq, which would be unsurprising given the relationship between Iraq and the USSR that had the potential to affect the military balance and developments in the region. Thus, there developed what was effectively an arms race between Iran and Iraq—and the Iraqi Kurds were in the middle, instrumental in affecting the balance insofar as they had the potential to debilitate and thereby prevent Iraq from properly fighting on a second front, which was again noted in internal US communications.[72]

By August 1972, Nixon had personally authorised what was a highly covert CIA operation to provide arms and financial assistance to Barzani's forces, and by

120 *1971–1975: Hope and betrayal*

March 29, 1973, according to the CIA, more than 1,000 tonnes of non-attributable essentialities, including medicine and blankets, had been supplied in addition to the monthly subsidy for Barzani in order to maintain his force of 25,000 Peshmerga, continuing from the year before. Iran also provided $4.8 million per year, together with an unspecified amount of arms and materials. The supplies from the US were all channelled through Iran.[73] Consistently, there was also at least a third actor involved in aiding the Kurds, the details of which are largely excised (not declassified) in the American archives, which we may again assume to have been Israel or Jordan, as explained earlier.

In March 1973, Kissinger made a request to Nixon for the President to authorise the continuation of the CIA operation, since he was satisfied that it was providing

> a strong buffer force against Iraqi-directed infiltration teams of saboteurs and terrorists; and worries the Baghdad regime, forcing it to deploy almost two-thirds of its ground forces in the north, reducing its capability for offensive adventures. The Ba'th [sic] regime continues to support radical subversion, recently even as far afield as Pakistan. It continues to finance Palestinian terrorist organizations and remains one of the most irreconcilable regimes against negotiated peace with Israel. It threatens to disrupt oil agreements which western companies may be able to negotiate with more moderate governments in the area. It is a regime whose instability we should continue to promote.[74]

From Kissinger's correspondence with Nixon, it is evident that the Shah was the pivotal factor behind this whole affair, although Kissinger also seemed to have come to loath the Iraqi regime by this time. Nixon approved Kissinger's proposal on the same day.[75] Meanwhile, according to the US Interest Section in Iraq, Baghdad had received more than $1 billion worth of Soviet military assistance since 1965 and over $500 million in economic assistance, making Iraq only second to Egypt in the Middle East in terms of Soviet aid received; the US and Iranian support for the Iraqi Kurds was thus simply incomparable to the Russia's backing of Iraq. The Section, unaware of the CIA operation, also added that 'A truce of March 1970 conceded regional autonomy to the Kurds... but the government is unwilling to grant it in practice and the Kurds refuse to settle for less'.[76]

Further explanation as to why US decision-makers decided to change their minds in this matter is provided in the record of a conversation between Kissinger and Helms and Saunders in which Kissinger stated the following:

> What I want is for the Politburo in Moscow to be in a frame of mind not to want to get involved in further adventures in the Middle East. I want them to recall that they were run out of Egypt and that Iraq turned out to be a bottomless pit. I want them to tell anyone who comes with a recommendation for renewed activity in the Middle East to go away. I want the Shah to help in

1971–1975: Hope and betrayal   121

this strategy. We do not want to push the USSR against the wall. We just want them in a frame of mind where they judge that the costs for activity in the Middle East seem excessive. We also want the Arabs in the area to feel that they cannot get a free ride by linking up with the Soviet Union. We want the Kurds to have enough strength to be an open wound in Iraq.[77]

The key figure in the US behind this decision to extend US military and financial assistance to the Kurds was Kissinger, for regional as well as international reasons, as established. Having being perceived as a trump card by the Shah of Iran from the early 1960s, the Iraqi Kurds were now similarly viewed by Kissinger. Meanwhile, the Shah clarified his intention in a meeting with Kissinger during his July 1973 state visit to Washington, when he said, 'We are preventing a coalition of the Baaths [sic], the Kurds, and the Communists. We are preventing this'.[78]

The Shah also noted that Turkey had been 'a little reluctant to cooperate,' and that it had 'always had a weakness for Iraq and a fear of the Kurds'.[79] The Kurds in Iraq requested more aid from the Shah, while also conveying that US backing was essential as they could 'see how clearly and completely the other front [Ba'ath] has the backing of the Soviet Union, and how hard they are trying to strengthen the influence of the Soviets and of Communism in the area'.[80] As indicated, however, this was also because the Kurds considered the Shah untrustworthy and thus not to be relied on alone. This appeal was subsequently forwarded to Kissinger.[81]

During his state visit, the Shah also conveyed to Kissinger that he had told Barzani that he did not want him to create an independent Kurdish state, for, according to the Shah, 'It would make the Turks terribly afraid. We don't want to frighten the Turks unnecessarily'.[82] What the Shah did not tell the Americans, however, was that he too did not want to see an independent Kurdish state. Regarding the Iraqi Kurds, the Shah told his hosts that they were 'a trump card' that they (the Iranians) did 'not want to let go'.[83] It should be recalled here that, since the early years of the Cold War, the Shah had been apprehensive about the Soviets creating a Kurdish state. The Shah also told Kissinger that the Kurds offered their only leverage in Iraq, and Kissinger replied by stating that the problem the Americans faced was that they did not know exactly what needed to be done (for the Kurds) and it was for this reason that the two sides (US and Iran) would have to cooperate on this. Essentially, therefore, Kissinger entrusted the Shah to take the lead, and he also conveyed Nixon's assent to this, not knowing of course that for the Shah the Kurds were simply a means to an end.[84]

In a separate meeting on July 27 between the Shah and Kissinger, among others, the Shah told Kissinger that he had told the Kurds 'absolutely not to participate in a coalition government' and to 'stop receiving Soviet representatives or the Ba'ath representatives from Baghdad'.[85] However, he added that if the two sides (Iran and the US) were going to ask that of the Kurds, then they must increase their financial assistance. Kissinger agreed to this request in principle, with Helms also concurring. It is to be noted that the initial request for increased assistance had come from the Kurds themselves, as indicated earlier. Furthermore,

122 *1971–1975: Hope and betrayal*

as a contingency plan and pertaining to regional politics, if Jordan were to be attacked by Iraq and Syria then, the Shah suggested, they 'could play the Kurdish card and encourage them to begin skirmishing'.[86] Again, we see the potential of the Kurds as a regional player, or rather, unfortunate for them, their usefulness for manipulation by the bigger powers.[87]

Not only was it the Shah who took the lead for the US in its change of policy regarding the Iraqi Kurds from 1972, but also, while the US had its own motivations for the covert operation, these were again instigated by the Shah, who convinced the Nixon administration that it was in the interest of the US to join him and back the Iraqi Kurds. But the Kurds, we know, were desperate to gain the support of America, and indeed it was Barzani who used the Soviet backing for Iraq and the importance of US 'moral support' to convince the Shah to bring the US on board. Thus, Barzani seems to have convinced the Shah that a superpower's might was essential to balance that of another (i.e. the US was needed to counteract the Soviets in Iraq); the Shah then argued this with the Nixon administration and the support was granted, although only for that limited objective. Neither the Shah nor the Nixon administration had in mind, as an objective, the establishment of the Kurdish entity that Barzani was fighting for, and neither were prepared to approve this.

In fact, although Kissinger was persuaded by the Shah, Kissinger was himself eminently biddable, for wider strategical reasons as seen from the US. Elsewhere, he confirmed his reasoning for why the US now wanted to back the Kurds after so many years of resisting this option. In the Senior Group Meeting (July 20, 1973), just days before the Shah visited the US, Kissinger told the Group that '[k]eeping the Kurds active in Iraq would not be contrary to our interest'.[88] Kissinger was responding to the Assistant Secretary of State for Near Eastern and South Asian Affairs, Joseph Sisco, who had argued that the US should continue its support for Iran and Jordan while 'keep[ing] the door open to Iraq and Syria'.[89] Kissinger agreed that the door should be kept open, but Iraq should be made to 'pay a price', namely, through the Kurds. This strategy was designed to essentially serve as a carrot and stick approach with Iraq in connection to the USSR's position in the region, and in this case, particularly in connection to Iran.

Thus, we should understand Kissinger as sending an indirect signal to Iraq and other regional states that relations with the Soviets would be counterproductive, so they should keep close to the US and not the USSR. Also when it came to the USSR itself, basically he confirmed that 'if we could get the Soviets to suffer a mis-adventure in Iraq it could curb the Soviet appetite in the Middle East'.[90] The matter had to be executed skilfully, however, for all parties concerned to buy into it. Indeed, the affair with the Shah and the Iraqi Kurds was so secret in the US that even both the Director of the Office of Iraqi *et al.* Affairs, David Korn, and the Country Officer for Iraq, Edward Djerejian, of the State Department were not aware of it.[91] Were the Russians to get wind of what was going on, see through the ruse and call the US's bluff, in essence, the Kurds could be rendered highly vulnerable—which was, basically, what happened.

1971–1975: Hope and betrayal   123

Following the Shah's July visit to the US and the request to increase the backing for the Kurds, the CIA presented the administration with four options. Kissinger then sought Helms' opinion on August 17, 1973, in an exclusive 'eyes-only' back channel message to ambassador Helms in Iran. Kissinger also wanted Helms to discuss the options with the Shah and relay back his views. Additionally, Kissinger also asked Helms to ascertain whether the Shah wanted to do more himself, to which Helms replied that the Shah had pledged to increase his own subsidy for the Kurdish movement by more than 50%. Helms recommended the first two of the options proposed, which were to replenish the CIA stocks of ordnance as a contingency measure and also to increase the Kurds' subsidy from the US by 50%, stating that 'the increase of our subsidy in response to the Shah's recommendation is symbolic of our support for the Shah and he likes this reassurance too'.[92]

As a result, the KDP rejected joining the National Front unless Baghdad fulfilled certain conditions.[93] At the behest of the US, Saudi Arabia also gave assistance in the summer of 1974, providing a one-off contribution estimated at $1 million.[94] Therefore, what was developing into a new phase of the Kurdish Revolution began with the backing of several parties. As shown here, however, each actor that came forward with material support for the KDP or the Iraqi Kurdish movement did so for different reasons and thus with different aims—and none actually supported the final goal held by the Kurds of democratically based autonomy, let alone independence.

Renewal of war and the great betrayal

In March 1974, a high-ranking Kurdish delegation met Saddam Hussein in Baghdad upon the latter's request. The Kurdish delegation offered a counter-proposal to Saddam's on how to resolve a number of contentious issues, which Saddam dismissed, and according to Masoud Barzani, thus:

> These proposals are not appropriate and are rejected. The only exit left is that you agree to the autonomy plan the way we [the government] have authored it and you have 15 days. During this period, we will have no activity and business. After that whoever does not agree to it, we will consider them an enemy of us.[95]

Saddam also warned the Kurdish delegation that if Iraq were pushed, then it would yield to the Shah, but—notably—'If we are forced to yield to the Shah you will then pay a high price'.[96] In other words, Saddam was quite open about involving the Kurds in the ongoing game with Iran. Tellingly also, the Soviet ambassador was present at the meeting, thus indicating Russia's support and, by implication, the larger Cold War game in play—its effect on the Iraqi Kurds. Clearly, the Ba'ath thus must have received Soviet backing for this push and was essentially seeking to renew the Kurdish War.

Two days later, Iraq unilaterally promulgated its version of an autonomy plan, which Saddam spoke about with the Kurdish delegation as mentioned, for

124   1971–1975: Hope and betrayal

Kurdistan and gave the Kurds until March 26 to accept it. This was effectively the end of the ceasefire agreed upon in March 1970. The Kurds objected to the Iraqi plan, since it did not include Kirkuk and was perceived as insufficient.[97] For its part, the USSR noted 'outside' interference as an impediment to a final settlement between the Iraqi government and the Kurds. In fact, according to a US embassy officer in Moscow who met a USSR official in March 1974, when it came to Iran–Iraq disputes and border clashes, the Soviets were not as supportive of Iraq as they were in its Kurdish policy and indicated their preference for a mutually agreed settlement.[98]

In retrospect, there appears to have been a key moment, which was that, according to the then head of *Parastn*, the KDP's intelligence agency, the Soviets had learnt about the Kurds' relations with the CIA. Quite when this occurred is not clear, but the main point is that the Russians were able and motivated to increase the stakes. Upon knowing this, they warned the Kurds through their envoys that travelled to Kurdistan against the course that the Kurds were taking, advising the Kurds 'not to believe the Americans' promises without actions to back up these promises'.[99] Meanwhile, Alexei Kosygin insisted that the Kurds join the National Front Government in Baghdad. The KGB discovery of the Kurds' relations with the CIA does seem to have gradually changed the Soviet perception of the Kurdish movement and, ultimately, its fully backing the Ba'ath against the Kurds. That said, however, it should also be noted that Soviet–Iraqi relations had already reached a new level with the Treaty of Friendship and Cooperation in 1972, so US support for the Kurds through the CIA essentially strengthened rather than changed the Soviets' resolve in backing Iraq, as evidenced by the developments that followed.[100]

The Kurdish leadership several times requested an increase in the US–Iranian subsidy and arms in anticipation of war.[101] On a number of occasions, the Kurds also wanted to unilaterally declare autonomy, but they were advised against this by the Shah and Kissinger because, as put by Kissinger's staff initially

> Up to now neither the Shah nor ourselves has [sic] wished to see the matter resolved one way or the other—either by Kurdish acquiescence or by the establishment of an unviable autonomous Kurdish government (particularly one pretending to speak for Iraqi Arab sentiment as well).[102]

Kissinger ultimately agreed to reject the Kurds' plan to declare a unilateral autonomy and instead forwarded a request to Nixon explaining the situation and then requesting an increase in the aid that the Kurds were receiving instead—essentially to keep the Kurds going and to 'reassure' them of the US backing. Of course, the other side of this was to tie down Iraq by its Kurdish War as explained earlier. Other reasons for why the US decision-makers did not look upon the Kurdish proposal for autonomy favourably was to avoid offending the Turks, the Arabs and also because this Kurdish plan went beyond a covert action—which was not in the US interest.[103] Meanwhile, in Kurdistan, by now, up

1971–1975: Hope and betrayal   125

to 250,000 people, including white-collar Kurds, from Kurdish areas under the control of the Iraqi government had migrated into Peshmerga-held territory, considering it a liberated area. The Kurds ultimately agreed to the advice of their supposedly allies.[104]

In early 1974, also, just as the four-year truce of March 11, 1970, was expiring, Soviet–Iraqi relations underwent a further enforcement, as indicated by the visit of several high-ranking Soviet officials. These included the Minister of Defence Marshal Grechko, who stayed in Iraq for three days, and the Ministers of Interior and Petroleum, among other officials.[105] The speedy developments and the well-planned Ba'ath schemes show that the Kurdish Issue must have been high on the agenda of these visits. Also, the type of equipment that the Soviets had provided to the Iraqis demonstrate the extent of the USSR's backing for Iraq in order to keep Iraq away from the West, this being listed by the US Interest Section in Baghdad thus:

> Soviet supply of Iraq with highly sophisticated military equipment; to [the] best of USINTS's knowledge Iraq is [the] only country outside USSR to have received TU-22 supersonic medium bombers and one of very few to receive MIG-23s and SU-20 fighter bombers. It has also received SA-2, SA-3, and SA-7 missiles.[106]

In late August 1974, the long-anticipated Iraqi ground invasion finally got underway, with eight Iraqi army divisions participating, according to the Kurds, in addition to other independent brigades.[107] The American *Newsweek* magazine put the number of Iraqi troops taking part in the assault to be an estimated 60,000, stating also that Iraq had 'undertaken round-the-clock bombing of civilians'.[108] Independent aid agencies as well as the UK Foreign Office were reporting the use of phosphorous and napalm bombs by the Iraqi troops.[109] In Masoud Barzani's words, the Army was 'not distinguishing between suckling children and fighting-men'.[110] Iraq's excessive and indiscriminate use of force was thus well known and widely reported by multiple sources.

Other sources, such as captured Iraqi pilots, reported that Russian pilots flew regular bombing sorties in their TU-22 supersonic bombers, and also that Russian pilots and planes were supporting Iraq in a total effort to overcome the Kurdish movement. One such report detailing this was published by the British *The Daily Telegraph* newspaper in September 1974. By September, British intelligence sources noted that Iraq had made some gains against the Kurds but that the cost of these gains had been high in terms of army casualties. A UK intelligent report, moreover, did not see it as unreasonable to infer that Russians were present among the Iraqi ground forces, if, indeed, the reports of Russian pilots and planes were true.[111]

In the meantime, large numbers of Kurds had already relocated to areas under Peshmerga control. The following excerpt from a memorandum in September from the US consul in Tabriz explained the morale on the Kurds' side; it is imperative to mention this here, as later the Shah would claim and tell the US that

126   *1971–1975: Hope and betrayal*

the Kurds were not fighting, and thus were basically to be blamed for their own sell-out. The memorandum stated that:

> Foreign correspondents, Iranians, and personal observations all agree that Kurdish morale [is] extremely high. According to doctor and Governor Otmishi, Kurds leave hospital as soon as they can move and return to front lines. More volunteers are supposedly available to join [the] Pish Merga [sic] than there are guns to supply them. Kurds said to be far more unified than in [the] past with heavy movement of urban educated Kurds to Barzani. [...] many Kurdish Communists [are] now fighting with Barzani side by side with Christian Kurds, some of whom I met.[112]

By December 1974, the above source reported that 'The Iraqi offensive [that] begun in August appears to have sputtered, flared and finally gone out'.[113] The consul noted that the Iraqis had not been able to push much beyond *Qelladze* and *Rewanduz*, with Barzani's headquarters in *Hacî Omeran* remaining secure. Indeed, the focus of the Iraqi assault was to capture the KDP headquarters in *Hacî Omeran* and also gain control of the Hamilton Road. Again, regarding Kurdish morale, the consul stated—emphatically—that there were 'no rpt [repeat] no signs of weakening of Kurdish morale or unity'.[114] He went on to convey that there was no reason to expect an early end to the war short of an Iranian change of policy or a change of government in Baghdad.[115] This fortitude was maintained despite the eyewitness accounts of aid workers from the UK and volunteers who had been to Kurdistan 'coming back to tell the press how badly Kurds are suffering' and that Iraqis were 'using "inhuman" methods such as phosphorus and napalm, etc., against some of which UN Resolutions exist'.[116] The use of phosphorus and napalm was also confirmed by Iranian hospitals treating Kurdish casualties.[117]

The British military attaché in Baghdad paradoxically confirmed the overall failure of the offensive. In stating that 'The Iraqi offensive has been a considerable success, although it failed, and in some cases failed very badly to accomplish its original goals'.[118] He was reporting success because the Iraqi army offensive had penetrated deeper into Kurdish territory than any before had been able to since the September Revolution began, in 1961. More importantly, however, it failed insofar as it did not achieve its primary aims of cutting Kurdish access to Iran and capturing Barzani's headquarters in *Hacî Omeran*. In addition to these, the areas it had captured were insecure, so the slow gains seem not to have been worth the losses. USINTS in Baghdad also countered Iraq's claims as magnifying its successes.[119]

Among Kurdish sources, there is to be found no talk of defeat or any such thing; in contrast, as indicated, morale was extremely high. In fact, the Iraqi army would have had to overcome five consecutive defensive zones that the Kurds had put in place in order to achieve its named objectives and had not even effectively broken through the first yet. The attitude on the Kurds' side was such that, by the end of 1974 they had devised a plan to encircle a large number of Iraqi troops in *Rewanduz* and take them as prisoners.[120] The Kurds had tried to acquire US

1971–1975: Hope and betrayal   127

backing and now that they achieved it, albeit ill-fated, they were fighting wholeheartedly.

The Iraqi losses were such that leading elements within the military began to blame Saddam Hussein for wanting to 'get rid of both the Kurds and the army'[121]—the claim being made in seriousness, the suggestion being that once the army had been so weakened that it would not be able to interfere in politics as before, Saddam would become the unchallenged ruler of Iraq. In short, Saddam's plan, like those before him, was going to backfire and the army turn on the government it seems, again, as it had done more than once since 1958. Saddam Hussein therefore seems to have put his own life on the line, as dependent on overpowering the Kurdish movement. Iraq by now had also taken a more reconciliatory approach towards the US, with top secret meetings taking place outside the country, from at least April 1974.[122]

Despite the Kurds' fighting ability, for which the evidence is overwhelming and consistent across multiple sources, by February 1975 the Shah was wavering— even according to his own Minister of the Royal Court, who confirmed that the Shah was the reason the Kurds had rejected joining the National Front Government in the first place.[123] Secret talks between Iran and Iraq, on the one hand, and the attempts of intermediaries, on the other, were giving the Shah pause for thought. This was after his November 1974 visit to Moscow; according to his own testimony, the Soviets had complained about Iran's support for the Kurds.[124] Assessing the evidence as a whole—and, of course, in addition to the secret talks and back-channel diplomacy by the intermediaries—this appears to have been a turning point in the diplomacy behind the ongoing conflict and thus, ultimately, in the Kurdish Revolution in Iraq, for thereafter the Shah's change of tune is apparent.

In a meeting with Kissinger in mid-February 1975, the Iranian leader stated that the Kurds had 'no guts left'[125] and that their resistance was weakening. Further, he admitted to Kissinger that he intended to meet Saddam Hussein, in response to an Iraqi overture. The following passage, from a report of Kissinger's meeting with Gerald Ford, now president upon Nixon's resignation in August, helps to clarify the Shah's real analysis of the situation:

> The Shah said he cannot accept an autonomous Kurdish state which would be under the dominance of a Communist Iraqi central government. He is suspicious that the Iraqis will stimulate some incidents along the Iraqi-Iranian border which could lead to an internationalization of the Kurdish question and its being brought before the United Nations Security Council, which he would consider most unhelpful. In short, he seems tempted to try to move in the direction of some understanding with Iraq regarding the Kurds, but is understandably sceptical that much is possible. In the meantime, he intends to continue his support for the Kurds.[126]

What the Shah was saying to Kissinger was clearly absurd; how would an autonomous Kurdish state sponsored by Iran and the US (and at war with Iraq)

128   *1971–1975: Hope and betrayal*

come under the dominance of the central Iraqi government? And also, for that matter, why would Iraq at this point have wanted an incident that would have resulted in the internationalisation of the Kurdish question? This would have been tantamount to shooting oneself in the foot.

As reported by another memorandum, Kissinger 'attempted to talk the Shah out of abandoning the Kurds'.[127] When they met, however, Kissinger also reported that the meeting was 'very satisfactory *in all major respects*' (emphasis added).[128] According to Masoud Barzani, Kissinger had assured Mustafa Barzani in 1972 that the Shah would remain faithful to the Kurds, regardless of developments.[129] He had made this commitment also, on behalf of the Nixon administration, but it is hard to believe and there is no evidence for the suggestion that American policy regarding Iraq and the Kurds veered wildly into a radically new direction following the inauguration of the new President Ford. On the contrary, there is clear evidence that it was the Shah who reneged on the agreement. This, manifestly, stands in sharp contrast to apparently pro-Iranian sources that attempt to vindicate the Shah, essentially by arguing that he had no other choice than to abandon the Kurds. In contrast to Alvandi, whose work was drawn upon in Chapter 1, Kimche also considers that Iran basically exchanged the Kurds for Iraq's compromise on the Shatt al-Arab boundary in the Algiers Accord, which Kimche refers to as a 'shameful agreement'.[130]

It is clear that the Iranian abandonment of the Kurds was actually the result of Iraq seeking to compromise with Iran as a *quid pro quo* to end Iran's backing for the Iraqi Kurds. With the Iraqis thrust in Kurdistan having being brought to a standstill and resulting in heavy Iraqi casualties, in early January, the Iraqi regime seems to have ignited a diplomatic frenzy to bring pressure to bear on Iran and seek a rapprochement. Iraq sent its Foreign Minister, Hammadi, to several Arab capitals during January 11–13, with a message from al-Bakr seeking assistance. The Iraqi minister also met Khalatbari, his Iranian counterpart, on the 16th of the same month, in Istanbul—but with this attempt at resolution failing over disputes in the Gulf.[131]

Debate around responsibility for the Kurdish defeat thus centres not so much on identifying the guilty party—clearly, that was the Shah, and this was a betrayal—but rather on attempts by the Shah to justify this betrayal. Dr Othman rejects the Shah's stated reasons for his shift in respect of the Kurds as fabrications and excuses. In the last few months before the betrayal, the Shah had also sent small units of his army, armed with artillery and anti-aircraft missiles, across the border in order to maximise Iraq's concessions in the secret talks that had begun, by means of increasing the pressure on Iraq's army in the War.[132] Therefore, as Saddam's *Plan A* was failing and his political ambitions were on the line, Arab countries, such as Egypt and Jordan, and even figures like the former French Prime Minister Jacques Chirac, at Iraq's behest, all tried to bring Iran and Iraq together to a settlement. Chirac conveyed messages from Iraq to Iran in his visit to Iran and discussed Iraq with the Shah. The rapprochement was further catalysed by the Shah's visit to Cairo in January of 1975, in which Sadat was apparently able to influence the Shah. These figures seem to have convinced the

1971–1975: Hope and betrayal   129

Shah that the Iraqi regime was a nationalist one and that it was not a Soviet tool—the Shah's main concern.[133]

Ultimately, following the mediation efforts, Saddam Hussein and the Shah met twice for lengthy talks during the OPEC Summit held in Algiers on March 4–6, 1973. In the communiqué that followed, on March 6, both sides committed to 'maintain strict and effective control over their joint borders in order to put a final end to all acts of subversion wherever they may come from'.[134] With that communiqué, one may say, the Revolution was effectively over—for now, at least. The Kurds depended on Iran for sustaining their resistance, for the inflow from the US, and with that lifeline cut, realistically, there was no way to continue it in its present form.[135]

On March 8, the head of SAVAK conveyed the following 'information'[136] to the US ambassador (Helms) who in turn forwarded it to Kissinger. The ambassador was scheduled to meet the Shah later that day, at 17.00 local time. The 'information' unveiled what had taken place in Algiers. Essentially, this was an explanation of the communiqué in which the Shah sought to make a partial justification for his decision—for why he had abandoned the Kurds. He essentially portrayed the Kurds as being unable to fight and Iran as no longer willing to send its own troops across the border to staff heavy weaponry. He claimed that the Kurds themselves had said they were unable to fight and that '[t]he Iraqi Army, with the equipment received from the Soviet Union could easily annihilate the Kurds this coming summer'.[137] The detail on the equipment could well speak of Moscow's input into this assessment of the situation, one may hazard, but there can be no doubt that the Shah was exaggerating this as the Kurds had already withstood everything in the Iraqi arsenal.

The Shah also informed Helms that 'President Boumedienne, President Sadat and King Hussein had told us the Iraqis were ready to settle all their disputes with us provided that we discontinue aid to the Kurds'.[138] Shah's own reporting that the Iraqis wanted to compromise on this issue and were ready to do what is stated proves that the Iraqis had lost hope of overcoming the Kurds militarily and thus it also refutes his own point that the Iraqis could easily annihilate the Kurds. If the Iraqis were so capable of annihilating the Kurds, then surely they wouldn't have approached Iran for a compromise of the nature explained.

Further, the Shah continued, it was not in Iran's interest to back the Kurds anymore. Only a few months earlier, in December 1974, he had ordered the head of his army to pull out their long-range guns from Kurdistan were the Kurds to prove to be incapable of withstanding further Iraqi army offensives (so that these guns would not fall into Iraqi hands).[139] However, the guns were not, in fact, withdrawn until the Algiers Accord—which actually constitutes further proof that the Kurds were capable of fighting on and Iran's army was aware of that.

When the Shah met Helms, he spoke to the ambassador thus:

> On the Kurds I got two promises from Saddam; one, that Barzani and his people would have one week to decide whether they wanted to stay in Iraq or come to Iran where they will have a haven, a decent life, and be able to

130   *1971–1975: Hope and betrayal*

withdraw without bloodshed... They will be given till the end of the month for their withdrawal.[140]

After this the border will be sealed, stated the Shah. The second *promise* was that the security services of both countries will work together to 'prevent the establishment of Communist Kurds in Barzani's territory'.[141] The Shah also told Helms that had he not done this, he might have been accused of having destroyed a chance of pulling the Iraqis out of the Soviet orbit and also importantly the Iraqis had not fully abided by the agreed deal already by taking military action against the Kurds while they were meant to ceasefire. In addition to these, allegedly, according to the Shah, the Kurds had said that they were unable to fight with the Iraqis with all the advanced Soviet equipment unless the support they receive is upgraded or else be allowed to declare independence.[142] Overall, however, the Shah's reasons here are quite inconsistent and entirely unconvincing as expounded upon earlier; it is very explicit that the Shah did not want the Kurds to become unmanageable in any way—by having an autonomous state of their own. This was unacceptable to the Shah and in order to prevent this he would have done anything—including this great sell-out. The fatal mistake that the Kurds made here seems to have been that they had underestimated the Shah's ruthlessness and overestimated the US policymakers' reliability. On the military sector, as evidenced by Saddam's yielding to the Shah, there was no hope for the Iraqis to overcome the Kurds militarily—hence approaching Iran for a compromise and this proves that the Shah's point of the Kurds not being able to fight is unconvincing, but in contrast the time had arrived for the Shah to trade the unfortunate Kurds for Iraq's compromise and also thus the recognition of Iran's prestige in the area. The Shah again played it very cunningly and used the *communist threat*, again, of Kurdistan becoming a communist entity to deceive US policymakers to acquiesce with his decision of selling out the Kurds.

The Shah then arranged to meet Barzani together with Mahmoud Othman, Mohsin Dizaei and Shafiq Qazaz, on March 11, 1974. The Shah only reluctantly met Barzani, as, according to his Minister of Royal Court, 'Naturally he was a little embarrassed to meet the man face to face'.[143] Indeed, given what he had done—was doing—one might easily imagine that he would feel a little awkward, that would be quite natural, or perhaps not. Othman believes that the Shah may have chosen this day (March 11) as a punishment to the Kurds for their declaration of the March 11, 1970 Accord with the Iraqi government, to which the Shah had strongly objected, and given the Shah's objection to the Accord, this is a reasonable assessment.

When the Shah met the Kurdish leaders, he spoke 'very arrogantly'.[144] He basically told them that the settlement was now a *fait accompli* and that Iraq had compromised regarding the Shatt al-Arab waterway.[145] Othman, who was among those that met the Shah that day, recalls it thus:

> We saw the Shah with Barzani in 1975. With regards to the Algiers Accord of 75, he told us face to face that, he said, in the past 42 years we [Iran] have

1971–1975: Hope and betrayal   131

had territorial problems with Iraq and no other Iraqi government has resolved this for us, not even that of Nuri Said. Saddam has come, and he is resolving it and I have accepted it. He told us face-to-face indirectly that you have lost, that is, you have become the sacrifice. He was straight forward in that, therefore, the matter [of Iran backing the Kurds until this point] was about interest [for Iran], it was not about pan-Iranism or any such thing, but some Iranian sources may think that way because they are not aware of the details.[146]

The Kurds were thus certainly the losers in the deal, and once again their fate had been decided for them elsewhere. For Othman, therefore, this was a clear-cut sell-out in return for Iran's settling with Iraq; this is consistent with the account given by Dizae who also participated in the meeting. On the other hand, as explicated, the reasons given by the Shah for this betrayal are unconvincing.

It may need to be mentioned here that Mukerem Tallebanî, a contemporary high-ranking Kurdish ICP official, refers to other unidentified sources claiming that Kissinger came to Baghdad secretly before the Algiers Accord and met with Saddam Hussein, thereby implying that the Accord had actually already been agreed upon as a result of this. Essentially, this implies that Kissinger was involved in the basic framing of the Accord.[147] However, this cannot be verified, which therefore is treated as no more than a claim (i.e. uncorroborated). Also in light of all the evidence consulted in this book, this claim is not likely to be factual. It should also be noted that Kissinger visited Iran on November 1, 1974 and met with the Shah for over three hours in a private meeting attended only by the American ambassador to Iran; even Iran's own Foreign Minister was excluded from this meeting—prompting the Minster of Iran's Royal Court to remark that he felt sorry for Iran's own Foreign Minister.[148] Whatever the unknown, we can be certain that the US had a profound relationship with the Shah and there are two possibilities when it comes to the Kurdish sell-out and the US: first, that the US was unaware of this, in which case the blame can be squarely put on the Shah; or that, second, Kissinger was indeed aware of this, given his thorough relationship with the Shah, in which case he is also to be equally blamed as the Shah.

There is no available evidence to suggest that the latter was the case—that Kissinger had prior knowledge on this; thus, according to the evidence, the Shah was the decision-maker here. Be that as it may, it does not vindicate the US from the charge of exploiting the Kurds for self-serving purposes and for leaving them to a bitter fate when it no longer needed them. On the contrary, it is apparent that the US, together with Iran and Israel, used the Kurds and then essentially betrayed them when the need was satisfied. The US also bears a particular responsibility as a superpower. At a minimum, it could have very easily threatened to bring the Kurdish plight to the international stage if the Kurds were to be sold out—together with its Western allies—but of course that was not in the interest of the US, either.

As the Kurdish leaders returned to Kurdistan, they decided to fight on without Iran, despite Iran having withdrawn its two artillery battalions and anti-aircraft

132   *1971–1975: Hope and betrayal*

batteries. However, a few days later, an Iranian representative visited the Kurds and informed them that Iran had agreed with Iraq for the latter to use Iranian territory to also attack the Kurds from behind. According to Mohsin Dizaei, he had personally seen Iraqi military officers on the Iranian side of the border, close to *Hacî* Omeran, with maps and planning an offensive from Iran. This therefore would have also pitted the Kurds against Iran by compelling them to fire on Iranian territory if they were to continue fighting the Iraqis and if the latter were to attack from Iranian territory too. It is not entirely clear whether the threat of Iraqi troops—behind Iranian territory—was just part of a psychological warfare intended to demoralise the Kurds, or not, but the Shah certainly had the means and the personality to do whatever it took to force a defeat on the Kurds to obtain his prize of an Iraqi compromise on the Shatt issue, and thus also the acceptance of Iran's regional significance. Whatever the facts on this, the Shah's manoeuvres were successful.

Under these circumstances, the Kurdish leadership took a majority decision to cease fighting, since continuation of the war in the present form would have led to unacceptable losses. It was thus decided that the struggle should be abandoned until resumption in the future, at a more favourable time. The issue was not only a military one, as the KDP also had the responsibility to care for large numbers of urban Kurdish families who had relocated to areas under its control, as mentioned (earlier).[149] In retrospect, the Shah simply seems to have sought to increase the pressure on the Kurds, by pretending that Iraq could attack from the rear, to force the Kurds to surrender so that his deal with Saddam Hussein would work out and he could obtain his prize.

Following the Accord, the CIA Director, William Colby, wrote to Kissinger and explained that the fundamental nature of US aid for the Iraqi Kurds was that it was channelled via the Iranians; this is how they disguised their relations with the Kurds. However, with the Shah scrupulously implementing the Accord 'by complete cessation of assistance to Kurds',[150] the US apparently faced a dilemma as to how to continue this effort, even assuming the Shah would permit it at all. And regardless, Colby stated, 'even if the Shah should prove amenable to continuing as funnel for our aid, there [was the] very serious question [of] whether it [is] justifiable for us to continue it'.[151] Colby also alluded to more desperate Kurdish pleas for help by the US in stating that the Shah's strict adherence to the Accord was further reflected by the 'impassioned character of Kurdish pleas to us for direct, unilateral, military and financial assistance'.[152] These 'impassioned pleas' by the Kurds also prove that even up to this point—after the signing of the Algiers Accord—the Kurds had intended to fight on but perhaps provided that the US continues its support as evidenced by their appeal to the US.

As to the fate of the Kurds, Colby wrote that

> In the meantime, Kurds have been caught short and are hurting badly. Their current emotionalism arising from feelings of abrupt abandonment by their allies creates possibility of undesirable indiscretions by the Kurds. We hope

1971–1975: Hope and betrayal   133

to avert this possibility by two interim steps intended to have some calming effect.[153]

The details of the first of these remain classified at present while the second was, with the Shah's consent, to still send the Kurds' March payment, which, he noted, was also justified on humanitarian grounds—although given the extent of the betrayal, this was largely to avert the possibility of the Kurds publicising the whole affair—as indicated by Colby himself. Subsequently, Colby also recommended that the decision on the US relationship with the Kurds be delayed due to its complexity pending further study of the situation.

The agreement not only gave the Shah what he wanted (abrogation of the 1937 treaty), which no other Iraqi government since then had been prepared to negotiate, but it also strengthened both of Iran's *de facto* and *de jure* prestige in the region as Saddam Hussein had now publicly agreed to Iran's demands.[154] And for Saddam, of course, his Kurdish Issue was now dealt with.

Among one of those impassioned pleas—made in vain—that Colby talked about was a letter from Barzani to Kissinger dated March 10, some of which is as follows:

> Your Excellency:
>
> Having always believed in the peaceful solution of disputes including those between Iran and Iraq, we are pleased to see that these two countries have come to some agreement in Algeria. However, our hearts bleed to see that an immediate by-product of this agreement is the destruction of our defenseless people in an unprecedented manner as Iran closed its border and stopped help to us completely and while the Iraqis began the biggest offensive they have ever launched and which is now being continued. Our movement and people are being destroyed in an unbelievable way with silence from everyone. We feel Your Excellency that the United States has a moral and political responsibility towards our people who have committed themselves to your country's policy. In consideration of this situation we beg Your Excellency to take action as immediate as possible on the following two issues.[155]

The issues that Barzani wanted action on were '1. Stopping the Iraqi offensive and opening the way for talks between us and Iraq to arrive at a solution for our people which will at least be face-saving'. And second

> Using whatever influence you have with the Iranian friends to help our people in these historically tragic and sad moments and at least in such a way that our people and Peshmergas could maintain some livelihood and perform at least partisan activities in Iraqi Kurdistan until our problem is also solved within the framework of the over-all Iranian-Iraqi agreement.[156]

Forwarding Barzani's message to Kissinger, Helms suggested that 'it may be desirable for you to send him some kind of comforting message',[157] being

134   *1971–1975: Hope and betrayal*

concerned, no doubt, about the risk of adverse publicity because basically the deal had already been done.

Consequently, when replying to Barzani via Helms on March 13—stating that he would respond later and sending his prayers to be with the Kurdish people—Kissinger also agreed that 'there would seem to be some responsibility not to cut them [the Kurds] off suddenly and completely', but he took no further action; nor did he attempt to do anything, apart from requesting Helms to ask the Iranians 'how Iran intends to handle its future relationship with the Kurds'. Kissinger asked further from Helms that

> [y]ou should find a tactful way to mention the problem both the Iranian and the US Governments will face in the US and elsewhere if there is a massacre and Barzani charges that he has been let down. The plight of the Kurds could arouse deep humanitarian concern. On the other, it would create an impossible situation if we were to be working at cross purposes with Iran.[158]

Ultimately, when the Kurdish leadership decided to abandon the struggle, some Peshmerga crossed the border and surrendered to Iran, some others to Iraq and some fled to Syria, while another faction went underground to renew the struggle at a later date. The sell-out was a catastrophe of a great magnitude for the Kurds. Finally, March was indeed the last month in which the US and Iran provided the Kurds with the monthly subsidy.[159]

In the meantime, with the Kurdish leadership having decided to abandon the war, Turkey moved troops to the border to prevent fleeing Kurds from crossing into Turkey. The UNHCR, the Dutch embassy and other actors approached Turkey to let in unarmed Kurds from Iraq before the two-week deadline given to the Kurds expired; these proved futile. Turkey did not let them even to merely transit to Iran via Turkey. Given the geography, some Kurds could make it to Turkey within that two weeks' time but not to Iran. Even Iran's own Foreign Minister, Khalatbari, the country that initially betrayed the Kurdish movement, described Turkey's attitude here—in preventing the movement of Kurdish refugees—as 'unreasonable and inhumane'.[160] Iraq later executed some of the Kurds that had taken advantage of a government amnesty and had surrendered. The Shah and Kissinger were personally aware of this; but when Kissinger was informed of it, he replied, 'Well, it could be true. In fact, it is inevitable, sooner or later. It doesn't surprise me'.[161]

Kissinger and his aides were now more concerned about hiding the operation from the public than anything else, and it was also for this reason that they allowed Barzani to receive treatment for cancer in the US upon the request of the Shah—so not to further embitter Barzani and push him to go public with the shameful secret. However, even when in the US, Barzani wanted to meet with a US official at policymaking level. In the words of the director of the CIA, William Colby,

> Barzani feels very strongly that he must present his people's case to such an official before he dies (estimated at six to eight months) and has indicated

1971–1975: Hope and betrayal   135

that it would be inappropriate for him to leave the United States until he has done so.[162]

In the aftermath, as reported by USINTS in Baghdad, Iraq's Minister of Information Tariq Aziz, citing the UK Baghdad Ambassador Graham, had told Gavin Young of _The Observer_ newspaper that the 'Shah had concluded march 6 accord against expressed desire of usg [USG]'.[163] The likelihood of this was examined earlier, but, regardless, it only demonstrates the callous attitude of the Shah towards the Kurds.

According to Saddam Hussein, the conflict had cost the Iraqis some 10,000 troops.[164] This is in addition to the misery and the loss that the conflict had caused the Kurds, of course. The exact scale of Kurdish losses will never be known, especially since these continued. Kimche has noted that

> The victorious Iraqi soldiers wreaked terrible vengeance on the abandoned Kurds. Hundreds were massacred; many thousands more were forcibly displaced from their homes and transported to camps in the arid south of the country while their own homes and villages were taken over by Iraqi Arabs.[165]

Back in the US, by early November 1975, news of the covert Kurdish operation had been leaked to the media and the House of Representatives established the House Select Committee on Intelligence (the Pike Committee) to investigate abuses by the US intelligence community. Asked about his betrayal of the Kurds, Kissinger is reported to have stated that 'Covert action should not be confused with missionary work'.[166] Throughout the whole affair, Israeli officials, including the Prime Minister Golda Meir and Israel's successive ambassadors to Washington petitioned the US and Kissinger for more assistance to what Golda Meir called 'our friends, the Kurds',[167] when she met Kissinger in Israel. Among some of the weapons that Israel sent to the Kurds included Sagger anti-tank and Strela anti-aircraft missiles, according to Yitzhak Rabin, but all these weapons essentially had to go through the Shah and Iran.[168] On another occasion, while working out the details of another weapons shipment for the Kurds, in January 1975, Israel's Deputy Prime Minister and Minister of Foreign Affairs Yigal Allon told Kissinger that to 'To abandon the Kurds is a crime'.[169] It seems that Allon was petitioning hard for the Kurds, hence his statement.

In fact, Israel had promised the Kurds that it would continue its supplies even if the Shah terminated his; that this would be via airdrops, and even two locations were chosen (the Qasre and the Hirt plains). However, after the Algiers Accord, Israel too informed the Kurds that it could not fulfil its commitment due to strategic and practical obstacles. It was following this, with all doors closed to them, that the Kurdish leadership decided to officially abandon the struggle.[170] Even countries like Jordan that had earlier promised support for the Kurds were implicit in the abandonment of the Kurds, specifically by mediating between Iran and Iraq with no regards for the Kurds' fate. Such was the effect of the Cold War and regional politics in Kurdistan.

136 *1971–1975: Hope and betrayal*

US foreign policy and the Iraqi Kurds in a wider context: from Nixon to Ford

Patrick Kiely has observed that when Nixon became President in January 1969, he inherited at least three major issues. These were the achievement of parity of strategic missiles with the USSR, dealing with the Vietnam War and handling the implications of the 1967 Arab–Israel War.[171] Through the Nixon Doctrine, the Administration sought to empower American allies, aiming to extricate the US from having to police communism. The way this was to be achieved was to extend military and economic aid to the allies, and Iran and Israel were among those that benefited. Meanwhile, Nixon pursued détente with the USSR. The purpose of simultaneously empowering allies while pursuing détente was to contain international communism while engaging in reconciliation with the USSR. Instead of US troops facing or confronting communist threats, therefore, US allies would be empowered to take on this role.[172] Increased Soviet encroachment in Iraq and the reluctance of the US (under both Nixon and Ford) to become involved in backing the Iraqi Kurds in any meaningful way, then becoming involved but clandestinely, only to abandon the Kurds after the Shah had (during Ford's presidency), must also be viewed against the backdrop of external and internal issues facing the US in the Cold War context for a better understanding of the topic.

Foremost among these major issues was the Vietnam War, which had cost some 59,000 American lives. Internally, therefore, there was no appetite for war among the US public in 1975. Moreover, following the 1973 ceasefire and communist takeover of South Vietnam in 1975, and repeal of the Gulf of Tonkin Resolution in 1971, Congress overrode Nixon's veto and passed the War Powers Act, which essentially required US presidents to consult with Congress before committing US troops to combat. In short, Congress reinstated its authority during Nixon's presidency, and open war was a less easy option. The USSR and the US also signed SALT 1 in 1972 as part of détente, while Nixon was also facing a potential impeachment over the Watergate Scandal. This political context—internal and international—notwithstanding Nixon's resignation in August 1974, may also help to explain why the US was unwilling or not in a position to escalate the Kurdish War in Iraq at the time, even against a Soviet ally (Iraq) and even if it had wanted to.[173] In this Cold War context, therefore, with the US both pursuing détente with the USSR and committed to contain communism through its allies—and in combination with the (post-)Vietnam framing—it is understandable that Kissinger might have wanted to push the Ba'ath government but not to the extent of escalating to a full conflict with the USSR.

In relation to the Iraqi Kurds, as examined, it was only from 1972 that the Nixon administration opted to offer support. While this was primarily due to the Shah's lobbying, it also fit very well with the overall strategy of empowering US allies to contain communism by themselves in the Cold War framework. The Nixon administration essentially assisted the Kurds because this meant backing the Shah who, in turn, was making his case to challenge Soviet hegemony over

1971–1975: Hope and betrayal   137

Iraq and consequently containing Iraq itself as a potential Russian client. The role of Israel also needs to be noted here. The Nixon administration never considered the Iraqi Kurds themselves as an ally, the evidence for which lies in the fact that once Iran turned its back on the Kurdish movement, the Nixon administration simply did the same. Iran was the ally that the US wanted to support, as per the Nixon Doctrine, not the Kurds.

When the period before 1972 is considered, the Nixon administration, like others before it, refused to look favourably on Kurdish pleas. Since the Nixon administration never considered the Iraqi Kurds as an ally, as stated, they could not benefit directly from the Nixon Doctrine of empowering US allies to confront communism. This could only happen through a third party—a state actor—as attested by the US only becoming involved in the Iraqi Kurd situation through Iran because the Shah convinced the Nixon administration that they needed to undermine Iraq's threat to Iran and the wider region and that the way to do this was to back the Kurds to weaken Iraq. This analysis thus shows the pivotal role of Iran in the matter, in its development as well as conclusion.

When Ford succeeded Nixon on August 9, 1974, he continued to view Iran as the central regional actor keeping the security of the Persian Gulf. Indeed, as Patrick Kiely has noted, 'Economic and military cooperation expanded [with Iran] significantly during Ford's tenure'.[174] The US regarded Iran as an observation post from which it could keep watch over the Soviet Union in the Middle East and, together with Turkey, form a block against any southwards movements by the USSR. Similarly, the US or Nixon and Kissinger wanted the June 1973 Arab–Israeli War and its aftermath to eliminate Soviet influence in the region. The US backed Israel during the war and Kissinger initiated a DEFCON 3 nuclear alert in response to the Soviet threat of intervention. Kissinger's 'shuttle diplomacy' had the same aim.[175] Therefore, US backing for the Iraqi Kurds through the Shah of Iran fits neatly into this broader US policy of containing 'international communism' in the region.

Regarding Iraq, once US decision-makers learnt that Iraq had compromised with Iran via the Algiers Accord and that Iran no longer needed its Kurdish card, the US no longer saw the need for the Kurds to be an 'open wound', as Kissinger expressed it, in Iraq. Additionally, Israel's backing for the Iraqi Kurds was to keep the Iraqi army busy at home; the Iraqi army being preoccupied with the Kurdish War meant that Iraq was not able to meaningfully join its Arab neighbours against Israel.

Notes

1 Alvandi, Roham, 'Nixon, Kissinger, and the Shah: The Origins of Iranian Primacy in the Persian Gulf', *Diplomatic History,* 36 (2012).
2 Ibid.
3 Ibid. Also, Othman, Mahmoud, in *Telephone Interview B.*
4 Stated in McDowall, David, *A Modern History of the Kurds* (London: I.B. Tauris, 2004), p. 339.

138 *1971–1975: Hope and betrayal*

5   See, for example, HRW, 'Claims in Conflict: Reversing Ethnic Cleansing in Northern Iraq: III. Background' (Human Rights Watch, 2004); and also McDowall, op. cit., p. 341.

6   'Airgram 222 From the Embassy in Lebanon to the Department of State, frus1969-76ve04/d292' (FRUS, July 16, 1971).

7   Ibid.

8   See, for example, Barzanî, Mes'ud, *Barzanî Û Bzutnewey Rizgarîxwazî Kurd: Bergî Sêyem, Beşî Yekem 1961–1975*, p. 17 (trans. by author).

9   Ibid.

10 Airgram 222 From the Embassy in Lebanon to the Department of State, frus1969-76ve04/d292.

11 Ibid.

12 Ibid.

13 FCO 17/408, Iraq: Political Affairs – Internal Kurdish Affairs, EQ1/4: 1966–1968.

14 'Kurdish Problem, 1973BAGHDA00214_b' (WPLUSD, April 17, 1973).

15 See Aziz, 'Mhemmed 'Ezîz – Beşî Sêyem', in *Pencemor*; Dzaei, 'Muhsîn Dzeyî – Nwênerî Pêşûy Mes'ud Barzanî – Beşî Sêyem', in *Pencemor*.

16 See 'Kurdish […], 1973BAGHDA00400_b' (WLPLUSD, July 7, 1973).

17 'Telegram 9689 From the Embassy in Lebanon to the Department of State, frus1969-76ve04/d293' (FRUS, November 3, 1971).

18 'Telegram 213299 From the Department of State to the Embassy in Iran, frus1969-76ve04/d294' (FRUS, November 24, 1971).

19 This analysis is drawn from US archives, such as: Telegram 213299 From the Department of State to the Embassy in Iran, frus1969-76ve04/d294.

20 For more on (American knowledge of) these projects, see the telegram from the US Embassy in Lebanon to the State Department, 'Airgram A-38 From the Embassy in Lebanon to the Department of State, frus1969-76ve04/d297' (FRUS, February 2, 1972).

21 See the assessment by Airgram A-38 From the Embassy in Lebanon to the Department of State, frus1969-76ve04/d297.

22 Airgram A-38 From the Embassy in Lebanon to the Department of State, frus1969-76ve04/d297.

23 Barzanî, *Barzanî Û Bzutnewey Rizgarîxwazî Kurd: Bergî Sêyem, Beşî Yekem 1961–1975*, pp. 73–83.

24 For SAVAKs and the Shah's repeated attempts in this, see 'Memorandum From Harold Saunders of the National Security Council Staff to the President's Deputy Assistant for National Security Affairs (Haig), frus1969-76ve04/d301' (FRUS, March 27, 1972); 'Memorandum From the Chief of the Near East and South Asia Division, Central Intelligence Agency (Waller) to the Director of Central Intelligence (Helms), frus1969-76ve04/d315' (FRUS, June 12, 1972); 'Memorandum From Harold Saunders of the National Security Council Staff to President Nixon, frus1969-76ve04/d211' (FRUS, July 12, 1972).

25 'Memorandum From Harold Saunders of the National Security Council Staff to the President's Deputy Assistant for National Security Affairs (Haig), frus1969-76ve04/d301' (FRUS, March 27, 1972); Memorandum From the Chief of the Near East and South Asia Division, Central Intelligence Agency (Waller) to the Director of Central Intelligence (Helms), frus1969-76ve04/d315; Memorandum From Harold Saunders of the National Security Council Staff to President Nixon, frus1969-76ve04/d211.

1971–1975: Hope and betrayal   139

26 See Memorandum From Harold Saunders of the National Security Council Staff to the President's Deputy Assistant for National Security Affairs (Haig), frus1969-76ve04/d301.

27 Ibid.

28 Ibid.

29 Airgram A-38 From the Embassy in Lebanon to the Department of State, frus1969-76ve04/d297.

30 'Memorandum From the Director of Central Intelligence (Helms) to the President's Assistant for National Security Affairs (Kissinger), Secretary of State Rogers, and Secretary of Defense Laird, frus1969-76ve04/d302' (FRUS, March 29, 1972).

31 Ibid.

32 'Memorandum From Andrew Killgore of the Bureau of Near Eastern and South Asian Affairs, Department of State to the Assistant Secretary for Near Eastern and South Asian Affairs (Sisco), frus1969-76ve04/d304' (FRUS, April 3, 1972).

33 Memorandum From the Director of Central Intelligence (Helms) to the President's Assistant for National Security Affairs (Kissinger), Secretary of State Rogers, and Secretary of Defense Laird, frus1969-76ve04/d302.

34 A copy of the original letter is available from Barzanî, *Barzanî Û Bzutnewey Rizgarîxwazî Kurd: Bergî Sêyem, Beşî Yekem 1961–1975*, p. 299; for a Kurdish version, see the same source, p. 84.

35 See, for instance, Memorandum From the Director of Central Intelligence (Helms) to the President's Assistant for National Security Affairs (Kissinger), Secretary of State Rogers, and Secretary of Defense Laird, frus1969-76ve04/d302.

36 Barzani also asked for scholarships for Kurdish students at Western universities; see Memorandum From the Director of Central Intelligence (Helms) to the President's Assistant for National Security Affairs (Kissinger), Secretary of State Rogers, and Secretary of Defense Laird, frus1969-76ve04/d302.

37 For more on these, see 'Memorandum From the Director of Central Intelligence (Helms) to the President's Assistant for National Security Affairs (Kissinger), Secretary of State Rogers, and Secretary of Defense Laird, frus1969-76ve04/d303' (FRUS, March 31, 1972).

38 Memorandum From Andrew Killgore of the Bureau of Near Eastern and South Asian Affairs, Department of State to the Assistant Secretary for Near Eastern and South Asian Affairs (Sisco), frus1969-76ve04/d304.

39 Ibid.

40 For a chronology of Nixon's visit see; Richard Nixon, 'Chronology of Visit […].

41 'Discussions with Shah of Iran […]' (DNSA, May 30, 1972), p. 3.

42 Ibid.

43 'Memorandum From Harold Saunders of the National Security Staff to the President's Assistant for National Security Affairs (Kissinger), frus1969-76ve04/d313' (FRUS, June 7, 1972).

44 Quoted in ibid.

45 Quoted in ibid.

46 Quoted in ibid.

47 Ibid.

48 See Barzanî, Mes'ud, *Barzanî Û Bzutnewey Rizgarîxwazî Kurd: Bergî Sêyem, Beşî Duwem 1961–1975*, (Hewlêr: Çapxaney wezaretî perwerde, [2004(?)]), pp. 99–102; also, the relevant footnote letter from Barzani's representative in Baghdad back to Barzani in Kurdistan in April 1973, in the same source (trans. by author).

140 *1971–1975: Hope and betrayal*

49 Memorandum From Harold Saunders of the National Security Staff to the President's Assistant for National Security Affairs (Kissinger), frus1969-76ve04/d313.
50 Alam, Asadollah, *The Shah and I: The Confidential Diary of Iran's Royal Court, 1968–77* (London: I.B. Tauris, 1991), p. 327.
51 Ibid., p. 327.
52 Memorandum From Harold Saunders of the National Security Staff to the President's Assistant for National Security Affairs (Kissinger), frus1969-76ve04/d313.
53 Ibid.
54 Ibid.
55 Ibid.
56 For this reply see 'Memorandum From the Chief of the Near East and South Asia Division, Central Intelligence Agency (Waller) to the Director of Central Intelligence (Helms), frus1969-76ve04/d315' (June 12, 1972).
57 See the following memo, for instance, which, from 1971, repeatedly shows at least another actor petitioning the US government to back the Kurds and whose name remains un-declassified: Memorandum From the Chief of the Near East and South Asia Division, Central Intelligence Agency (Waller) to the Director of Central Intelligence (Helms), frus1969-76ve04/d315.
58 'Memorandum of Conversation, frus1969-76ve04/d319' (FRUS, July 5, 1972); Othman, in *Telephone Interview B*.
59 'Memorandum of Conversation, frus1969-76ve04/d319'.
60 Ibid.
61 Ibid.
62 'Memorandum From the President's Deputy Assistant for National Security Affairs (Haig) to the President's Assistant for National Security Affairs (Kissinger), frus1969-76ve04/d321' (FRUS, July 28, 1972).
63 Ibid.
64 Ibid.
65 Ibid.
66 Ibid.
67 Ibid.
68 'Telegram 7605 From the Embassy in Lebanon to the Department of State, frus1969-76ve04/d320' (FRUS, July 13, 1972).
69 Ibid.
70 'Memorandum From the President's Assistant for National Security Affairs (Kissinger) to President Nixon, frus1969-76ve04/d325' (FRUS, October 5, 1972).
71 Ibid.
72 See, for example, 'Telegram 210666 From the Department of State to the Embassy in Iran, frus1969-76ve04/d234' (FRUS, November 18, 1972). And also 'Memorandum From David A. Korn, NEA/IRN, to the Assistant Secretary of State for Near Eastern and South Asian Affairs (Sisco), frus1969-76ve04/d324' (FRUS, September 20, 1972); 'National Intelligence Estimate 36.2–72 frus1969-76ve04/d330' (FRUS, December 21, 1972).
73 See, for example, 'Memorandum From the President's Assistant for National Security Affairs (Kissinger) to President Nixon, frus1969-76v27/d207' (FRUS, March 29, 1973).
74 Ibid.
75 See ibid.

1971–1975: Hope and betrayal 141

76 'Telegram From the Interests Section in Baghdad to the Department of State, frus1969-76v27/d208' (FRUS, March 31, 1973).
77 'Memorandum of Conversation, frus1969-76v27/d24' (FRUS, July 23, 1973).
78 'Memorandum for the President's File by the President's Assistant for National Security Affairs (Kissinger), frus1969-76v27/d25' (FRUS, July 24, 1973).
79 Ibid.
80 'Memorandum From Acting Director of Central Intelligence Walters to the President's Assistant for National Security Affairs (Kissinger), frus1969-76v27/d225' (FRUS, July 26, 1973).
81 See ibid; and also 'Memorandum From Director of Central Intelligence Colby to the President's Assistant for National Security Affairs (Kissinger), frus1969-76v27/d227' (FRUS, August 7, 1973); 'Minutes of Senior Review Group Meeting, frus1969-76v27/d23' (FRUS, July 20, 1973).
82 '27. Memorandum of Conversation, frus1969-76v27/d27' (FRUS, July 24, 1973).
83 Ibid.
84 Ibid.
85 'Memorandum of Conversation, frus1969-76v27/d30' (FRUS, July 27, 1973).
86 Ibid.
87 Ibid.
88 Minutes of Senior Review Group Meeting, frus1969-76v27/d23.
89 Ibid.
90 Ibid.
91 The following memo is indicative of this: 'Memorandum of Conversation, frus1969-76v27/d226' (FRUS, July 27, 1973).
92 'Backchannel Message From the President's Assistant for National Security Affairs (Kissinger) to the Ambassador to Iran (Helms), frus1969-76v27/d229' (FRUS, August 16, 1973). Also, see ibid for the Four Options recommended by the CIA.
93 Ibid.
94 Othman, in *Telephone Interview B*.
95 Quoted in Barzanî, *Barzanî Û Bzutnewey Rizgarîxwazî Kurd: Bergî Sêyem, Beşî Duwem 1961–1975*, p. 112 (trans. by author).
96 Barzanî, *Barzanî Û Bzutnewey Rizgarîxwazî Kurd: Bergî Sêyem, Beşî Duwem 1961–1975*, p. 111 (trans. by author). Also, Aziz, 'Mhemmed 'Ezîz – Beşî Sêyem', in *Pencemor*; Othman, in *Telephone Interview B*.
97 See, for example, 'Memorandum From Director of Central Intelligence Colby to the President's Assistant for National Security Affairs (Kissinger), frus1969-76v27/d243' (FRUS, March 21, 1974). Also, Barzanî, *Barzanî Û Bzutnewey Rizgarîxwazî Kurd: Bergî Sêyem, Beşî Duwem 1961–1975*, p. 112.
98 This position was indicated by the Soviet Ministry of Foreign Affairs-Deputy Chief for Near East Countries (Pyrlin) in his meeting with a US Embassy officer in Moscow on March 16, 1974; see 'Soviet Views on Kurdish Problem and Iraqi-Iranian Frontier Clashes, =1974MOSCOW03744_b' (WikiLeaks, March 16, 1974); also, Pravda's Middle East Specialist (Demchenko) expressed a similar view on March 13; see 'Pravda Supports Iraqi Government […], 1974MOSCOW03590_b' (WikiLeaks, March 14, 1974); this was also the take of the US Embassy in Moscow as based on the actual meeting with Pyrlin.
99 Barzanî, *Barzanî Û Bzutnewey Rizgarîxwazî Kurd: Bergî Sêyem, Beşî Duwem 1961–1975*, p. 92 (trans. by author). For more on these, see ibid., p. 300 for a letter

142   *1971–1975: Hope and betrayal*

written in Kurdish by Talabani to Barzani on June 22, 1972. For more on the names of the envoys, see p. 92.

100 Barzanî, *Barzanî Û Bzutnewey Rizgarîxwazî Kurd: Bergî Sêyem, Beşî Duwem 1961–1975*, pp. 207–208.

101 See Memorandum From Director of Central Intelligence Colby to the President's Assistant for National Security Affairs (Kissinger), frus1969-76v27/d243.

102 'Backchannel Message From the President's Deputy Assistant for National Security Affairs (Scowcroft) to the Ambassador to Iran (Helms), frus1969-76v27/d244' (FRUS, March 26, 1974).

103 See, for example, 'Backchannel Message From the Ambassador to Iran (Helms) to Secretary of State Kissinger, frus1969-76v27/d247' (FRUS, April 17, 1974); 'Memorandum From the President's Assistant for National Security Affairs (Kissinger) to President Nixon, frus1969-76v27/d246' (FRUS, April 11, 1974); 'Backchannel Message From the President's Deputy Assistant for National Security Affairs (Scowcroft) to the Ambassador to Iran (Helms), frus1969-76v27/d244' (FRUS, March 26, 1974).

104 'Backchannel Message From the Ambassador to Iran (Helms) to Secretary of State Kissinger, frus1969-76v27/d248' (FRUS, April 22, 1974). Also see Barzanî, *Barzanî Û Bzutnewey Rizgarîxwazî Kurd: Bergî Sêyem, Beşî Duwem 1961–1975*, pp. 167–183.

105 'Soviet-Iraqi Relations, 1974BAGHDA00317_b' (WLPLUSD, May 15, 1974).

106 'Telegram From the Interests Section in Baghdad to the Department of State, frus1969-76v27/d263' (FRUS, October 24, 1974). For more indications of the USSR's support for Iraq up until the collapse of the Kurdish resistance in March 1975 see: Barzanî, *Barzanî Û Bzutnewey Rizgarîxwazî Kurd: Bergî Sêyem, Beşî Duwem 1961–1975*, pp. 162–165.

107 For more on the plan of the invasion by the Iraqis see 'Telegram From the Consulate in Tabriz to the Department of State, frus1969-76v27/d261' (FRUS, September 4, 1974).

108 See 'FCO 8/2534: Soviet Involvment in the Iraqi-Kurdish War' (United Kingdom: The National Archives, n.d.), p. 2.

109 Ibid.

110 Barzanî, *Barzanî Û Bzutnewey Rizgarîxwazî Kurd: Bergî Sêyem, Beşî Yekem 1961–1975*, p. 17 (trans. by author).

111 'FCO 8/2534: British Embassy Tehran' (United Kingdom: The National Archives, January 9, 1975).

112 Telegram From the Consulate in Tabriz to the Department of State, frus1969-76v27/d261.

113 'Iraqi Kurdish War: Failure of Iraqi Summer Offensive, 1974TABRIZ00032_b' (WLPLUSD, December 2, 1974).

114 FCO 8/2534: Soviet Involvement in the Iraqi–Kurdish War.

115 Ibid.

116 'Pro-Kurdish Lobby stirring in Britan, 1975LONDON01382_b' (WLPLUSD, January 29, 1975).

117 Ibid. and also 'Kurdish War: Temporary Quiet, 1975TABRIZ00008_b' (WLPLUSD, February 2, 1975).

118 'Letter From the Consul in Tabriz (Neumann) to the Consular Coordinator at the Embassy in Iran (Bolster), frus1969-76v27/d269' (FRUS, December 26, 1974).

119 Ibid.

1971–1975: Hope and betrayal   143

120 Barzanî, *Barzanî Û Bzutnewey Rizgarîxwazî Kurd: Bergî Sêyem, Beşî Duwem 1961–1975*, pp. 162–165.

121 For more on these details, including the names of Soviet advisors mentioned, see ibid.

122 For a full account of this and Iraq's 'desire' to improve relations with the US, see 'Telegram From the Mission at the United Nations to the Department of State, frus1969-76v27/d252' (FRUS, June 5, 1974). Also 'Telegram From the Interests Section in Baghdad to the Department of State, frus1969-76v27/d251' (FRUS, May 30, 1974); 'Telegram From the Interests Section in Baghdad to the Department of State, frus1969-76v27/d255' (FRUS, June 25, 1974); 'Telegram From the Interests Section in Baghdad to the Department of State, frus1969-76v27/d257' (FRUS, August 9, 1974).

123 Alam, op. cit., p. 418.

124 Ibid., p. 398.

125 Quoted in 'Memorandum From the President's Deputy Assistant for National Security Affairs (Scowcroft) to President Ford, frus1969-76v27/d103' (FRUS, February 19, 1975).

126 Ibid.

127 See footnotes of ibid.

128 Ibid.

129 Barzanî, *Barzanî Û Bzutnewey Rizgarîxwazî Kurd: Bergî Sêyem, Beşî Duwem 1961–1975*, pp. 167–183.

130 Kimche, David, *The Last Option: After Nasser, Arafat & Saddam Hussein: The Quest for Peace in the Middle East*, pp. 189–200. Also see, for instance, Alvandi, Nixon, Kissinger, and the Shah: The United States and Iran in the Cold War, pp. 110 and 112.

131 'Telegram From the Interests Section in Baghdad to the Department of State, frus1969-76v27/d271' (FRUS, February 1, 1975).

132 Othman, in *Telephone Interview B*.

133 As reported by the Egyptian Ambassador to Baghdad and others: see Telegram From the Interests Section in Baghdad to the Department of State, frus1969-76v27/d271.

134 Quoted in 'Defense Intelligence Notice Prepared in the Defense Intelligence Agency, frus1969-76v27/d273' (FRUS, March 7, 1975).

135 Ibid.

136 Quoted in 'Backchannel Message From the Ambassador to Iran (Helms) to the President's Deputy Assistant for National Security Affairs (Scowcroft), frus1969-76v27/d275' (FRUS, March 8, 1975).

137 Ibid.

138 Ibid.; Also, see Alam, op. cit., p. 382.

139 Alam, op. cit., p. 400.

140 'Backchannel Message From the Ambassador to Iran (Helms) to the President's Deputy Assistant for National Security Affairs (Scowcroft), frus1969-76v27/d276' (FRUS, March 8, 1975).

141 Ibid.

142 For the Shah's account, see ibid.

143 Alam, op. cit., p. 418.

144 Dzaei, 'Muhsîn Dzeyî – Nwênerî Pêşûy Mes'ud Barzanî – Beşî Sêyem', in *Pencemor*.

145 Ibid.

144 *1971–1975: Hope and betrayal*

146 Othman, in *Telephone Interview B* (trans. by author).

147 Talabani, 'Mukerem Tallebanî 3', in *Pencemor*.

148 Alam, op. cit., p. 174.

149 Dzaei, 'Muhsîn Dzeyî – Nwênerî Pêşûy Mes'ud Barzanî – Beşî Sêyem', in *Pencemor*.

150 'Message From the Central Intelligence Agency to the President's Deputy Assistant for National Security Affairs (Scowcroft), frus1969-76v27/d280' (FRUS, March 13, 1975).

151 Ibid.

152 Ibid.

153 Ibid.

154 This is derived from Helms' analysis from Iran to the State Department, see; '279. Telegram From the Embassy in Iran [...]' (FRUS, March 13, 1975).

155 Barzani's letter as provided by the State Department is accessible via: 'Backchannel Message From the President's Deputy Assistant for National Security Affairs (Scowcroft) to Secretary of State Kissinger, frus1969-76v27/d278' (FRUS, March 10, 1975).

156 Ibid.

157 Ibid.

158 '281. Backchannel Message From the President's Deputy Assistant for National Security Affairs (Scowcroft) to the Ambassador to Iran (Helms), frus1969-76v27/d281' (FRUS, March 16, 1975).

159 '282. Backchannel Message From the Ambassador to Iran (Helms) to the President's Deputy Assistant for National Security Affairs (Scowcroft), frus1969-76v27/d282' (FRUS, March 19, 1975); '284. Telegram From the Embassy in Iran to the Department of State, frus1969-76v27/d284' (FRUS, March 25, 1975).

160 'Deadline Extended for Refugee Kurds Returning to Iraq, 1975TEHRAN02887_b' (WLPLUSD, March 31, 1975). For more details on other relevant events at this time, see also 'Iran- Iraq Border Closes, but Iraq Extends Deadline for Returning Kurds, 1975TEHRAN02932_b' (WLPLUSD, April 1, 1975); 'Hoveyda's Trip to Baghdad; Border Closure Approaches, 1975TEHRAN02857_b' (WLPLUSD, March 30, 1975); 'GOI Actions to Solve Kurdish Problem, 1975BAGHDA00360_b' (WLPLUSD, April 2, 1975); 'Pacification of Kurdish Areas, 1975BAGH-DA00384_b' (WLPLUSD, April 7, 1975); 'Iraqi Kurds in Iran: Situation and Request, 1975TABRIZ00017_b' (WLPLUSD, April 10, 1975); 'Assistance to Kurds, 1975BAGHDA00341_b' (WLPLUSD, March 30, 1975); 'Human Rights Reporting [...],1975STATE074981_b' (WLPLUSD, April 3, 1975); 'Turkish Policy On Kurdish Refugees. Cable: 1975ANKARA02858_b' (April 10, 1975); 'Barzani Appeal, 1975BAGHDA00303_b' (WLPLUSD, March 24, 1975); 'Minutes of National Security Council Meeting, frus1969-76v26/d166' (FRUS, March 28, 1975); Ronald Neumann, 'Iraqi Kurds in Iran: Situation of Request' (DNSA, April 10, 1975). '300. Defense Intelligence Agency Intelligence Appraisal, frus1969-76v27/d300' (FRUS, October 6, 1975). 'Kurdish Refugees in Iran, 1975TAB-RIZ00022_b' (WLPLUSD, April 23, 1975); 'Memorandum From Director of Central Intelligence Colby to the President's Assistant for National Security Affairs (Kissinger), frus1969-76v27/d289' (FRUS, June 4, 1975); 'Discussion with Iraqi Foreign Minister Saadoun Hammadi' (DNSA, December 17, 1975).

161 '[Secretary's Staff Meeting; Attached to Decision Summary]' (DNSA, May 16, 1975).

1971–1975: Hope and betrayal   145

162 'Memorandum From Director of Central Intelligence Colby to the President's Assistant for National Security Affairs (Kissinger), frus1969-76v27/d299' (FRUS, September 26, 1975). Also see '[NATO Event; Kurds in Iran; Thomas Morgan]' (DNSA, July 17, 1975). 'Memorandum From Rob Roy Ratliff of the National Security Council Staff to Secretary of State Kissinger, frus1969-76v27/d293' (FRUS, July 24, 1975).

163 'Pacification of Kurdish Areas, 1975BAGHDA00384_b' (WLPLUSD, April 7, 1975).

164 'Paper Prepared in the Office of Current Intelligence, Central Intelligence Agency, frus1969-76v27/d286' (FRUS, May 1, 1975).

165 Kimche, op. cit., p. 195.

166 Quoted in Pike Committee Report Full (1976). Retrieved from https://archive.org/details/PikeCommitteeReportFull/page/n11. Also See Daniel Schorr (1996) Telling It Like It Is: Kissinger and the Kurds. Retrieved from https://www.csmonitor.com/1996/1018/101896.opin.column.1.html; 'Telegram From the Embassy in Iran to the Department of State, frus1969-76v27/d301' (FRUS, November 3, 1975); '[Discussion with President Ford [...]' (DNSA, October 31, 1975).

167 '[Meeting with Israeli Officials; Includes Israeli Memorandum Entitled 'The Situation in Kurdistan']' (DNSA, May 7, 1974). Also see e.g. 'Discussion with Israeli Leaders in Jerusalem; Attachments Not Included', (DNSA, November 7, 1974); '[Talk with Simcha Dinitz; Includes Tabs A and B; Tab C Not Included]' (DNSA, December 23, 1974); '[Meeting with Israeli Ambassador Dinitz]' (DNSA, March 21, 1974).

168 'Discussion with Israeli Leaders in Jerusalem; Attachments Not Included' (DNSA, November 7, 1974).

169 '[Discussion with Yigal Allon on Military Aid; Includes Tab A; Tabs B and C Not Included]' (DNSA, January 16, 1975).

170 Barzanî, *Barzanî Û Bzutnewey Rizgarîxwazî Kurd: Bergî Sêyem, Beşî Duwem 1961–1975*, pp. 167–183.

171 Kiely, Patrick, 'Through Distorted Lenses [...]', in *America and Iraq: Policy-Making, Intervention and Regional Politics,* ed. by Patrick Kiely and David Ryan (London: Routledge, 2009), pp. 36–55.

172 For more on the Nixon administration's foreign policy, see Hahn, Peter L., *Missions Accomplished? The United States and Iraq since World War I* (New York, NY; Oxford: Oxford University Press, 2012), pp. 102–108; Kaufman, Joyce P., *A Concise History of US Foreign Policy* (Lanham, MD: Rowman& Littlefield, 2006); Crabb, Cecil Van Meter, *The Doctrines of American Foreign Policy: Their Meaning, Role, and Future* (Baton Rouge, LA: Louisiana State University Press, 1982), pp. 278–324.

173 For more on these issues see Kaufman, op. cit., pp. 278–324.

174 Kiely, op. cit., pp. 36–54 (p. 47).

175 For more on these issues and US relations with Iran during the Ford administration see ibid., pp. 46–49.

Conclusion

This consideration of the effect of the Cold War and regional politics on the Iraqi Kurds, with particular emphasis on US policy, during the time period covered, from 1958, the overthrow of the Hashemite monarchy and establishment of the Republic of Iraq to 1975, the ending of the September Revolution, or *Şorrşî Eylul*, has involved large numbers of both primary and secondary sources, consisting of US and UK documents and Kurdish language sources, among others. Many of these sources are not previously synergistically introduced in a theme such as that of this book. It has, consequently, been a complex work, but one that I believe has produced some new insights as well as confirmed various suspicions and claims.

Despite a clear structural organisation—chronologically, the period being divided into four consecutive time periods, one for each chapter—the narrative has inevitably involved repeated backtracking and overlapping of themes and issues, with at other times no sharp lines between one topic and another. Indeed, the complexity of the subject and the involvement of several actors with their different stakes in the subject studied meant that the various strands of this research had to be constantly interlinked. Overall, the intention has been to strike a balance among the range of perspectives and considerations in the narrative presentation. With that in mind, the following paragraphs review the main concerns of each chapter and, thereby, the collective findings.

Chapter 1 started with a background of the Kurdish Issue from WWI to late 1963, with a focus from 1958. The attention here was largely on the Iraqi Kurds, and how, from the early years of the Cold War, Iran and Turkey, both US allies, had inflated the risk of the Soviets sponsoring a Kurdish state and thus indicating the potential for a profound Soviet gain in the region in relation to the Cold War. Iran, in particular, sought to convince US policymakers of Russia's *grand design*, which was supposed to gain the Soviets a land bridge to the Middle East through a putative Kurdish state to be established as a result of a Soviet intercession and neutralisation of US allies, such as Iran. The US, it appears, really did believe that the USSR could destabilise the region by exploiting the Kurds.

The Iraqi Revolution of 1958 had a striking effect on Iran's relations with the Iraqi Kurds. During the time period covered here, however, Iran was quite uninterested in the Iraqi Kurds' winning any sort of autonomy or self-rule, since it simply wanted to exploit their needs in this regard so as to affect developments in

Iraq and counteract Iraqi governments that it did not approve of—for instance, by presenting them to America as communists or (pro-Nasser) Arab nationalists. Another long-term effect of the revolution, following from its own linkage to the onset of hostilities in Kurdistan between its Peshmerga and the Iraqi army under the Qasim government—the September Revolution (*Şorrşî Eylul*) of 1961—was for outside powers, such as the USSR and Egypt, to form relations with the Kurds in order to hold a *Kurdish card* in Iraq.

An assessment of US foreign policy from Truman to Kennedy in Chapter 1 found the way the US viewed the (issue of the) Iraqi Kurds, as a strictly internal Iraqi matter, to be quite compatible with the Truman and the Eisenhower Doctrines as well the policies of the Kennedy administration. Essentially *anticommunism* was the primary US strategic consideration under these presidents, so not only were the regional politics unfavourable for the Iraqi Kurds and their cause, due to nationalist and territorial integrity concerns as well as ethnic enmity, but US global policy also was unaccommodating—because the US viewed the Kurds in the light of their potential to destabilise its Cold War allies of Iran and Turkey, as well as the post-Ottoman framework for the Middle East generally.

With regards to US policy, the argument of Chapter 1 was that the US did have a policy on the Iraqi Kurdish Issue—that it was to be regarded as an internal Iraqi matter—and that this policy was well established among US officials, it was well developed and it was based on conscious decisions. One other factor that this chapter took into account was the fact that the Iraqi Kurds did not count as a state actor and thus were not accorded policy considerations equal to those of state actors. Under Barzani and the KDP, the Kurds themselves had essentially offered to pledge themselves as a US client in the Middle East were it to assist them with money and arms for their struggle. On its side, the US was well aware that the Kurds wanted democracy for Iraq and autonomy for Kurdistan.

Setting off from the Ba'athists' putsch of February 1963, where it was found that the US essentially sacrificed the Kurds in order to win the favour of the Ba'ath government and pull it towards the West's side in the Cold War, Chapter 2 emphasises the importance for the US of keeping out *international communism* from Iraq. This was the priority, and the Kurds were expendable. In fact, it is argued, the US was oversensitive in its worries about offending the Ba'ath government in relation to the Kurds, with the Kennedy administration going so far even as to provide Baghdad with ammunition and military hardware to be used against the Kurds. Of course, Cold War politics was the rationale.

The Iraqi Kurds were not only unfortunate victims of the Cold War but also caught in a bitter regional power rivalry between Arab and Persian nationalisms. Here, it was US ally, the Shah of Iran, who exploited the Iraqi Kurds. The primary function of the Kurds for Iran was as a means through which to challenge the government in Baghdad, then comprising the pro-Nasser nationalists, who had overthrown the (first) Ba'ath regime in November 1963. Similarly, Egypt and Nasser also developed their relations with the Iraqi Kurds, basically for the same reason as Iran, to influence the course of politics in Iraq. The relationship of all external powers with the Iraqi Kurds, therefore, was functional, to instrumentalise

148   *Conclusion*

them in order to shape the politics of Iraq in the broader regional struggles for influence and power.

As a rather small, non-state actor, and landlocked to boot, the Iraqi Kurdish movement had little choice but to cooperate with any power that showed an interest in assisting them in their resistance against Baghdad, which meant, essentially, their fight against racial and cultural assimilation into Arab Iraq. Outside powers, therefore, exploited this for their own advantage. The Iraqi state also brought its own, complex considerations, with, further to local rivalries, an important role as a regional player in the Cold War. Iran, for instance, was partly motivated also by the need to circumvent Soviet backing for the Kurds in indirectly seeking to persuade the Kurdish leadership to seek help from Tehran, the aim being to not leave an opening that the USSR could fill.

Lastly, this chapter also argued that the US interest in containing communism and securing its allies was in overall tension with the Iraqi Kurds' ambitions. The US, during this time, under Kennedy and Johnson, saw the Kurds as potentially destabilising its regional allies, Iran and Turkey. Therefore, the interests of its allies and keeping the Soviets out were important for the US, but not the ambitions of the Iraqi Kurds themselves. The attempts of Barzani's emissaries to entreat the US thus fell on deaf ears. Those ears, moreover, were relatively low level; the Kurds were not given access to the higher reaches of the successive US administrations. Essentially, they were kept at a distance, in order that Washington was not to be seen as in any way compromised in its important relations, with its regional allies, the state actors.

Continuing this theme, Chapter 3 examined how the Iraqi Kurds tried in vain in 1965 to secure the backing of the US. The reasons behind US reluctance to do so were confirmed (the US wanted to avoid offending regional powers and sought not to give a reason for the Soviets to meddle) as was, therefore, an effect of the Cold War on the Iraqi Kurds (that the latter were victims of the former). In fact, rather than garnering support, the Kurds saw the US State Department succumb to Iraqi demands later in 1965 for it to intervene to stop the flow of arms from Iran that was supplying them in their still ongoing military conflict with Baghdad. Kurdish appeals to the US multiple times and through multiple channels gained nothing.

Next, this chapter identified a significant link between Britain's withdrawal from the Gulf and the position of the Iraqi Kurds. Basically, the British withdrawal in 1971 left a power vacuum that resulted in an Iranian sense of regional instability which in turn led to the Shah's further support for the Iraqi Kurds; Iran endeavoured to ensure that the Iraqi government and military were kept busy in Kurdistan and thus unable to consider adventures elsewhere, such as in the Gulf. Thus also, Iran desperately tried to prevent the KDP under Barzani from signing a peace agreement with the second Ba'ath government, which had come to power in 1968 and was seeking to resolve its Kurdish Issue but in a way that it wanted. The Iranian attempt failed, and the agreement was eventually to become the March 11, 1970 Accord. Israel had also offered to intensify its military backing for the Kurds if they did not sign the agreement. Israel was another regional power named in this work as basically using the Kurds for its own, strategic

Conclusion 149

benefit, essentially by preoccupying Iraq. In this case, the aim was to ensure that the Iraqi army could not join other Arab countries against it, as indeed was the case in the 1967 war, in which Iraqi forces did not significantly contribute.

This chapter also investigated the growing influence of the USSR. While the US had feared Soviet influence in the region through the Kurds as a loose cannon, as it were, the change of government in Baghdad meant that this actually transpired at state level, through Iraq. The crucial role of the USSR in bringing the KDP together with the Ba'ath government for the agreement was thus emphasised here. The pressure the Soviets brought to bear on all parties was detailed, to the extent that the Accord could be said to have been forced through and sponsored by the USSR—for its own Cold War interests, of course.

Still, US policy regarding the Iraqi Kurds had essentially seen no change since 1960. There was simply no incentive for the US to intervene in the Kurdish Issue in any positive way, all the more so since it would have offended Iraq, Iran and Turkey, in addition to the Arab world. This was also while the USSR and Nasser (before his death) preferred a peaceful solution to the Kurdish Issue in Iraq, and while the Soviets acted to ensure this; the US, however, was not willing to intervene for a peaceful solution, primarily directed by the duplicitous considerations of Iran, which wanted to foment Kurdish ambitions in Iraq but only to a certain point, to occupy Baghdad, and not to give succour to any wider Kurdish ambitions (i.e. inside Iran itself).

Barzani made several attempts to have President Johnson use his influence to resolve the Kurdish Issue within Iraq and also to prevent the supply of arms to Baghdad. Barzani clearly conveyed the Kurds' ambition for the establishment and promotion of democracy and human rights; he did not simply ask the US to aid the Kurds militarily or economically but also requested assistance in finding a just and peaceful solution. To all intents and purposes, the US rejection of the Iraqi Kurds' pleas came from the White House.

Importantly, the totalitarian nature of the Ba'ath regime failed to result in a change to US Kurdish policy. Such a change could have been expected, but it did not materialise. Even though the Ba'ath search for an external enemy as a bogeyman scapegoat included the deployment of America and its regional allies for the role, the US refused to back joint initiatives, which included the Kurds, to overthrow the Ba'ath, mainly because it did not see the likelihood of a replacement government that would be any friendlier to US interests than the Ba'ath.

The US did not mislead the Kurds by giving them false hope; that seems clear. Nevertheless, it did keep the Kurds on friendly terms while also being quite prepared to sacrifice them for good relations with the regional state actors. Thus, Iraq's brutal actions in Kurdistan, such as indiscriminate bombings and the use of banned weapons, had no noticeable effect on the US position, even though Washington was well aware of what was going on. Strong evidence for all these findings was produced in this chapter, which showed that by late 1971, the US was fully aware of the nature of the Iraqi regime, that it was backtracking on the March 1970 Accord and that this would not last long—none of which had any effect on US policy regarding the Iraqi Kurds.

150   *Conclusion*

Chapter 4 detailed the failure of the Kurds to convince the US to back an anti-Ba'ath initiative to topple the regime—or rather, the US reluctance to become entangled in this. This was in addition to Kurdish demands and plans for a democratic Iraq, which also failed to induce any support from the US, now under the Nixon administration. The chapter then moved on to explore the strengthening of relations between the USSR and Iraq and the impact of this.

Crucially, this rapprochement failed to raise alarm signals in the US, mainly because US diplomats still believed that Iraq's internal instability (the Kurdish War) would prevent it from posing a threat in the region. Iran was considerably less convinced of this, however—and correctly so, in that although the USSR enjoyed cordial relations with the Kurdish leadership, as the Kremlin–Ba'athist relationship solidified, the Kurds were gradually sidelined by the Soviets. Barzani's faith in the Soviets faded, and his messages to the US became increasingly desperate. The chapter then moved on to scrutinise how, from 1972, Barzani responded to the Soviet backing of the Ba'athists in Baghdad.

Barzani sought to persuade Iran and Jordan of the dangers that the Soviet influence could pose. The USSR had pressed the KDP to join a coalition government with the Ba'ath and the ICP and, therefore Barzani was stuck between joining this government or winning sufficient support outside of Iraq in the case of a resumption of hostilities. For Barzani and the KDP, the Ba'ath was untrustworthy and over time would seek to control all of Kurdistan, while rejecting the Soviet proposal would inevitably lead to renewal of the Kurdish War. Barzani's assessment seems to have been depressingly accurate.

The Kurdish leader made one final direct appeal to the US and also to Iran, Jordan and Israel, attempting to convince the US of the seriousness of the situation. Iran in particular advanced Barzani's argument with the Nixon administration for why the US needed to receive his petition favourably. Consequently, in August 1972, the Nixon administration finally agreed that the US would receive a Kurdish representation at a high level. The upshot was the provision of ordnance and financial assistance to the Kurdish movement under Barzani. The Shah and Kissinger were the key figures in this decision.

The purpose of the pivot to the Kurds was again essentially to *absorb* Iraq's energies and limit its capacity for offensive action abroad. This was, essentially, the Iranian agenda. If anything, Iran was even more highly motivated to prevent a *national front* government comprising the KDP and ICP with the Ba'ath than it had been to prevent the 1970 Accord. In conjunction with this and in reference to the Cold War, however, Kissinger also wanted to make the cost of the Soviet move in Iraq so high that that it would come to consider this, and consequently Middle Eastern incursions generally, not to be worth the high price paid. In his own words, Kissinger wanted the Kurds to be strong enough to 'be an open wound in Iraq',[1] constantly sucking in Soviet resources (the parallel with Vietnam is manifest).

This chapter then examined how the Kurdish War was reignited from August 1974 by the Iraq army's total assault on KDP-held areas of Iraqi Kurdistan. It covered the various actors' interests in this, emphasising the absolutely crucial

Conclusion   151

role of Iran, ultimately, in closing the border and cutting off supplies to the Kurds. The chapter went on to look at the events that led up to the Algiers Accord of March 1975 in what was, indeed, a huge betrayal of the Kurds by Iran, and also the US.

Essentially, it can be inferred that it was lack of good relations between Iran and Iraq that had originally led the Shah of Iran to support the Kurds. However, the Shah and also Jordan sold this as a Cold War and a regional security issue to the Nixon administration and thus managed to involve the US. The US was primarily involved to contain and eventually reduce the Soviet influence in Iraq and thus, opportunistically, in the Middle East, too. It thus became involved behind the scenes in empowering one of its allies (Iran) to stand up to what it saw as the communist threat. As related to the Cold War, therefore, this was in line with the Nixon Doctrine and then later, after 1974, with the US policy under Ford.

It could be contended that the Shah not only misled and sold the Kurdish national liberation movement but it also deceived the US to advance his country's interests with Iraq. The Kurds also insisted on the US involvement if they were to reject Soviet demands of the Kurds to join the coalition government. The timing of the change in the Shah's position—following a visit to Moscow and prior to its effective declaration in—indicates the USSR as instrumental in the Iranian leader's volte face; basically, it would appear, Russia was among those that brokered a deal between Iraq and Iran in which both parties gained—the latter in relation to a longstanding territorial dispute with its neighbour and the former through a resolution by force of its Kurdish Issue—for a while, at least. This is not to dismiss the role of the other actors mentioned. The US, one may conclude, was the loser in this Cold War game, but the Kurds paid the price, for all.

Chapter 4 also presented multi-sourced evidence to challenge and dismiss suggestions that the Shah had no choice but to betray the Kurds. On the contrary, Iraq's military campaign in Kurdistan was shown to be unsuccessful, with all-out war backed by the USSR failing to dislodge the autonomy-seeking Kurds from their mountain strongholds, who were even growing in confidence at the end. Indeed, the continuation of the conflict may have well brought about the end of Saddam Hussein's political career as it had done to other Iraqi leaders before; the reason that Saddam Hussein had to yield to the Shah's territorial demands was precisely *because* of Iraq's military failure.

In backing the Iraqi Kurds from 1972 to 1975, albeit rather lightly in material terms and highly covertly through the CIA, the US, as a Cold War superpower, had three fundamental objectives: to contain and punish Iraq for its Soviet links, as well as making this a lesson to other Arab states; to counter and ultimately smoke the Soviets out of Iraq, and thus the Middle East; and to support an ally in need (Iran). This chapter substantiated these as Kissinger's views at the time. Lastly, the overarching global foreign policies of the Nixon and Ford administrations were studied, and the Iraqi Kurds' place in these identified. What this chapter established in terms of the Nixon administration's backing for Iran and ultimately (covertly) the Iraqi Kurds was in accordance with the broader US

152 *Conclusion*

foreign policy of the time, namely, to back its allies to face communism by themselves as opposed to having US troops take up this role.

Overall, I would argue, this book has substantively shown that the combined effect of internal Iraqi and regional Middle Eastern politics in complex combinations with Cold War calculations on the Iraqi Kurds was such that their political fate was essentially decided outside of Kurdistan—and somewhat outside of Iraq even—with little regard, if any, to the desires of the people there. Human rights as a legal–judicial consideration—let alone an ethical one—were hardly a consideration.

US involvement in the history of the Iraqi Kurdish struggle during this period was dominated by Cold War considerations as they played out in the regional context, mostly through a policy of sympathetic disengagement, and at the end through a failed covert support. The US policy towards the Iraqi Kurds was also dependent on what was happening in Baghdad, although not, it is suggested, sufficiently well when the USSR started to gain influence there (i.e. during the years that the second Ba'ath government established itself). By its own parameters, that is, US assessments were found wanting, its policies thus inefficient and the end result a failure.

Iran was found to be a pivotal player in what was examined in this book—and this is while Israeli, and Jordanian officials, sought to advance the Kurdish Issue with US officials, in particular in the post-1970 period leading to the Algiers Accord of March 1975. The regional dimension of the Iraqi Kurdish Issue in the Middle East and the attempts of various powers to exploit it to advance their own interests in the area combined with the overarching Cold War considerations in the end led to a quite tragic conclusion for the Kurds. It would be some years before the Kurds could continue their quest for territorial self-determination and, ultimately, the sovereignty of statehood. As for the Kurds in all this history, they were not the pawns of any party, but they too were taking their national interests into account and acting upon it, in their struggle for self-rule or self-determination. As put by Mustafa Barzani in an interview before his death from cancer in 1979, 'We do not want to be anybody's pawns. We are an ancient people. We want our autonomy. We want sarbasti—freedom. I do not know who will take my place one day. But they cannot crush us'.[2]

Notes

1 Memorandum of Conversation, frus1969-76v27/d24.
2 Quoted in Daniel Schorr (1991) '1975 Background to Betrayal'. Retrieved from https://www.washingtonpost.com/archive/opinions/1991/04/07/1975-background-to-betrayal/aa973065-ea5e-4270-8cf9-02361307073c/.

Bibliography

Note: All translations of material quoted from interviews and in videos made by the author; Latin alphabet transliterations of Kurdish (Sorani) language titles made using the open-access software available at http://chawg.org/kurdi-nus/.

Unpublished

Author interviews

Telephone Interview (A) from the UK with Dr Mahmoud Othman (October 14, 2015).
Telephone Interview (B) from the UK with Dr Mahmoud Othman (October 15, 2015).

Documents

US archival sources

Archives Unbound – Gale.
Declassified Documents Reference System (DDRS, Gale Digital Collections).
Digital National Security Archives (DNSA).
FRUS (State Department and also documents from the Presidential libraries, Departments of State and Defense, National Security Council, Central Intelligence Agency, Agency for International Development, and others).
National Security Archives (George Washington University).
The Cold War International History Project.
The National Archives, US (www.archives.gov).
WikiLeaks (The WikiLeaks Public Library of US Diplomacy's 'The Kissinger Cables').

UK archival sources

British National Archives (in Kew, London Borough of Richmond upon Thames).

Published

Audio-visual (Videos)

Aziz, Mohammed, 'Mhemed 'Ezîz', in *Pencemor*, ed. by Kawa Emin (Kurdistan, Iraq: Rudaw, 2015a).

154 Bibliography

Aziz, Mohammed, 'Mhemmed 'Ezîz – Beşî Sêyem' [Mhemmed Eziz – Part Three], in *Pencemor*, ed. by Kawa Emin (Kurdistan, Iraq: Rudaw, 2015b).

Dzaei, Mohsin, 'Muhsîn Dzeyî – Nwênerî Pêşûy Mes'ud Barzanî – Beşî Duwem' [Muhsin Dzeyi – Masoud Barzani's Former Representative – Part Two], in *Pencemor*, ed. by Kawa Emin (Kurdistan, Iraq: Rudaw, 2015a).

Dzaei, Mohsin, 'Muhsîn Dzeyî – Nwênerî Pêşûy Mes'ud Barzanî – Beşî Sêyem' [Muhsin Dzeyi – Masoud Barzani's Former Representative – Part Three], in *Pencemor*, ed. by Kawa Emin (Kurdistan, Iraq: Rudaw, 2015b).

Othman, Omar, 'Umer 'Usman, Endamî Serkirdayetî Partî' [Umar Usman, Member of the KDP Leadership Committee], in *Pencemor*, ed. by Kawa Emin (Kurdistan, Iraq: Rudaw, 2016).

Talabani, Mukaram, 'Mukerem Tallebanî 3', in *Pencemor*, ed. by Kawa Emin (Kurdistan, Iraq: Rudaw, 2015).

Written (Books, Articles, Memoirs, Newspapers, etc.)

Abrahamian, Ervand, *Iran between Two Revolutions* (Princeton, NJ: Princeton University Press, 1982).

Aburish, Said, *Saddam Hussein: The Politics of Revenge* (London: Bloomsbury, 2001).

Alam, Asadollah, *The Shah and I: The Confidential Diary of Iran's Royal Court, 1968–77* (London: I.B. Tauris, 1991).

Alder, Emanuel, 'Seizing the Middle Ground: Constructivism in World Politics', *European Journal of International Relations*, 3 (3) (1997), 319–363.

Ali, Hawraman, 'Self Determination for the Kurds?', *Coventry University Law Journal, 16* (2011), 30–43.

Allain, Jean, *International Law in the Middle East: Closer to Power than Justice* (England & United States: Ashgate Publishing Limited, 2004).

Alvandi, Roham, 'Nixon, Kissinger, and the Shah: The Origins of Iranian Primacy in the Persian Gulf', *Diplomatic History, 36* (2012), 337–372.

Alvandi, Roham, *Nixon, Kissinger, and the Shah: The United States and Iran in the Cold War* (New York, NY: Oxford University Press, 2014).

Barrett, Roby Carol, *The Greater Middle East and the Cold War: US Foreign Policy under Eisenhower and Kennedy* (London: I.B. Tauris & Co Ltd, 2010).

Barzani, Massoud, *Mustafa Barzani and the Kurdish Liberation Movement (1931–1961)* (New York, NY: Palgrave, 2003).

Barzani, Massoud, *Barzanî Û Bzutnewey Rizgarîxwazî Kurd: Bergî Sêyem, Beşî Duwem 1961–1975* [Barzani and the Kurdish Libration Movement, Part iii, Vol. ii: The September Revolution 1961–1975], trans. by Hawraman Ali (Hewlêr: Çapxaney wezaretî perwerde, 2004[?]).

Barzani, Massoud, *Barzanî Û Bzutnewey Rizgarîxwazî Kurd: Bergî Sêyem, Beşî Yekem 1961–1975* [Barzani and the Kurdish Libration Movement, Part iii, Vol. i: The September Revolution 1961–1975], trans. by Hawraman Ali (Hewlêr: Çapxaney wezaretî perwerde, 2004[?]).

Barzani, Massoud, *Barzanî Û Bzutnewey Rizgarîxwazî Kurd: Bergî Yekem 1931–1958* [Barzani and the Kurdish Libration Movement, Part i: 1931–1958], trans. by Hawraman Ali (Hewlêr: Çapxaney wezaretî perwerde, 2012a).

Barzani, Massoud, *Barzanî Û Bzutnewey Rizgarîxwazî Kurd: Bergî Duwem 1958–1961* [Barzani and the Kurdish Libration Movement, Part ii: 1958–1961], trans. by Hawraman Ali (Hewlêr: Çapxaney wezaretî perwerde, 2012b).

Bibliography 155

Bengio, Ofra, *The Kurds of Iraq: Building a State within a State* (Boulder, CO: Lynne Rienner Publishers, Inc., 2012).

Bengio, Ofra, 'Surprising Ties between Israel and the Kurds', *Middle East Quarterly, 21* (2014).

Brown, L. Carl, ed., *Diplomacy in the Middle East: The International Relations of Regional and Outside Powers* (London: I. B. Tauris, 2004).

Bull, Hedley and Hurrell, Andrew, *The Anarchical Society: A Study of Order in World Politics* (New York, NY: Columbia University Press, 2002).

Charountaki, Marianna, *The Kurds and US Foreign Policy: International Relations in the Middle East since 1945* (London & New York, NY: Routledge, 2011).

CIA, 'Kurdish Areas in the Middle East and the Soviet Union' (The University of Texas at Austin, 1986).

CIA, 'Kurdish_Lands_92.jpg', University of Texas at Austin (1992) Retrieved from <http://www.lib.utexas.edu/maps/middle_east_and_asia/kurdish_lands_92.jpg> [Accessed August 20, 2015].

Costigliola, Frank, 'US Foreign Policy from Kennedy to Johnson', in *The Cambridge History of the Cold War Volume 2: Crises and Détente*, ed. by Arne Westad and Melvyn Leffler (Cambridge: Cambridge University Press, 2010), pp. 112–133.

Crabb, Cecil Van Meter, *The Doctrines of American Foreign Policy: Their Meaning, Role, and Future* (Baton Rouge, LA: Louisiana State University Press, 1982).

Doyle, Michael W., 'Liberalism and Foreign Policy', in *Foreign Policy: Theories, Actors, Cases*, ed. by Steve Smith, Amelia Hadfield and Timothy Dunne (Oxford & New York, NY: Oxford University Press, 2008), p. 50.

Eagleton, William, *The Kurdish Republic of 1946* (London & New York, NY: Oxford University Press, 1963).

Entessar, Nader, *Kurdish Ethnonationalism* (Boulder, CO: Lynn Rienner Publishers, 1992).

Entessar, Nader, 'Kurdish Politics in Regional Context', in *Kurdish Politics in the Middle East* (Lanham, MD: Lexington Books, 2010a), pp. 155–170.

Entessar, Nader, *Kurdish Politics in the Middle East* (Lanham, MD: Lexington Books, 2010b).

Faiaz, Mae'hd, *Beşêk Le Bîreweryekanî Mam Celal* [Some of Mam Jalal's Memories], trans. by Hawraman Ali (Erbil: Aras Press, 2009).

Fawcett, Louise, *International Relations of the Middle East* (Oxford: Oxford University Press, 2013).

Ghareeb, Edmund, *The Kurdish Question in Iraq* (New York, NY: Syracuse University Press, 1981).

Gibson, Bryan R., *Sold Out? US Foreign Policy, Iraq, the Kurds and the Cold War* (New York, NY: Palgrave Macmillan, 2015).

Gunter, Michael M., *The Kurds of Iraq: Tragedy and Hope* (New York, NY: St. Martin's Press, 1992).

Gunter, Michael M., 'The Five Stages of American Foreign Policy Towards the Kurds', *Insight Turkey, 13* (2011), 93–106.

Hahn, Peter L., *Missions Accomplished? The United States and Iraq since World War I* (New York, NY & Oxford: Oxford University Press, 2012).

Halabi, Yakub, *US Foreign Policy in the Middle East: From Crises to Change* (Farnham, Surrey: Ashgate Publishing Limited, 2009).

Halliday, Fred, *Nation and Religion in the Middle East* (London: Saqi Books, 2000).

Halliday, Fred, *The Middle East in International Relations: Power, Politics and Ideology* (Cambridge: Cambridge University Press, 2005).

156   Bibliography

Hartley, Anthony, 'John Kennedy's Foreign Policy', *Foreign Policy, 4* (1971), 77–87.

Hinnebusch, Raymond and Ehteshami, Anoushiravan, eds., *The Foreign Policies of Middle East States* (London: Lynne Rienner Publishers, 2002).

Hinnebusch, Raymond, *The International Politics of the Middle East* (Manchester: Manchester University Press, 2003).

Hogan, Michael J. and Paterson, Thomas G., eds., *Explaining the History of American Foreign Relations* (Cambridge: Cambridge University Press, 2004).

HR-NET, 'The Treaty of Peace between the Allied and Associated Powers and Turkey Signed at Sèvres August 10, 1920' (1995–2016). Retrieved from <http://www.hri.org/docs/sevres/part3.html> [Accessed September 15, 2014].

HRW, 'Claims in Conflict: Reversing Ethnic Cleansing in Northern Iraq: iii. Background', Human Rights Watch, (2004). Retrieved from <http://www.hrw.org/reports/2004/iraq0804/4.htm> [Accessed September 15, 2014].

IranWire, 'Israelis and Kurds Love Each Other', IranWire, (2014) . Retrieved from <http://en.iranwire.com/features/5888/> [Accessed September 10, 2014].

Jacobs, Matthew F., *Imagining the Middle East: The Building of an American Foreign Policy, 1918–1967* (Chapel Hill, NC: University of North Carolina Press, 2011).

Jacobsen, Eric, 'A Coincidence of Interests: Kennedy, US Assistance, and the 1963 Iraqi Ba'th Regime', *Diplomatic History, 37* (2013), 1029–1059.

Jentleson, Bruce W., *American Foreign Policy: The Dynamics of Choice in the 21st Century* (New York, NY: Norton, 2004).

Kane, Thomas M., 'Realism', in *New Directions in US Foreign Policy*, ed. by Inderjeet Parmar, et al (Oxfordshire & New York, NY: Routledge, 2009), pp. 5–17.

Kaufman, Joyce P., *A Concise History of US Foreign Policy* (Lanham, MD: Rowman & Littlefield, 2006).

Keddie, Nikki and Richard, Yann, *Modern Iran: Roots and Results of Revolution* (New Haven, CT: Yale University Press, 2006).

Kiely, Patrick, 'Through Distorted Lenses [...]', in *America and Iraq: Policy-Making, Intervention and Regional Politics*, ed. by Patrick Kiely and David Ryan (London: Routledge, 2009), pp. 36–55.

Kiely, Patrick and Ryan, David, eds., *America and Iraq: Policy-Making, Intervention and Regional Politics* (London: Routledge, 2009).

Kimche, David, *The Last Option: After Nasser, Arafat & Saddam Hussein: The Quest for Peace in the Middle East* (London: Weidenfeld & Nicolson, 1991).

Lawrence, Quil, *Invisible Nation: How the Kurds' Quest for Statehood Is Shaping Iraq and the Middle East* (New York, NY: Walker & Co., 2008).

Lesch, David W., *The Middle East and the United States: A Historical and Political Reassessment* (New York, NY: Westview Press, 2007).

Little, Douglas, 'His Finest Hour? Eisenhower, Lebanon, and the 1958 Middle East Crisis', *Diplomatic History, 20* (1996), 27–54.

Little, Douglas, 'The Cold War in the Middle East: Suez Crisis to Camp David Accords', in *The Cambridge History of the Cold War Volume 2: Crises and Détente*, ed. by Arne Westad and Melvyn P. Leffler (Cambridge: Cambridge University Press, 2010a), pp. 305–326.

Little, Douglas, 'The United States and the Kurds: A Cold War Story', *Journal of Cold War Studies, 12* (2010b), 63–98.

Mack, David L., 'The United States Policy and the Iraqi Kurds', in *Kurdish Identity: Human Rights and Political Status*, ed. by G. Charles, et al (Gainesville, FL: The University Press of Florida, 2007).

Bibliography 157

Macmillan, John, 'Liberal Internationalism', in *International Relations Theory for the Twenty-First Century: An Introduction* (London & New York, NY: Routledge, 2007).

Majeed, Mohammed Shareef Jalal, 'President George W. Bush's Policy Towards Iraq: Change or Continuity?' (PhD, University of Durham, 2010).

McDonald, Matt and Jackson, Richard, 'Constructivism, US Foreign Policy and the War on Terror', in *New Directions in US Foreign Policy*, ed. by Inderjeet Parmar, et al (Oxfordshire & New York, NY: Routledge, 2009).

McDowall, David, *A Modern History of the Kurds* (London: I.B. Tauris, 2004).

McGlinchey, Stephen, 'Richard Nixon's Road to Tehran: The Making of the US–Iran Arms Agreement of May 1972', *Diplomatic History, 37* (2013), 841–860.

McKiernan, Kevin, *The Kurds: A People in Search of Their Homeland* (New York, NY: St. Martin's Press, 2006).

Mearsheimer, John J., *The Tragedy of Great Power Politics* (New York, NY; London: Norton, 2001).

Meho, Lokman, *The Kurdish Question in US Foreign Policy: A Documentary Sourcebook* (Westport, CT & London: Praeger, 2004).

Milton-Edwards, Beverley and Hinchcliffe, Peter, *Conflicts in the Middle East since 1945*. The Making of the Contemporary World (London: Taylor & Francis/Routledge, 2004).

Mitchell, David, *Making Foreign Policy: Presidential Management of the Decision-Making Process* (Aldershot: Ashgate Publishing Limited, 2005).

Mitrokhin, Vasili and Andrew, Christopher, *The World Was Going Our Way: The KGB and the Battle for the Third World* (New York, NY: Basic Books, 2005).

Morgenthau, Hans and Thompson, Kenneth W., *Politics among Nations: The Struggle for Power and Peace* (New York, NY: Knopf, 1985).

Mylroie, Judith and Mylroie, Laurie, *Saddam and the Crisis in the Gulf* (New York, NY: Times Nooks, 1990).

O'Ballance, Edgar, *The Kurdish Struggle, 1920–94* (Basingstoke: Macmillan, 1995).

Observer, ProQuest Historical Newspapers: The Guardian (1821–2003) and The Observer (1792–2003). Retrieved from <http://search.proquest.com/hnpguardianobserver/index> [Accessed September 11, 2014].

Osgood, Kenneth, 'Eisenhower and Regime Change in Iraq: The United States and the Iraqi Revolution of 1958', in *America and Iraq: Policy-Making, Intervention and Regional Politics*, ed. by Patrick Kiely and David Ryan (London: Routledge, 2009), pp. 4–27.

Parmar, Inderjeet, 'Foreign Policy Fusion: Liberal Interventionists, Conservative Nationalists and Neoconservatives – The New Alliance Dominating the US Foreign Policy Establishment', *International Politics, 46* (2009), 177–209.

Parmar, Inderjeet, et al, *New Directions in US Foreign Policy* (Oxfordshire & New York, NY: Routledge, 2009).

Parmar, Inderjeet, and Cox, Michael, eds. *Soft Power and US Foreign Policy Theoretical, Historical and Contemporary Perspectives* (Hoboken, NJ: Taylor & Francis, 2010).

Parsi, Trita, *Treacherous Alliance: The Secret Dealings of Israel, Iran, and the United States* (New Haven, CT: Yale University Press, 2007).

Pauly, Robert J., ed., *International Relations Theory and US Foreign Policy* (Farnham: Ashgate Publishing Limited, 2010).

Rafaat, Aram, 'US-Kurdish Relations in Post-Invasion Iraq', *MERIA: The Middle East Review of International Affairs, 11* (4) 2007, 79–89.

Randal, Jonathan, *Kurdistan: After Such Knowledge, What Forgiveness?* (London: Bloomsbury, 1998).

158   Bibliography

Refugees International, '*Buried Alive: Stateless Kurds in Syria*' (2006) Retrieved from <http://www.refworld.org/docid/47a6eba80.html> [Accessed April 4, 2017].

Rehmany, Wirya, *Şorrşî Eylul Le Bellgename Nhêneyekanî Emrîkada* [The September Revolution in then Secret Documents of America] (Tehran: [no pub.], 2013).

Reşîd, Selah, *Mam celal: dîdarî temen, le lawêtyewe bo koşkî komarî, beşî yekem* (Kurdistan, Iraq: Karo, 2017) p. 256 (trans. by author).

Reus-Smit, Christian and Snidal, Duncan, *The Oxford Handbook of International Relations* (Oxford: Oxford University Press, 2008).

Romano, David, *The Kurdish National Movement: Opportunity, Mobilization and Identity* (New York, NY: Cambridge University Press, 2006).

Sayigh, Yezid and Shlaim, Avi, eds., *The Cold War and the Middle East* (Oxford: Clarendon Press, 1997).

Shareef, Mohammed, *The United States, Iraq and the Kurds: Shock, Awe and Aftermath* (Oxfordshire & New York, NY: Routledge, 2014).

Smith, Steve, et al, *Foreign Policy: Theories, Actors, Cases* (Oxford & New York, NY: Oxford University Press, 2008).

Stansfield Gareth, *Iraqi Kurdistan: Political Development and Emergent Democracy* (London: Taylor & Francis, 2004).

Stansfield, Gareth, *Iraq: People, History, Politics* (Malden, MA: Wiley, 2007).

Takeyh, Ray and Simon, Steven, *The Pragmatic Superpower: Winning the Cold War in the Middle East* (London & New York, NY: W.W. Norton, 2016).

Tripp, Charles, *A History of Iraq* (Cambridge: Cambridge University Press, 2007).

Washington Post, ProQuest Historical Newspapers: The Washington Post (1877–1997). Retrieved from <http://search.proquest.com/hnpwashingtonpost> [Accessed September 11, 2014].

Westad, Odd Arne, *The Global Cold War: Third World Interventions and the Making of Our Times* (Cambridge: Cambridge University Press, 2005).

Wittkopf, Eugene, et al, *American Foreign Policy: Pattern and Process* (Belmont, CA: Thomson/Wadsworth, 2008).

Wolfe-Hunnicutt, Brandon, 'Embracing Regime Change in Iraq: American Foreign Policy and the 1963 Coup D'état in Baghdad', *Diplomatic History, 39* (2015), 98–125.

Index

Note: Page numbers followed by "n" denote endnotes and italic represent figures.

Abrahamian, Ervand 12
Adams, J. Wesley 77
Ahmad, Ibrahim 50, 85
Alam, Asadollah 16, 91, 95
al-Bakr, Ahmed Hassan 86, 87, 90
al-Bazzaz, Abd al-Rahman 49, 67, 75; and
  Kurdish Issue 80–82
Algiers Accord 1, 15, 61, 100, 106–107,
  128–130, 132, 135
Alvandi, Roham 4–6, 9–10, 14
anti-communism 147
Arab Federation 50
Arab Iraqi society 50
Arabisation Campaign 107
Arab–Israel hostilities 98
Arab–Israeli wars 1
Arab–Kurd peace 56
Arab nationalism 61–62, 67
Arab–Persian power 93
Aram, Abbas 77
Arif, Abdul Salam 49, 65
Atherton, Alfred L. 83
Averell, Harriman W. 55
Aziz, Mohammed 15
Aziz, Tariq 135

Ba'ath government 10, 12, 15, 49–53,
  70n101, 106; Arab–Israel hostilities 110;
  Arab nationalism 110; Kurdish Society
  principles 108; Peshmerga's control
  108–109; post 1970 110–111;
  'pro-American' government 110; self-
  determination 108; US documentation
  109

Ba'athists after Qasim: Arab–Kurd peace
  56; Ba'ath–Kurdish negotiations 57;
  institutionalised policy 54; Interim Policy

Guidelines 58; Kurd–Arab relations 53;
  Kurd campaign 57; *Kurdish problem* 55;
  Kurdish War 55–56; NSC 53, 56;
  Qasim-period policy 58; regional politics
  60; Republic of Iraq 59; Soviet
  exploitation 56; Tabriz consul 59; US
  allies 56, 57; US *vs.* USSR 56
Ba'athists block: anti-Ba'ath non-Kurdish
  elements 117; CIA 120, 123; coalition
  government 121; KDP 116, 123; Kurdish
  factionalism 119; regional politics 122;
  SAVAK 116; Soviet military assistance
  120; US 'moral support' 122; US
  regional allies 117–118
Baghdad 1, 2, 7, 10, 26–27, 33, 34, 49–51,
  55–58, 78; embassy 64; Kurdish War 63
Bakhtiar, Teymur 86
Ball, George W. 65
Barrett, Roby 14
Barzani, Idris 98, 107, 113, 116
Barzani, Masoud 1, 5, 7–9, 15, 27, 33, 35,
  49–50, 65, 69, 76, 88–92, 106–114,
  119–123, 128–129, 133–135
Barzani memoir-series publications 5
Barzani, Mustafa 5, 15, 22–23, 33, 37, 38,
  40, 50, 52–55, 58–61, 63, 68, 69, 76, 77,
  82, 83, 85, 98, 152
Battle of Mount Handren (1966) 83
Bazzaz Declaration 49, 75, 83
Bengio, Ofra 6, 80
Bowling, John W. 56
Brezhnev, Leonid 92
British withdrawal, Iraqi Kurds
  implications: Arab–Israel hostilities 98;
  Arab–Persian power 93; Ba'ath Party
  rule 99; CENTO 93; international
  community 93–94; Iranian–Iraqi
  agreement 95; *Kurdish autonomy* 99;

160 *Index*

Kurdish buffer zone 96; Peshmerga 96, *96*; regional and international politics 93; regional tensions 94; Russian pressure 95; SAVAK 98–99; Shaykhdoms 94–95; USSR 97
Brown, L. Carl 12
Bundy, McGeorge 53–54, 59, 61
Bush, George W. 2, 3

Central Intelligence Agency (CIA) 66, 120, 123
Central Treaty Organisation (CENTO) 51–52, 86, 93
Charountaki, Marianna 2–6
Chirac, Jacques 128
Colby, William 132
Cold War's regional delineation: American intelligence 26; Kurdish independent movements 25; NSC 24; parent state, CIA 24; post-Ottoman framework 25; self-determination 24; Soviet–Kurdish relations 26; Soviet power 25
Costigliola, Frank 70
Crabb, Cecil V. 41

Declassified Documents Reference System (DDRS) 14
Digital National Security Archives (DNSA) 14
Diplomatic History (Little) 14
Djerejian, Edward 122
Douglas, William Orville 56, 69
Dulles, Allen 31
Dulles, John Foster 26, 31

Egypt 1, 2, 23, 27, 35, 62; mountain warfare 63
Ehteshami, Anoushiravan 12
Eisenhower, Dwight D. 8, 9, 11, 29–31, 41, 56, 69, 93, 147
Entessar, Nader 6–7, 22, 49, 63, 69, 90

Faisal's accession 22
Fawcett, Louise 12

Five Stages of American Foreign Policy Towards the Kurds (Gunter) 7
Foreign Relations of the United States (FRUS) 14

Gallman, Waldemar J. 37
Ghareeb, Edmund 6, 25

Gibson, Bryan R. 2, 3, 5, 6, 10, 11, 12
Grechko, Marshal 125
1991 Gulf War 3
Gunter, Michael M. 2, 5–8

Hahn, Peter L. 5, 6
Haig, Alexander 112, 118–119
Halabi, Yakub 14
Halliday, Fred 12
Hare, Raymond A. 83
Hart, Parker T. 30
Hashemite accession 22
Helms, Richard 116–118, 120, 123, 129, 133, 134
Herz, Martin F. 77
Hinchcliffe, Peter 12
Hinnebusch, Raymond 12
Hogan, Michael J. 14
hostilities, Kurdistan 23; KDP 33; Kurdish rebellion scheme 34; Kurdish tribes 35, 36; Kurds' September Revolution 33; Mitrokhin Archive 34; Soviet–Kurdish relations 34; Soviet Trojan 35–36; Treaty of Friendship and Cooperation 33–34; UAR 34
Hughes, Thomas 84
human rights 82–85
Human Rights Watch 108
Hussein, Saddam 4–5, 7, 15, 42, 86, 91–92, 94, 112, 113, 123, 127–131, 133, 135

Interim Policy Guidelines 58
international communism 41, 42, 147
international politics 23
intra-Kurdish politics 2
Iran 1, 15, 23, 25, 28, 35–37, 39, 42, 50; Kurdish trump card 66–69; military assistance 29; Shatt al-Arab demands 8
Iran–Egypt tensions 1
Iran's Secret War with Iraq (Alvandi) 10
Iraq 13; civil war 9; Hawker Hunter bombers 12; Kurdish liberation movement 1; military failure 4; political class tensions 1, 2; pro-Nasserites *see* pro-Nasserites, Iraq; Shatt al-Arab issue (1975) 4, 19n32; *United States and the Kurds, The* (Little) 8; US policy 2–3
Iraqi Communist Party (ICP) 5
Iraqi Kurdistan: Political Development and Emergent Democracy (Stansfield) 6
Iraq–Iran tensions 1
Iraqi Revolution (1958) 7, 41, 45n26, 146; approach and policy 27; Baghdad Pact

28–30; collective defence planning 28; FRUS 30; Iran's relations 27; Kurdish anxiety 31; Kurdish population 31, *32*; military assistance 29; pro-Western Arab regimes 29; regional politics 32; self-determination 27; USIA 29; US inter-departmental Special National Intelligence Estimate 29
Israel 1, 9–10, 23, 66, 84, 85
Israel–Kurdish relations 40

Jackson, Richard 14
Jacob, Matthew F. 14
Jacobsen, Eric 14
Jentleson, Bruce W. 14
Jernegan, John D. 77
Johnson, Lyndon B. 11, 61–63, 69–70, 74n101, 82–84, 149
Jordan 1, 28

Kane, Thomas M. 14
Kaufman, Burton 14
Kaufman, Joyce P. 14, 69
KDP *see* Kurdistan Democratic Party (KDP)
Keddie, Nikki R. 12
Kennedy administration 7–9, 11–12, 35, 36, 43, 52–59, 69–70, 70n101, 116–118, 120, 147
Kiely, Patrick 6, 14, 136, 137
Kimche, David 6, 11, 61, 135
Kissinger, Henry 8, 112, 114–117, 119–121, 124, 127–128, 131–134, 137, 150
Komer, Robert W. 56–57, 61
Kosygin, Alexei 124
Kurdish buffer zone 96
Kurdish factionalism 119
Kurdish Mehabad Republic 81
Kurdish memoir-series publications (1975) *see* Barzani memoir-series publications
Kurdish national liberation movement 12, 107
Kurdish rebellion scheme 34
Kurdish tribes 35, 36
Kurdistan 8, 12, 15, 22, 49–51, 53; Bazzaz Declaration 75; CIA involvement 13–14; Cold War allies 65; communists 38, 52, 130; democratic system 108; destruction 11; hostilities 16, 147 *see also* hostilities, Kurdistan; independent 25, 27, 29, 31; Iraqi army 9, 63, 83, 90, 98, 117; Iraqi bombings 43; Iraqi Kurdish–Iraqi

government settlement 97; Kurdish refugees 84; legislature 109; 'liberation' government 114; political developments 6; population 31, *32*; Soviet intervention 57; Soviet 'land bridge' 31; war in 10, 16; wireless communication station 69
Kurdistan Democratic Party (KDP) 15, 23, 38, 49, 52–53, 75, 91, 106, 116, 147–150
Kurds' September Revolution 33, 107
Kuwait, mountain warfare 63

language barriers 3, 5
Lawrence, Quil 6
Lebanon, mountain warfare 63
Lesch, David W. 12
Little, Douglas 5, 6, 8–9, 14

MacArthur, Douglas 97
Mack, David L. 5, 6
Macmillan, Harold 31
Mahabad Republic (1946) 9
McDonald, Matt 14
McDowall, David 6
McKesson, John 59
McNamara, Robert 36, 57
Meho, Lokman 5, 6
Meyer, Armin H. 78, 81
Michael Gunter 7–8
military assistance 12
Milton-Edwards, Beverley 12
Mitrokhin Archive, Soviet archival source 16, 34
Modern History of the Kurds (McDowall) 6
Mofti, Shamsaddin 76

Nasser, Gamal Abdel 2, 11, 15, 27–29, 34, 36, 50, 51, 56, 57, 60, 62–65, 79, 81, 93, 147
Nasseri, Nematollah 98
National Security Council (NSC) 24, 53, 56
Nixon, Richard 8–10, 89, 114–120, 122, 124, 127, 128, 136–137, 150, 151

O'Ballance, Edgar 6
Osgood, Kenneth 3, 5
Othman, Mahmoud 15, 68, 107, 128, 130, 131
Othman, Omar 15, 33
Ottoman Empire 22

Parsi, Trita 12
Paterson, Thomas G. 14
Pauly, Robert J. 14

162   *Index*

Pike House Committee Report 7–8
politics and struggle (1965–1971): Arab
anti-Americanism 79; Arab nationalism
78; Ba'ath government 90; Ba'athists
return 85–90; Ba'ath–Kurdish
negotiations 91; Ba'ath leadership 92;
Bazzaz Declaration 75; British
withdrawal *see* British withdrawal, Iraqi
Kurds implications; Cold War victims
76–77; human rights 82–85; international
communism 79; KDP 75, 91; Kurdish
legislative assembly 75; Kurdish
Mehabad Republic 81; 'predatory'
powers 78; regional communism 79;
SAVAK 92; Soviet embassy, Baghdad
91; Soviet satellite 80; Treaty of
Friendship and Cooperation (1972) 92;
US Iran embassy 77; US Iraq embassy
77; US regional allies 79
post-Ottoman framework 147
Primakov, Yevgeny 33, 91
pro-Nasser Arif regimes' 40
pro-Nasser Iraqi government 50, 51
pro-Nasserites, Iraq: Agents of international
communism 62; Algiers Accord 61; Arab
nationalism 61–62; Ba'ath regime
60–61, 62; Baghdad's allegiance 65;
Cold War allies 65; GOI–Kurdish
negotiations 61; Kurdish Issue 63;
Kurdish problem 66; regional Cold War
struggle 64; self-determination 65; Soviet
agents 64

Qasim, Abd al-Karim 11, 12, 23, 25, 27,
30, 35, 37, 49, 50, 53, 60, 62, 110 *see
also* Ba'athists after Qasim

Rafaat, Aram 6
Randal, Jonathan 6
regional politics 23
Rehmany, Wirya 6
Republic of Iraq 26, 146
Republic of Mongolia 51
Republic of Turkey 22
Ricciardone, Francis 5, 6
Romano, David 6
Rusk, Dean 64, 84
Russia 118; *Kurdish plans* 50; policies 2
Ryan, David 6

Sadat, Anwar 115
Saunders, Harold H. 53–54, 57, 112, 113,
115–116

Sayigh, Yezid 12
Sāzemān-e Ettelā'ātvaAmniyat-e Keshvar
(SAVAK) 92, 98–99, 106, 112, 116, 129
self-determination 22, 49, 152
Shareef, Mohammed 2–5, 6, 7, 43
Shatt al-Arab issue 35
Shelepin, Aleksandr 34
Shlaim, Avi 12
Simon, Steven 14
Sisco, Joseph J. 99
Soviet–Iraqi rapprochement 112–116
Soviet–Kurdish relations 26, 34
Soviet Trojan 35–36
Stansfield, Gareth 6, 12
Strong, Robert C. 38, 39, 66, 76, 78
Syria 1, 29, 35, 42; mountain warfare 63

Takeyh, Ray 14
Talabani, Jalal 15, 25, 34, 49, 50, 54, 62
Talabani, Mukaram 15, 85, 131
Talbot, Phillips 38, 39
Talib, Naji 64, 76, 83
Tehran embassy 82
Treaty of Friendship and Cooperation
(1972) 8, 33–34, 92, 106
Treaty of Lausanne (1923) 22
Treaty of Sèvres 22
Tripp, Charles 12
Truman Doctrine 41, 43, 70, 147
Turkey 1, 8, 23, 25, 28–30, 36–37, 39;
Soviet Union/communism 41

UK 23, 51; British National Archives
14
United Arab Republic (UAR) 29, 34
United Nations Security Council 127
United States and the Kurds, The (Little) 8
United States Diplomatic authorities 58
US Information Agency (USIA) 29
US inter-departmental Special National
Intelligence Estimate 29
US-Iraqi relations, Cold War 3, 5
US Special Intelligence Estimate 61
USSR–Arab relations 52
US/USSR 1, 5, 6, 11, 15, 23, 148, 150;
American intelligence 26; anti-Arab
resentments 8; 'Arab Iraq' 7; Baghdad
Pact 38; CIA activities 8; foreign
policy 2, 6, 10, 11, 30, 40–43, 69–70,
136–137, 151–152; GOI 37;
institutionalised policy 39; internal
matter 38; Iran embassy 77; Iraq
embassy 77; Iraqi Kurds, assistance

Index 163

to 33–34; Israel–Kurdish relations 40; KDP 38; Kurdish leadership 107; policy 76; pro-Nasser Arif regimes' 40; regional allies 79; satellite Kurdish state 24; Soviet-client Kurdish state 26; USSR 38

Vanli, Ismet Sherif 76–77
Vietnam War 69, 136

Wailes, Edward 28
war renewal: Algiers Accord 128–130, 132, 135; British intelligence sources 125; CIA 124; "inhuman" methods 126; Iranian-Iraqi agreement 133; KDP's intelligence agency 124; Kurdish delegation 123–124; Kurdish leadership 134; Kurdish Revolution 127; SAVAK 129; Soviet–Iraqi relations 125; US intelligence community 135; USSR 124; Western allies 131
Westad, Odd Arne 12
Wolfe-Hunnicutt, Brandon 14
World War II, US foreign policy 6

Yahya, Tahir 84
Yemen 66; mountain warfare 63

Zorlu, Fatin Rüştü 30